# GEOGRAPHY, POWER, STRATEGY & DEFENCE POLICY

## ESSAYS IN HONOUR OF PAUL DIBB

# GEOGRAPHY, POWER, STRATEGY & DEFENCE POLICY

## ESSAYS IN HONOUR OF PAUL DIBB

Edited by Desmond Ball and Sheryn Lee

Australian
National
University

# PRESS

**ANU PRESS**

Published by ANU Press
The Australian National University
Acton ACT 2601, Australia
Email: anupress@anu.edu.au
This title is also available online at press.anu.edu.au

National Library of Australia Cataloguing-in-Publication entry

| | |
|---|---|
| Title: | Geography, power, strategy and defence policy : essays in honour of Paul Dibb / editors: Desmond Ball, Sheryn Lee. |
| ISBN: | 9781760460136 (paperback) 9781760460143 (ebook) |
| Subjects: | Dibb, Paul, 1939---Criticism and interpretation. Defensive (Military science) Military planning--Australia. Festschriften. Australia--Military policy. Australia--Defenses. |
| Other Creators/Contributors: | |
| | Ball, Desmond, 1947- editor. Lee, Sheryn, editor. |
| Dewey Number: | 355.033594 |

Cover design and layout by ANU Press.
Cover photograph: SDSC Photograph Collection.

# Contents

# Acronyms

| | |
|---|---|
| ADF | Australian Defence Force |
| ADMI | area of direct military interest |
| ADSCS | Australian Defence Satellite Communications Station |
| AEW&C | airborne early warning and control |
| ALP | Australian Labor Party |
| AM | Member of the Order of Australia |
| ANU | The Australian National University |
| ANZUS | Australia, New Zealand, United States |
| APSI | area of primary strategic interest |
| ARF | ASEAN Regional Forum |
| ASEAN | Association of Southeast Asian Nations |
| ASIO | Australian Security Intelligence Organisation |
| ASPI | Australian Strategic Policy Institute |
| ASW | anti-submarine warfare |
| AUSTEO | Australian eyes only |
| BAE | Bureau of Agricultural Economics |
| CBM | confidence-building measure |
| CDAA | circularly disposed antenna array |
| CDF | Chief of Defence Force |
| CIA | Central Intelligence Agency (US) |
| CINCPAC | Commander in Chief, Pacific (US) |
| CNS | Chief of Naval Staff |
| COMSAT | communications satellite |
| CPSU | Communist Party of the Soviet Union |
| DDG | guided missile destroyer |

| | |
|---|---|
| DDS&T | Deputy Director for Science and Technology, CIA |
| DFAT | Department of Foreign Affairs and Trade |
| DIO | Defence Intelligence Organisation |
| DOA | Defence of Australia |
| DRM | Donald Ralph Marshall |
| DSB | Defence Security Branch |
| DSD | Defence Signals Directorate |
| DSTO | Defence Science and Technology Organisation |
| EEC | European Economic Community |
| EEPs | ARF Experts and Eminent Persons group |
| FFG | guided missile frigate |
| FORNSAT | foreign satellite |
| FPDA | Five Power Defence Arrangements |
| GCHQ | Government Communications Headquarters |
| GCSB | Government Communications Security Bureau |
| GDP | gross domestic product |
| HF | high frequency (3–30 MHz) |
| HF DF HF | interception and direction-finding |
| HQ ADF | headquarters of the Australian Defence Force |
| ICBM | inter-continental ballistic missile |
| IISS | International Institute for Strategic Studies |
| INTERFET | International Force for East Timor |
| JDA | Japan Defense Agency |
| JIO | Joint Intelligence Organisation |
| JORN | Jindalee Operational Radar Network |
| KGB | Committee for State Security (Soviet) |
| LHD | landing helicopter dock |
| MOFA | Ministry of Foreign Affairs (Japan) |
| NAS | National Assessments Staff |
| NATO | North Atlantic Treaty Organization |
| NCO | non-commissioned officer |
| NIC | National Intelligence Committee |
| NRO | National Reconnaissance Office |

| | |
|---|---|
| ONA | Office of National Assessments |
| OSCAR | Office of Special Clearances and Records |
| OSCE | Organization for Security and Co-operation in Europe |
| OSO | Office of SIGINT Operations |
| OTHR | over-the-horizon radar |
| PLA | People's Liberation Army |
| PNG | Papua New Guinea |
| PRC | People's Republic of China |
| RAAF | Royal Australian Air Force |
| RAN | Royal Australian Navy |
| RANTACS | RAN Tactical School |
| RMA | revolution in military affairs |
| RSPacS | Research School of Pacific Studies, ANU |
| RSPAS | Research School of Pacific and Asian Studies, ANU |
| RSSS | Research School of Social Sciences, ANU |
| SB83 | The Strategic Basis of Australian Defence Policy, 1983 |
| SDF | Self-Defense Force (Japan) |
| SDSC | Strategic and Defence Studies Centre |
| SIGINT | signals intelligence |
| STOVL | short take-off and vertical landing |
| UKUSA | United Kingdom United States of America SIGINT agreement |
| USSR | Union of Soviet Socialist Republics |
| VCDF | Vice Chief of the Defence Force |

# Contributors

Robert Ayson is Professor of Strategic Studies and directs the Centre for Strategic Studies: New Zealand. He has held academic positions with The Australian National University, Massey University and the University of Waikato, and official positions in Wellington with the Foreign Affairs, Defence and Trade Select Committee and the External (now National) Assessments Bureau. He has written books on two of the twentieth century's leading thinkers in strategic studies and international relations, Hedley Bull and Thomas Schelling, and is a frequent media commentator on Asia-Pacific security, nuclear issues and New Zealand and Australian defence policy. Robert is also Honorary Professor at the New Zealand Defence Force Command and Staff College.

Desmond Ball AO is Emeritus Professor at The Australian National University's Strategic and Defence Studies Centre having been head of the Centre from 1984 to 1991. Professor Ball is the author of more than 40 books or monographs on technical intelligence subjects, nuclear strategy, Australian defence, and security in the Asia-Pacific region. His publications include *Breaking the Codes: Australia's KGB Network, 1944–50* (with David Horner); *Death in Balibo, Lies in Canberra* (with Hamish McDonald); and *Australia and Cyber-Warfare* (with Gary Waters and Ian Dudgeon). He has also written articles on issues such as the strategic culture in the Asia-Pacific region and defence acquisition programs in the region. Professor Ball was elected a Fellow of the Academy of Social Sciences of Australia in 1986. He served on the Council of the International Institute for Strategic Studies from 1994 until 2000, and was co-chair of the Steering Committee of the Council for Security Cooperation in the Asia-Pacific from 2000 until 2002.

**Geoffrey Barker** is a former foreign affairs and defence correspondent for the *Australian Financial Review*. He has previously been a visiting fellow at the Strategic and Defence Studies Centre, The Australian National University. Now semi-retired, he was a European and Washington correspondent for Fairfax and News Ltd newspapers. From Washington he covered the end of the Cold War and of the Soviet Union, including all of the summit meetings between President Reagan and Premier Gorbachev.

**Admiral (Retired) Chris Barrie AC** has been a visiting fellow at the Strategic and Defence Studies Centre at The Australian National University since 2003. He joined the Royal Australian Navy in 1961, serving for 41 years. He served during the 1990s as Director of the RAN Surface Warfare School and Commanding Officer of HMAS *Watson*; Deputy Maritime Commander and Chief of Staff at Maritime Headquarters in Sydney; Deputy Chief of Naval Staff; and Vice Chief of the Defence Force. He was Chief of the Defence Force (CDF) from July 1998 to July 2002. As CDF, he directed and commanded the operation to secure East Timor in 1999–2000. Following his retirement in 2002, he spent a year at Oxford University, where he has continued to be involved in its Strategic Leadership programs.

**The Hon. Kim C. Beazley AC** has recently retired as Ambassador to the United States of America (appointed in February 2010). He was a member of the Australian Parliament (House of Representatives) from 1980 to 2007. He served as Minister for Defence in the Hawke Labor Government in 1984–90, and was Deputy Prime Minister in 1995–96. He was leader of the Australian Labor Party (ALP) and Leader of the Opposition in 1996–2001 and 2005–06. After retiring from politics in 2007, Mr Beazley was appointed Winthrop Professor in the Department of Politics and International Relations at the University of Western Australia. In July 2008 he was appointed Chancellor of The Australian National University, a position he held until December 2009.

**Richard Brabin-Smith AO** is a visiting fellow at the Strategic and Defence Studies Centre of The Australian National University, where he follows his interests in Australian and regional security. Before this he spent some 30 years in the Australian Department of Defence in a wide variety of analytical, policy and corporate management positions. These included Chief Defence Scientist and Deputy Secretary Strategic Policy. In the mid-1980s, he worked with Paul Dibb to help with the drafting of the 1986 *Review of Australia's Defence Capabilities* (the Dibb Review). In the mid-1990s, he was the Defence civilian member of the senior review panel of the *Defence Efficiency Review* (the McIntosh Review).

**Allan Hawke AC FAICD FAIM FIPAA** is a retired senior Australian public servant. He has a Bachelor of Science (First Class Honours) and a Doctor of Philosophy degree from The Australian National University (ANU). He served as Deputy Director of the Defence Signals Directorate in 1990–91, Deputy Secretary Strategy and Intelligence in the Department of Defence from 1991 to 1993, Chief of Staff to Prime Minister Paul Keating in 1993–94, Deputy Secretary in the Department of the Prime Minister and Cabinet in 1994, Secretary of the Department of Veterans Affairs in 1994–96, Secretary of the Department of Defence in 1999–2002, Australian High Commissioner to New Zealand in 2003–05, and was Chancellor of ANU in 2006–08.

**Raoul Heinrichs** teaches international politics and security at the Strategic and Defence Studies Centre, The Australian National University (ANU). He is a former Sir Arthur Tange Scholar and Lowy Institute research associate. Previously, he was the founding coordinator of the Lowy Institute's MacArthur Asia Security Project and, before that, the Institute's inaugural Michael and Deborah Thawley Scholar in international security, with a research placement at the Center for Strategic and International Studies in Washington, DC. He has a Masters degree from ANU, where he was a TB Millar Scholar in Strategic and Defence Studies, and a First Class Honours degree from Monash University. Throughout 2007, he worked on foreign and security policy in the office of then Opposition leader Kevin Rudd.

**Peter Jennings PSM** has been Executive Director of the Australian Strategic Policy Institute since 30 April 2012. He previously served as Defence adviser to the Federal Opposition (1990–93), Chief of Staff to the Minister for Defence (1996–98), and head of the Strategic Policy Branch in the Department of Defence (1998–99). In late 1999, he was co-director of the East Timor Policy Unit, responsible for developing Australia's policy approaches to the international peacekeeping operation in East Timor. He was appointed the Deputy Director of the Defence Imagery and Geospatial Organisation in 2002. He was a senior adviser in the Prime Minister's office responsible for developing a strategic policy framework for Cabinet in 2002–03. He was the

Deputy Secretary Strategy in the Department of Defence in 2010–12. He was awarded the Public Service Medal in the Australia Day 2013 Honours List for outstanding public service through the development of Australia's strategic and defence policy, particularly in the areas of Australian Defence Force operations in East Timor, Iraq and Afghanistan.

**Sheryn Lee** is an associate lecturer in Security Studies at the Department of Security Studies and Criminology, Macquarie University. She is also a PhD candidate at the Strategic and Defence Studies Centre, The Australian National University, and a non-resident WSD Handa Fellow at Pacific Forum, Center for Strategic and International Studies, Honolulu. She holds an MA in Political Science from the University of Pennsylvania, where she was a Benjamin Franklin Fellow and Mumford Fellow. Previously, she has been a researcher, tutor, and TB Millar Scholar at the Strategic and Defence Studies Centre, and Robert O'Neill Scholar at the International Institute of Strategic Studies–Asia in Singapore. She has previously published in *Asian Security* and *Survival*, and co-edited *Insurgent Intellectual: Essays in Honour of Professor Desmond Ball* (with Brendan Taylor and Nicholas Farrelly) and *Power and International Relations: Essays in Honour of Coral Bell* (with Desmond Ball).

**Peter J. Rimmer** is an Emeritus Professor in the School of History, Culture and Language, ANU College of Asia and the Pacific, The Australian National University. Formerly a lecturer at Monash University between 1965 and 1967, he was a member of the Department of Human Geography in the Research School of Pacific and Asian Studies between 1967 and 2000, a colleague of Paul Dibb in 1969–70 and elected a Fellow of the Academy of the Social Sciences of Australia in 1992. An economic geographer, he specialises in urban and regional development within the Asian-Pacific Rim with a particular emphasis upon the role of telecommunications and transport (road, rail, sea and air). He has undertaken research work in China, Hong Kong SAR, Japan, Korea, Indonesia, Malaysia, Papua New Guinea, the Philippines, Singapore, Taiwan, Thailand and Vietnam. His publications include *Rikisha to Rapid Transit: Urban Public Transport Systems and Policy in Southeast Asia*, *Cities, Transport & Communications: The Integration of Southeast Asia Since 1850* (with Howard Dick), *The City in Southeast Asia: Patterns, Processes and Policy* (with Howard Dick), and *Asian-Pacific Rim Logistics: Global Context and Local Policies*.

The last study, published in 2014–15, stems from the period when he was the Distinguished Professor of Global Logistics in the Graduate School of Logistics at Inha University, Incheon, Korea.

**Benjamin Schreer** is Professor of Security Studies and Head of the Department of Security Studies and Criminology, Macquarie University. He was previously a senior analyst for defence strategy at the Australian Strategic Policy Institute, and the deputy head of the Strategic and Defence Studies Centre, The Australian National University. He has also held positions as the deputy director of the Aspen Institute in Berlin, leader of a Centre of Excellence at Konstanz University, and deputy head of a research unit at the German Institute for International and Security Affairs (Stiftung Wissenschaft und Politik) in Berlin. He has published in leading academic journals such as *International Affairs*, *Survival*, *Asia Policy* and *Contemporary Security Policy*.

**Brendan Taylor** is Associate Professor and Head of the Strategic and Defence Studies Centre, The Australian National University. He is a specialist on great power strategic relations in the Asia-Pacific, economic sanctions, and Asian security architecture. His publications have featured in such leading academic journals as *International Affairs*, *Survival*, *Asian Security*, *Review of International Studies* and the *Australian Journal of International Affairs*. He is the author of *Sanctions as Grand Strategy*, which was published in the International Institute for Strategic Studies *Adelphi* series, as well as *American Sanctions in the Asia Pacific* (2010). He is also the editor of *Australia as an Asia-Pacific Regional Power* (2007), *Insurgent Intellectual: Essays in Honour of Professor Desmond Ball* (2012), and *Bilateralism, Multilateralism and Asia-Pacific Security* (2013).

**William T. Tow** is Professor and Head of the Department of International Relations at The Australian National University's Coral Bell School of Asia Pacific Affairs. His research interests are alliance security politics, Asia-Pacific regional security architectures and US security policy in that region. He has authored or edited more than 20 books, 10 working papers and over 100 journal articles/book chapters on various aspects of these subjects. He was editor of the *Australian Journal of International Affairs* (2001–06) and a member of the Australian–American Fulbright Commission's Board of Directors (1992–97). He has been a Visiting Professor at the Rajaratnam School of International Studies in Singapore (2008 and 2012), a visiting fellow at Stanford University (1999) and a visiting research associate at the International Institute for Strategic Studies (1994). His recent research has been funded by the Australian Research Council, the MacArthur Foundation, the Japan Foundation, and Australia's Department of Foreign Affairs and Trade.

R. Gerard Ward is Emeritus Professor at The Australian National University, was formerly Professor of Human Geography (1971–98), Research School of Pacific Studies, and director of the Research School from 1980 to 1993. Before 1971 he lectured at the University of Auckland and University College London, and was Foundation Professor of Geography, University of Papua and New Guinea (1967–71). His publications include *Land Use and Population in Fiji* (1965); *American Activities in the Central Pacific, 1790–1870* (8 vols, 1966–67); *The Settlement of Polynesia: A Computer Simulation* (1973); *South Pacific Agriculture: Choices and Constraints* (1980); *Land, Custom and Practice in the South Pacific* (1995); *Samoa: Mapping the Diversity* (1998); and many papers and reports on the Pacific Islands. He was elected a Fellow of the Academy of Social Sciences of Australia in 1971. From 1995 to 2003 he was Vice-President and President of the Pacific Science Association.

Hugh White AO is Professor of Strategic Studies at the Strategic and Defence Studies Centre, The Australian National University. He has worked on Australian and regional strategic, defence and foreign policy issues since 1980. He has been an intelligence analyst, journalist, ministerial adviser, departmental official, think tanker and academic. In the 1990s he served as international relations adviser to Prime Minister Bob Hawke and as Deputy Secretary of Defence for Strategy and Intelligence. He was the principal author of Australia's 2000 Defence White Paper. From 2004 to 2011 he was head of The Australian National University's Strategic and Defence Studies Centre. His recent publications include *Power Shift: Australia's Future between Washington and Beijing* published as a Quarterly Essay in September 2010, and *The China Choice: Why America Should Share Power*, first published by Black Inc. in 2012. In the 1970s he studied philosophy at Melbourne and Oxford universities.

# Photographs and Maps

Photo 1: Pontefract, the coalmining settlement in Yorkshire where Paul Dibb was born
Source: Paul Dibb

Photo 2: Paul Dibb visiting the 6th Army at Badaling near Beijing, August 1978. The first visit to China by a declared senior intelligence officer
Source: Paul Dibb

Photo 3: Dr Fedor Mediansky, Paul Dibb and Desmond Ball at an SDSC conference outside the H.C. Coombs Lecture Theatre,  c. 1984
Source: SDSC Photograph Collection

Photo 4: Senior Research Fellow at SDSC, 1984
Source: SDSC Photograph Collection

Photo 5: Official photo at the time of the release of Dibb's *Review of Australia's Defence Capabilities* (public version), June 1986
Source: Paul Dibb

Photo 6: Cartoon by Pascal Locanto, *Sydney Morning Herald*, 4 June 1986

Source: Fairfax Media

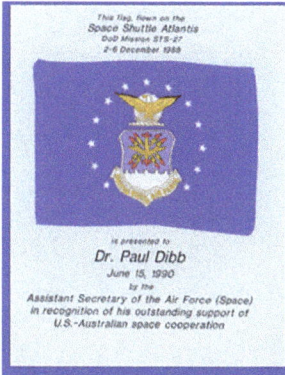

Photo 7: Award presented to Dr Paul Dibb, 'in recognition of his outstanding support of US–Australian space cooperation', 15 June 1990

Source: Paul Dibb

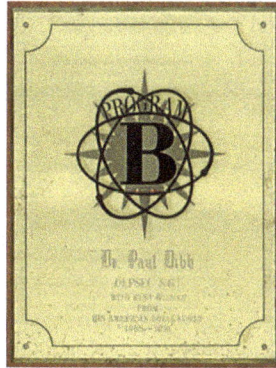

Photo 8: Award presented to Dr Paul Dibb by the NRO's Program B for his support during his period as Deputy Secretary (Strategy and Intelligence), 1988–91

Source: Paul Dibb

Photo 9: Visit of Try Sutrisno (Vice-President of Indonesia), at Tindal Air Force Base, Katherine, 1989

L to R: Kim Beazley, General Peter Gration, Try Sutrisno, Air Commodore Peter Nicholson and Dr Paul Dibb

Source: Paul Dibb

**Photo 10: Lunch at the Pentagon with Kim Beazley and Paul Wolfowitz, Washington DC, 1989**

L to R: Dr Paul Dibb, unnamed, Kim Beazley, Paul Wolfowitz

Source: Paul Dibb

**Photo 11: Deputy Secretary of Defence (Strategy and Intelligence), 1990**

Source: Paul Dibb

Photo 12: Signing ceremony marking amendment to Nurrungar
agreement, 1990
Source: Paul Dibb

Photo 13: Head of SDSC, Kioloa, 1992
Source: SDSC Photogaph Collection

Photo 14: Hosting a visit to Australia by Indonesia's retired Defence Minister and PANGAB Leonardus Benjamin (Benny) Moerdani, Adelaide, 21 July 1993

L to R: Sabam Siagian (Indonesian Ambassador to Australia), Admiral Alan Beaumont, Benny Moerdani, Robert Ray (Australian Defence Minister), Allan Hawke (Secretary of Department of Defence), General John Baker (Chief of Defence Force), unnamed, Professor Paul Dibb, Pat Carroll (Assistant Secretary, Asia Branch, Department of Defence)

Source: Paul Dibb

Photo 15: Hosting a visit to Australia by Indonesia's retired Defence Minister and PANGAB Benny Moerdani, Adelaide, 21 July 1993

L to R: Professor Paul Dibb, unnamed, Benny Moerdani, Sabam Siagian

Source: Paul Dibb

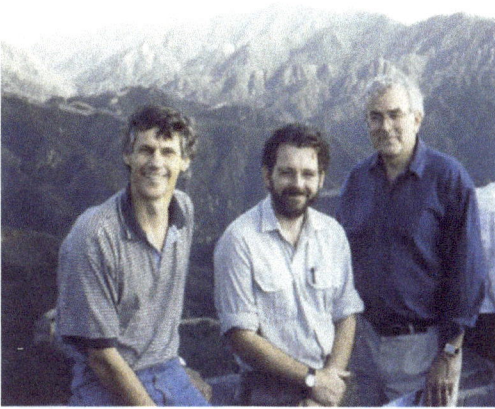

Photo 16: At the Great Wall of China with Rory Steele (DFAT) and Hugh White (ONA), during a 1.5 Track with China led by Paul Dibb, 1992

Source: Paul Dibb

Photo 17: Speech to the National Press Club, Canberra, September 1993

Source: Paul Dibb

Photo 18: Alexander Downer (Minister for Foreign Affairs and Trade), Professor Paul Dibb and Professor Robert O'Neill at the SDSC's 30th anniversary, 1996

Source: Darren Boyd/Bob Cooper

Photo 19: Professor Robert O'Neill, Professor Paul Dibb, Yukio Satoh (Japanese Ambassador to Australia) and Professor Desmond Ball at the SDSC's 30th anniversary, 1996

Source: Darren Boyd/Bob Cooper

Photo 20: Speech to the National Press Club, Canberra, 2003
Source: Paul Dibb

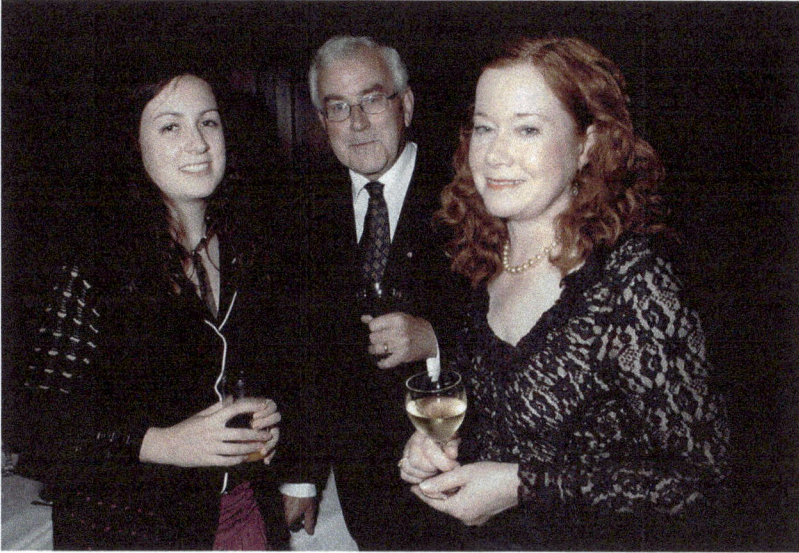

**Photo 21: Retirement dinner and Emeritus occasion, 23 May 2005**
L to R: Katya Dibb, Emeritus Professor Paul Dibb and Rhondda Nicholas
Source: Paul Dibb

**Photo 22: Retirement dinner and Emeritus occasion with the Hon. Kim Beazley, 23 May 2005**
Source: Paul Dibb

Photo 23: Retirement dinner and Emeritus occasion with the Hon. Kim Beazley and Professor Hugh White, 23 May 2005
Source: Paul Dibb

Photo 24: Paul in his Porsche 911RS, Wakefield Park, June 2006
Source: Paul Dibb

Photo 25: Outside the Hedley Bull Centre, ANU, November 2013
Source: SDSC Photograph Collection

Photo 26: The 9th Meeting of the ARF Experts and Eminent Persons, Helsinki, 12–13 March 2015

Source: 9th ARF EEPs, Helsinki, Finland, 12–13 March 2015

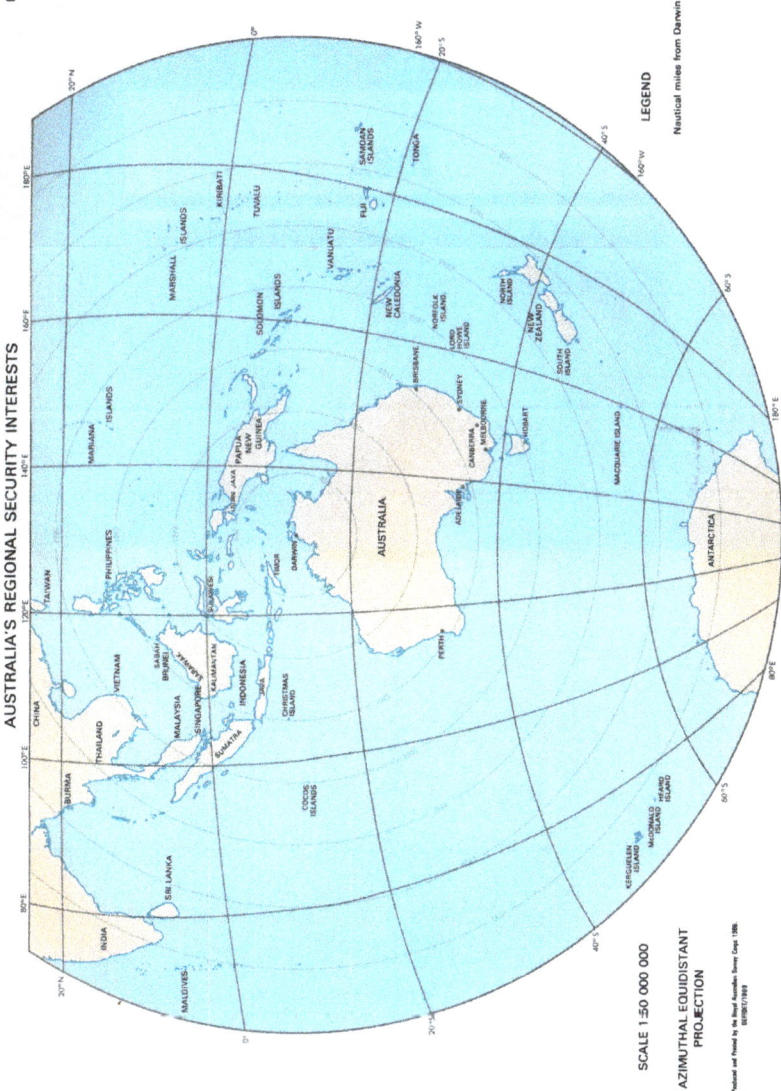

Map 1: Australia's regional security interests

Source: Paul Dibb, *Review of Australia's Defence Capabilities*, report to the Minister for Defence (Canberra: Australian Government Publishing Service, 1986)

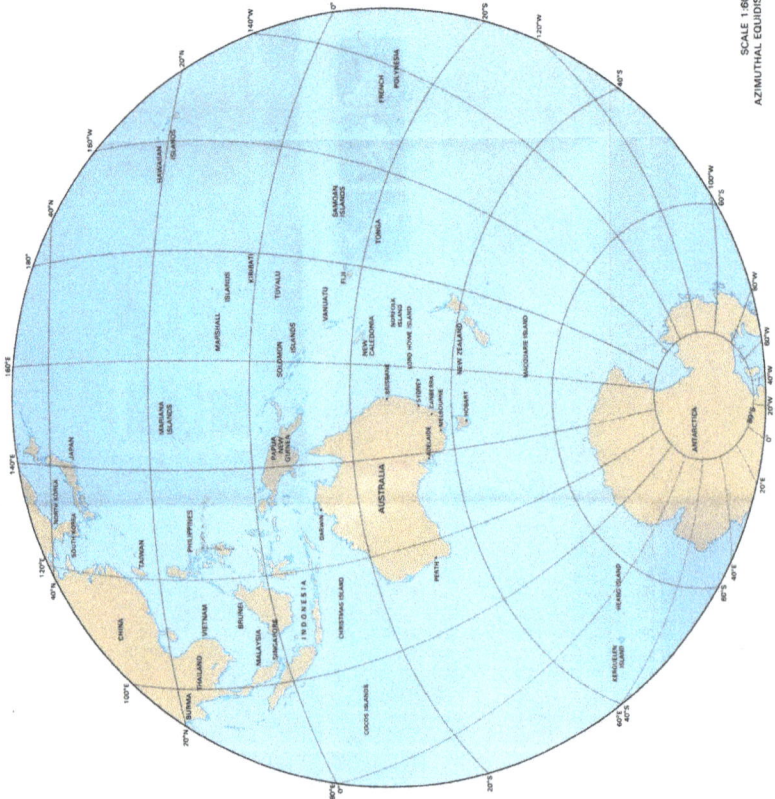

**Map 2: Australia's sphere of regional interests**

Source: *The Defence of Australia 1987*, Presented to Parliament by the Minister for Defence the Honourable Kim C. Beazley, M.P. (Canberra: Australian Government Publishing Service, 1987)

# Introduction

Desmond Ball and Sheryn Lee

Paul Dibb has enjoyed an unusual career. He has earned and maintained an international scholarly reputation of the highest order, while at the same time he has done much distinguished public service. He was a pioneer in moving back and forth between posts in government departments, notably the Department of Defence, and academia. He has published more than a dozen books and monographs, about 100 chapters and articles in scholarly books and journals, and produced six official reports for government. He has happily engaged in vigorous public debate about important and controversial strategic and defence issues. Since 2006 he has written more than 40 op-ed articles for the *Australian*, each involving rigorous and succinct analyses of current issues than usually appears on those pages.

In January 1989, having just been appointed Deputy Secretary (Strategy and Intelligence) in the Department of Defence, he was awarded a Member of the Order of Australia (AM) in 'recognition of service to the Public Service'. Much of this service involved matters of the highest secrecy, but his public activities included the role from November 1986 to December 1988 of director of the Joint Intelligence Organisation (JIO), where he had previously spent 11 years. From 1974 to 2004, he was one of the handful of Defence officials fully cleared for entry into the US–Australian 'joint facilities', including Pine Gap, the CIA's most important technical intelligence collection station in the world. He also worked for the Australian Security Intelligence Organisation (ASIO) on counterintelligence operations from 1964 to 1991. Over 1985–86, he produced the *Review of Australia's Defence Capabilities*, which became known as the Dibb Review, for Minister for Defence Kim Beazley.[1] There are few others in this country who are as comfortable with robust public debate while maintaining such professional intimacy with core elements of the intelligence community as Dibb.

This collection of essays, by more than a dozen of his friends and colleagues, is intended to review Dibb's work, including his public service and his academic publications. The unusual combination of governmental experience and keeper of secrets on the one hand, and prolific academic and public commentator on the other hand, is a particularly interesting aspect of Dibb's career. His academic writings are tempered by geostrategic and political realities, while his strategic analyses and policy advice are informed by academic discourse.

Two of Paul's closest friends, Allan Hawke and Admiral (Retired) Chris Barrie, both of whom worked with him in Defence, have contributed personal perspectives on him. In Chapter 1, Hawke describes Paul's upbringing in the coalmining villages in West Yorkshire, and his determination to avoid coalmining as a career. He graduated from Nottingham University in 1960 with a Bachelor of Arts in economics and geography with honours, but that was not good enough for entry into Britain's Civil Service. He was from the wrong class. However, as Hawke notes, 'Britain's loss was to turn out to be Australia's gain'. He joined the Australian Public Service in Canberra in January 1962, starting in the Department of Trade and later moving to the then Bureau of Agricultural Economics (BAE). Having studied Russian at Nottingham, the BAE wanted him to work on Soviet agricultural economics, which prompted his long-term professional interest in the Soviet Union/Russia.

Chris Barrie, in Chapter 2, relates that he first met Paul in 1985, when Paul was working on the Dibb Review and Chris was 'a relatively junior Navy officer', but their friendship only blossomed after 2003, when Chris joined the Strategic and Defence Studies Centre (SDSC) at The Australian National University (ANU), having retired as Chief of the Defence Force (CDF) the previous year. He describes working

---

1   Paul Dibb, *Review of Australia's Defence Capabilities*, report to the Minister for Defence (Canberra: Australian Government Publishing Service, 1986).

with Paul as 'an enriching experience'. He also highlights Paul's 'deep commitment to … nurturing, encouraging and mentoring [younger people] in the strategic studies field'.

Desmond Ball, who has known and worked closely with Dibb since the mid-1980s, provides further personal reflections in Chapter 3. He describes the major milestones in Dibb's career, but also tries to shed light on the personality of a man who has earned international academic prominence, been honoured for his government service, and negotiated the interstices between these very different realms before anyone else attempted anything similar. Ball describes Dibb as being highly motivated and with the courage to seek out new pastures — characteristics that might also explain his penchant for driving fast cars. He was able to attract the support of superb mentors, such as Bob Furlonger and Bob Mathams in the JIO; Sir Arthur Tange, Secretary of the Department of Defence; Kim Beazley; and professors Harry Rigby and J.D.B. Miller at ANU. He has always focused on the critical issues of the time, but also ones selected for their enduring and consequential implications, such as the central role of the 'joint facilities' in the US–Australian alliance, the impact of deficiencies in Soviet human geography that brought into question its status as a superpower in the 1980s, the determinate role of geography in shaping Australia's defence strategy and capabilities, the balance of power in East Asia, and the strategic competition between China and the United States. As Robert Ayson depicts him in Chapter 6, drawing on Isaiah Berlin's typology, Dibb is 'more of a hedgehog (a thinker who focuses on one big idea) and less of a fox (who knows many)'.[2]

Dibb's work on Soviet agricultural economics led him to visit the Soviet embassy in Canberra and thence to his acquaintance with Don Marshall, a young member of ASIO's counterespionage branch, who Dibb has called 'the person who changed my life'. In 1964, Marshall persuaded him to cultivate several officials in the embassy (most particularly Nikolai Poseliagin, Igor Saprykin and Yuri Pavlov) to get their views on issues concerning the central strategic nuclear balance and to discern their real interests and priorities and, possibly, persuade one or other of them to defect. He failed to 'turn' any of them; he says that 'they were either too smart or they had a mole deep

---

2    Isaiah Berlin, *The Hedgehog and the Fox: An Essay on Tolstoy's View of History*, 2nd edn (Princeton University Press, 2013), p. 1.

inside ASIO'. The first detailed account of this side of Dibb's life was published by Geoffrey Barker in January 2007.[3] That article forms the basis for Chapter 4, in which Barker situates Dibb's counterintelligence work for ASIO and his personal and professional relationship with Marshall in the broader context of the unabashed 'realism' of his understanding of international relations and his appreciation of the magnitude of the threat posed to Western interests and, indeed, Western survival by the Soviet Union.

Marshall was instrumental in Paul becoming an Australian citizen in February 1970. Paul was in the Department of Human Geography at ANU at that time, but was anticipating a position in JIO. Marshall said 'if you're going to join the Australian intelligence community, you should be a citizen, mate', and produced a form for Paul to fill in. A week later, without any further formalities, Marshall gave him his citizenship certificate.

Dibb left Nottingham University not only with a deep and abiding interest in the Soviet Union/Russia but also, and even more fundamentally, he had been intellectually framed in its very good Geography Department. In 1964–65, he had an Australian Public Service scholarship to study part-time in the Department of Geography in the School of General Studies at ANU where, as Peter J. Rimmer and R. Gerard Ward note in Chapter 5, he 'would have inculcated in Dibb the need for the greater use of statistics and model-building in geographical analysis'. In 1969–70, he spent a year in the Department of Human Geography in the Research School of Pacific Studies (RSPacS) at ANU, where he was further exposed to 'the development of a scientific approach to geographical problems'. As Rimmer and Ward show, Dibb's geographical training is the foundation on which his views about power, strategy, and Australian defence planning rest. He is a solid member of 'the pantheon of geostrategists who have long recognised geography as a decisive factor in the fortunes of nation states'; his studies of the Soviet Union/Russia and China are underpinned by geographical analysis; his 'arc of instability' is inherently a geographic construct; and geography has infused his approach to Australian defence policy and planning, with his concepts of the 'area of direct military interest' (ADMI) and surrounding 'area of primary strategic

---

3    Geoffrey Barker, 'The Person Who Changed My Life', *Weekend Australian Financial Review*, 25–28 Jan. 2007, pp. 27–29.

interest' (APSI), and his appreciation of the sea–air gap as the key to Defence of Australia (DOA), and hence his prioritising of maritime and air forces in terms of capabilities. For Rimmer and Ward, Dibb exemplifies 'the power of geography in public policy and discourse'.

In Chapter 6, Robert Ayson traverses some of the same terrain as Rimmer and Ward in the previous chapter but, with the eye of a strategist, he concentrates mainly on the period since the 1980s, or just the latter half of the Rimmer–Ward excursion. Ayson says that 'it is difficult to exaggerate the importance of geographical considerations in Dibb's approach to strategy and defence policy decision-making, especially, but not only, in the case of Australia'. Geography shapes our abiding (and truly vital) national interests, and it should be a primary determinant of Australia's strategic policy and defence capabilities. Ayson notes that 'there is more than a hint of material determinism' in some of Dibb's writings about Australian defence. Further, however, he argues that some of the principal geographic themes that Dibb articulated with respect to Australia's defence in 1986 were derived from his Soviet studies. There, Dibb found that Soviet priorities could be depicted in terms of 'an area of primary strategic interest defined by one's immediate geography'; that geography contained both assets and liabilities, which successful planning required be adroitly leveraged; and that the Kremlin's anxieties about the distant, vast, sparsely populated and resource-rich Siberia had implicit resonance with concerns in Canberra about Australia's northern stretches and approaches.

The mid- and late 1980s was the 'golden age' of Australian national security policymaking, defence planning and force-structure development. The Dibb Review in 1986 and the government's 1987 White Paper, *The Defence of Australia*, produced for the first time a clear and coherent basis for Australian defence planning and capability development. New strategic concepts were developed for contingency planning and warning-time analysis. Clear and coherent guidance was articulated that provided the Australian Defence Force (ADF) with the capability to control the sea–air gap, that ocean moat to our north, and thus effect the defence of Australia on a self-reliant basis. This conceptual transformation in Australian defence policy was directed by Beazley, at that time Minister for Defence, but Dibb was largely responsible for developing the strategic concepts and defining the criteria for capability planning and force-structure development, as well as integrating it into the strategic guidance. Beazley observes in Chapter 7 that the 'remorseless' and 'systematic' logic of Dibb's constructs 'has never been bettered'.

Three chapters of this book are devoted to examining Dibb's work on Australian defence policy and planning. In Chapter 7, Beazley describes Dibb as 'the creative spirit behind the 1980s Labor Government's defence strategy, which prioritised the defence of Australia'. He believes that understanding the 'essence of our strategic geography' was fundamental to Dibb's contribution. The strength of his logic derived from the 'disciplined linkages that he forged between national strategy, military strategy, geography and force structure'. Geography dictates that defence of the air and maritime approaches should be the most important determinant of the ADF's force structure.

Maps, which are now invariably integrated with high-resolution digital imagery, are essential tools in geography. Sir Arthur Tange told the CDF conference at Canungra, Queensland, in August 1986 that 'a map of one's own country is the most fundamental of all defence documentation'.[4] The maps that accompanied the Dibb Review in 1986 and the 1987 *Defence of Australia* White Paper, and which were novel as well as controversial in their geostrategic implications, are reproduced prior to this Introduction (Maps 1 and 2).

Richard Brabin-Smith, in Chapter 8, provides a first-hand account of the development of the concepts that comprised Dibb's logic for the defence of Australia. He was a member of the five-person Department of Defence Review Team, which was organised to support Dibb with respect to the preparation and production of the review. As a specialist in force-structure analysis, Dibb had already been exploring some of these concepts. The Dibb Review was a feast for defence academics, policymakers, force planners and the media, being replete with ideas and a cascade of concepts publicly explicated for the first time: 'enhanced self-reliance' as a national strategy; 'denial' through defence of the 'sea–air gap' as a military strategy; concepts pertaining to different levels of contingency ('low level', 'escalated low level' and

---

4    Arthur Tange, 'The Reorganization of the Defence Group of Departments: Reflections Ten Years On', address to CDF [Chief of Defence Force] Conference, Canungra, Queensland, 26 Aug. 1986, in Arthur Tange, *Defence Policy Administration and Organization: Selected Lectures, 1971–1986* (Canberra: University College of New South Wales, 1986), p. 90.

'higher level') and associated warning times (and henceforth expansion times); ADMI and APSI; and a host of 'operational concepts' that were largely derived from geographical considerations.

Brabin-Smith also provides an insightful critique of the impact of the conceptual framework and the specific capability recommendations of the Dibb Review on the subsequent service force structure developments. Resistance to some elements of the logic was widespread, not only involving the Army. The Navy has never accepted the argument in the review that greater priority should be accorded to the anti-submarine warfare (ASW) capabilities of the surface fleet. Having served as Deputy Secretary (Strategy) in 2000–02, and then having had more than a decade of academic rumination, Brabin-Smith still strongly believes that 'the imperatives of Australia's strategic geography need to remain the foundation upon which Australian defence planning continues to build'.

Peter Jennings, in Chapter 9, addresses 'the politics and practicalities of designing Australia's force structure'. He focuses on the interaction of defence policymaking and politics, at the intersection of the political decision-making process, involving the cabinet room and ministerial suites in Parliament House, and the force-development process at Russell Hill. He argues that the Dibb Review 'set the model' that has been followed to greater or lesser extents by successive governments in the development of Defence white papers ever since and, after reviewing the 1976, 1987, 1994, 2000, 2009, 2013 and 2016 publications, concludes that the 'Dibb model' is likely to remain the 'favoured way of making defence policy'.

'Politics and practicalities' also mean, however, that the demands of the political parties for 'product differentiation' are just as compelling as changes in the strategic environment with respect to shaping the policy guidance. Both factors figured in the policy of 'DOA plus' articulated by Defence Minister Ian McLachlan in 1996–98 in the first conservative Coalition Government under John Howard, who said that 'Australia's defence does not begin at the coast-line' but could involve operations further forward of the island archipelago (or sea–air gap), including 'proactive operations' against 'military assets and installations which could be used to attack Australia' and the ability to defeat an enemy 'on land' at substantial distances from Australia.

Jennings, who was involved in the development of the 'DOA plus' policy, notes in Chapter 9 that it involved 'extension of the DOA concept further into the region', while retaining the geographically based DOA as its core. He notes that '[the policies of] DOA and "forward defence" meet at some point in the archipelago of islands to Australia's north and further into South-East Asia', whereat another geographical space is in effect added to the DOA's ADMI and APSI. The new space extended from around 2,500 to around 3,500 kilometres north-west and north-east of Darwin, and potentially as far as 5,000–6,000 kilometres north into north-east Asia. Parts of this large area are a long way from Australia's shores. As Jennings also notes, 'the requirements for an effective "DOA plus" policy are practically identical to what is needed to sustain an expeditionary force'. Indeed, 'DOA plus' effectively opened the door for the Services, and particularly the Army, to justify new capabilities not required by narrower definitions of DOA. In the late 1990s the Army dropped its focus on the defence of northern Australia and adopted a strategic concept which 'reflects Australia's experience in the south-west Pacific campaign of World War II'.[5] In practice, 'DOA plus' involved much more than a simple geographic extension of DOA; it was the first fracture in a succession of increasingly fraught policy statements, beginning with the 2000 White Paper but more haphazard in the 2009, 2013 and 2016 exercises.

The US alliance is inevitably a central consideration in Australian defence planning and, as Benjamin Schreer states in Chapter 10, it 'has been of singular importance to Paul Dibb's professional life'. In Chapter 7, Kim Beazley says that the alliance is 'a verity to which Dibb always paid obeisance'. Indeed, Dibb has consistently argued, both as a senior official and an academic, that the alliance is 'irreplaceable' and that its benefits are 'priceless'. A 'self-reliant' defence posture is not possible without access to US technology, intelligence and logistics support. As Schreer describes, the US– Australian 'joint facilities', originally comprised of the naval communications station at North West Cape, the early warning satellite ground station at Nurrungar and the ground control station for the CIA's geostationary signals intelligence (SIGINT) satellites

---

5    Australian Army, *Fundamentals of Land Warfare* (Canberra, Dec. 1998), at www.army.gov. au/Our-future/Publications/Key-Publications/Land-Warfare-Doctrine-1. See also Robert Garran, 'Army has Foreign Shores in its Sights', *Australian*, 4 Mar. 1999, p. 2; and 'Australia: Army Casts Eye at Offshore Ops', *Jane's Defence Weekly*, 7 Apr. 1999, pp. 30–33.

at Pine Gap, with only the latter in operation from 1999, constitute the strategic essence of the alliance. For Dibb, Pine Gap has not only provided Australia with extraordinary intelligence, it is also the essence of US extended deterrence guarantees. Moreover, hosting Pine Gap manifests Australia's interest in committing the United States to the Asia-Pacific region and encouraging the United States to act as a 'balancer' in the region and 'to check against hegemonic ambitions of a hostile major power'. Schreer observes that Dibb is 'a "classical realist" when it comes to alliance politics: he stresses the importance of values and traditions that tie the two allies together'.

As Schreer carefully recounts, however, Dibb has also expressed grave concerns about some aspects of the alliance. He has noted that the threat perceptions of the two allies are not always aligned, that 'the United States is a global power with a variety of interests, none of them centred on Australia', that 'there are potential situations where we would not expect the United States to commit combat forces on our behalf', and that America, as a unilateral power, had become dismissive of the norms of international behaviour. He was critical of George Bush's decision to invade Iraq in 2003, and of the Howard Government's willingness to support it. He accepts that there are costs and risks associated with the joint facilities (including the assessment that they likely ranked as Soviet nuclear targets during the Cold War).

Importantly, Dibb is a vigorous contestant of the view that US power is in decline and that Australia should be more 'accommodating' to the rising China. As he argued in 2011:

> We should not be in the business of accommodating China on key issues of our own security just because of some narrow mercantile views of the relationship. Neither should we eschew opportunities to enhance our longstanding alliance with the US because of premature notions of that great nation's decline.[6]

For Dibb, a rising China increases the need for Australia to tighten and strengthen its relationship with Washington.

Dibb began his career as a student of Soviet economic geography and the Soviet Union, and Russia since 1991, has remained a perennial interest. His first publication on the region, on the economics of

---

6    Paul Dibb, 'US Build-up No Threat to Peace', *Australian*, 15 Nov. 2011.

the Soviet wheat industry, was in 1966, now just on 50 years ago.[7] His widely acclaimed book on the Soviet Union as 'the incomplete superpower' was published 30 years ago in 1986.[8] He included Russia as a party to the emerging balance of power in Asia in his monograph published by the International Institute for Strategic Studies (IISS) in London in 1995, a time when other analysts (including Hugh White) thought that it could be omitted from relevant calculus.[9] In 2006, in an influential article published in Washington, he argued that 'the Bear is back'; that is, that Russia was making 'a comeback' as a major power, that it was already exhibiting the 'contemporary will to re-establish and reassert great power status', that Vladimir Putin had reversed its post-Soviet military decline, and that a resurgent Russia would be strong, assertive, unafraid of clashing with the North Atlantic Treaty Organization (NATO) and insistent on obtaining 'Russian dominance in its neighbourhood, especially in Ukraine, the Baltics and eastern Europe'.[10] He thought that Russia's invasion of Georgia in 2008 and its invasion of Ukraine and annexation of Crimea in March 2014 signified the return to 'a world where the sanctity of internationally recognised borders is ignored, the use of force is back in command and where a nuclear-armed major power acts with impunity in its own neighbourhood'.[11] He said in July 2014 that Putin acted from 'the traditional perspective of a former KGB colonel', and that his policies are imbued with 'a classical KGB colonel's deception, disguising (*maskirovka*) his true intent'.[12]

Hugh White, in Chapter 11, uses *The Soviet Union: The Incomplete Superpower* as a case study to elucidate Dibb's approach to 'unravelling the enigma of Soviet power' — a country at once 'weak and mighty', and its policies cloaked in deception. For Dibb, the fundamental methodological premise for understanding both Soviet motivations and capability developments was to see events as they would be

---

7    Paul Dibb, *The Economics of the Soviet Wheat Industry* (Canberra: Bureau of Agricultural Economics, 1966).

8    Paul Dibb, *The Soviet Union: The Incomplete Superpower* (London: International Institute for Strategic Studies and Macmillan, 1986).

9    Paul Dibb, *Towards a New Balance of Power in Asia*, Adelphi Paper No. 295 (London: International Institute for Strategic Studies, 1995).

10   Paul Dibb 'The Bear is Back', *The American Interest*, Vol. 2, No. 2, 1 Nov. 2006, pp. 78–85, www.the-american-interest.com/2006/11/01/the-bear-is-back/.

11   Paul Dibb, *The Geopolitical Implications of Russia's Invasion of Ukraine*, Centre of Gravity Paper, No. 16, Jun. (Canberra: Strategic and Defence Studies Centre, 2014).

12   Paul Dibb, 'Putin's Hand is All Over the MH17 Catastrophe', *Australian*, 21 July 2014.

perceived in Moscow — perceptions that 'are derived from unique cultural and historical traditions'. Central to these is a sense of its own weakness and vulnerability. Dibb's exploration of the 'weak' side of the equation identified the pressures that were so quickly to bring about the collapse of the Soviet Union. White concludes that assessment of a resurgent Russia must be based on appreciation of the 'resolve and determination, borne of the deep historical, cultural and geographical factors' that Dibb explained in *The Incomplete Superpower*.

As an avowed realist, Dibb regards power as the ultimate determinant of conflicts between nation-states involving their respective vital interests. Geographical considerations, involving the domains of both human geography (including economic parameters, demographic factors and political structures) and physical geography (borders and approaches, distances and major terrain features), are among the most important ingredients of national power. As Brendan Taylor says in Chapter 12, Dibb is a 'classical realist' in that he appreciates the importance of domestic economic and political dynamics in affecting social stability and shaping inter-state power dynamics.

Taylor is concerned in Chapter 12 with Dibb's analysis of the Asian balance of power and, most particularly, his Adelphi Paper entitled *Towards a New Balance of Power in Asia*, published by the IISS in 1995, which he regards as still being '*the* classic academic treatment of the Asian balance'. He is struck by the prevalence of Australian scholars in writings on this subject, notably Coral Bell, Hedley Bull and Hugh White as well as Dibb. He attributes this, 'first and foremost', to Australia's strategic geography and, in particular, its proximity to Asia. As Bell wrote in 1968, 'Australians are the only group of Westerners who must remain fully and inescapably vulnerable to the diplomatic stresses arising in Asia, on whose periphery they live or die'.[13] On the other hand, Australia's distance from the major powers in north-east Asia perhaps allows Australian scholars 'to look at the Asian balance more objectively and systematically' than scholars and practitioners from within that subregion. Taylor is impressed by the 'remarkable degree of prescience' in Dibb's analysis 'when seen in the context of the shifting power dynamics that are evident in Asia today'.

---

13    Coral Bell, *The Asian Balance of Power: A Comparison with European Precedents*, Adelphi Paper No. 44, Feb. (1968), p. 1.

He believes that Dibb's treatment of the Asian balance demonstrates the benefits of his 'crossbreeding' in government service/intelligence assessment and academic scholarship.

Dibb is unquestionably a 'passionate realist', but he is also a strong advocate of regional engagement and a dedicated participant in certain important multilateral processes. His involvement in regional diplomacy began, as Raoul Heinrichs and William T. Tow describe in Chapter 13, with bilateral intelligence exchanges and security dialogues with regional counterparts. For example, he initiated intelligence exchanges with the Chinese People's Liberation Army (PLA) in August 1978 (see Photo 2). He initiated the bilateral security dialogue between Australia and Japan in March 1990, when together with Admiral Alan Beaumont, Vice Chief of the Defence Force (VCDF), he led an Australian party to Tokyo for official talks. Australia became the second country, after the United States, with which Japan engaged in regular bilateral security dialogues. The initial talks were hosted by Yukio Satoh, then the director-general of the Information Analysis, Research and Planning Bureau in the Ministry of Foreign Affairs (MOFA), and one of Japan's foremost official exponents of multilateralism. The discussion was limited on the Japanese side to MOFA and Japan Defense Agency (JDA) civilians, as the JDA was at that stage unwilling to approve direct military–military talks between Japan's Self-Defense Forces (SDF) and other defence forces (apart from the United States). This series of exchanges, referred to as the Dibb–Beaumont talks, continued until 1995, when the Japanese side agreed to the institution of annual political–military and military–military consultations. The initial exchanges mainly involved assessments concerning the strategic nuclear balance between the United States and the Soviet Union and the implications of strategic arms control negotiations.[14]

In the early 1990s, as regional discourse about post-Cold War security arrangements boomed, Dibb invented the concept of Track 1.5 diplomacy to refer to bilateral and multilateral security agenda-setting and participation dialogues dominated by officials — participating in their private capacities.[15] In coining the term, he became an exemplar

---

14  Desmond Ball, 'Whither the Japan–Australia Security Relationship?', Nautilus Institute for Security and Sustainability, *APSNet Policy Forum*, 21 Sep. 2006, nautilus.org/apsnet/0632a-ball-html/.
15  See 'Track One-and-a-Half', in David Capie & Paul Evans, *The Asia-Pacific Security Lexicon* (Singapore: Institute of Southeast Asian Studies, 2002), pp. 211–12.

practitioner. He organised the first Australia–China bilateral Track 1.5 meeting in Beijing in 1992, at which he was accompanied by Rory Steele from Department of Foreign Affairs and Trade (DFAT) and Hugh White from the Office of National Assessments (ONA) (see Photo 16).

In 1994, he co-authored with Foreign Minister Gareth Evans the path-breaking *Australian Paper on Practical Proposals for Security Cooperation in the Asia Pacific Region*, which infused the concept paper adopted by the Association of Southeast Asian Nations (ASEAN) regional forum (ARF) at its second meeting in Brunei in August 1995. Since 2006, he has served as an Australian representative on the ARF Experts and Eminent Persons (EEP) group, where, Heinrichs and Tow note, 'he has been a tireless agitator for the need to approach Asia's multilateral security architecture in ways that lead from dialogue to practical cooperation'. In particular, 'he has worked assiduously to gain support for a regional "incidents at sea" accord'.[16] Complementing his expertise with respect to 'hard power', his contributions to regional diplomacy have been matched by few of his peers. His help to shape Australia's strategic position in the region, and the region's agenda for multilateral security cooperation, is truly an extraordinary legacy.

## Acknowledgements

The editors are indebted to Paul Dibb, who was supportive of this project from the outset. He provided most of the photographs reproduced herein.

We are grateful to Fairfax Media for permission to reproduce the cartoon of Paul (Photo 6) by Pascal Locanto, first published by the *Sydney Morning Herald* on 4 June 1986.

Our sincere thanks also to our copyeditor, Dr Justine Molony, for her meticulous work on the manuscript and preparing it for publication. We also wish to thank Raoul Heinrichs, a teacher and research scholar in the Strategic and Defence Studies Centre, who provided research assistance for several of the contributors, including Kim Beazley, Benjamin Schreer, Brendan Taylor and Hugh White.

---

16    Paul Dibb, 'Treaty May Steer China, Japan to Safer Waters', *Australian*, 1 Apr. 2013.

# 1

# Introducing Paul Dibb (1): Britain's Loss, Australia's Gain

Allan Hawke

Emeritus Professor Paul Dibb AM is notoriously protective of his private life, so this introductory note tries to give some insight into the man behind the legend without trespassing too far into his privacy.

In a reflection on his own life as an intellectual, Des Ball quoted Karl Mannheim's explanation that it is difficult for intellectuals to separate their work and domestic domains. In a veiled reference to the price that is sometimes exacted in personal relationships, Des went on to say that thinking doesn't stop at home in the evenings or on weekends.[1]

Paul was appointed a Member of the Order of Australia (AM) on Australia Day 1989 for 'public service'. He has made a sustained, significant and enduring contribution to defence, intelligence and national security for over 30 years.

The articles that follow showcase this claim, although much of his work in the intelligence area is necessarily not in the public arena. They provide a glimpse of his intellect, analytical skills, lectures and writing in all these fields.

---

1    Desmond Ball, 'Reflections of a Defence Intellectual', in Brij V. Lal & Alison Ley (eds), *The Coombs: A House of Memories*, 2nd edn (Canberra: ANU Press, 2014), p. 149.

When I was a teenager, my father (who Paul knew when they were in the Department of Trade) took me out to the laundry, filled a bucket with water, put my arm in it up to the elbow and then removed it. He said, 'Son, that's the mark that most men leave on the world'. Not so with Paul. One measure of the worth and legacy that Paul will leave can be found in the calibre of the authors in this testimonial — a veritable galaxy of people whose life work has been devoted to serving Australia's defence and national interests.

I first met Paul in 1985 when the Defence Secretary, Sir William Cole, asked me to make the necessary arrangements for the *Review of Australia's Defence Capabilities*, better known as the Dibb Review.[2]

We have been colleagues, collaborators and mates ever since — even after my remarks at his 60th birthday at the Burrawang pub — and we have shared dinners and visits in Canberra and at his Robertson farm together with Paul's spouse Rhondda Nicholas.

Defence Minister Kim Beazley described Paul's work as '... the most important appraisal of Australia's Defence capabilities since the end of World War Two'. The 1987 White Paper, *The Defence of Australia*, written largely by Paul, set the standard for those that have followed. The conceptual architecture of the self-reliant Defence of Australia (DOA) doctrine, which Paul developed then, still stands Australia in good stead and should remain the basis for future capability reviews and force-structure decisions.

Fast forward to 1991 when I was transitioning from Deputy Director of the Defence Signals Directorate to succeed Paul as Deputy Secretary (Strategy and Intelligence) in Defence. I had the great fortune to be the 'roadie' on Paul's farewell world tour before he left Defence in July 1991 to become head of The Australian National University's (ANU) Strategic and Defence Studies Centre (SDSC).

The legendary Sir Arthur Tange said in support of Paul's appointment that he had 'rare versatility' and 'there is none inside or outside the Defence community better equipped at present to understand the issues in contention and the policy choices'. Rare praise indeed from the Great Mandarin.

---

2    Paul Dibb, *Review of Australia's Defence Capabilities*, report to the Minister for Defence (Canberra: Australian Government Publishing Service, 1986).

After doing the rounds of the Washington agencies and departments, where Paul inter alia reprised his work and influence on US officials about the Soviet Union, we flew into Manchester airport on a Friday evening with three day's grace before a set of appointments in London.

We based ourselves in York from where, as fellow members of the High Church of England, we attended the evening service at York Minster seated in the bishop's row of chairs. We also undertook a pilgrimage to Beverley to call on Paul's Uncle Jack and Aunty Paula. Jack, who was on his last legs suffering from emphysema, got out of bed, took off his oxygen mask and came to the lounge room where he promptly lit a cigarette while sharing a large glass of whisky with us. There were tears all round when we departed for dinner at Paul's mother's house.

While in York, we took a side trip to have a look at the UK–US intelligence base at Menwith Hill. We got lost when going there and pulled in to a housing estate to seek directions from an old lady who was walking along the street. 'Oh you mean spy base', she said in a broad Yorkshire accent and pointed the way. Almost as soon as we arrived and drove around the outskirts, we were pulled over by the police, questioned about why we were there and asked to show our passports (which we didn't have with us).

On arriving in London to see the head of UK Government Communications Headquarters, Sir John Adye, we found that our visit had already been reported to him, leading to some friendly banter about the different arrangements with the United States between the UK and Australian joint facilities.

A further call on Sir Malcolm McIntosh, the Australian-born head of the UK Procurement Office, led to an exchange where Malcolm in his broadest Australian accent said, 'On behalf of her Majesty's United Kingdom Government, I have to tell you ...' Paul, reverting to his Yorkshire accent, replied, 'Well, I'm authorised to tell you that the Australian Government ...'.

Paul, an only child, was born on 3 October 1939. His mother Ethel who was 'in service' as a maid to a local solicitor was evacuated — from Hull where they lived during the war — to live with her sister while awaiting Paul's arrival. We paid homage by visiting 4 William Street in Fryston, the coalmining village where Paul was born.

Ethel's marriage to Paul's father, Cyril — a trolley-bus driver who died in the early 1970s — didn't last and she remarried Alec Harbottle who was a Merchant Navy captain during the Second World War. After the war, Alec resumed his occupation as a coalminer, becoming a pit bottom deputy. When Paul was 17, Alec took him down the pit, following which, the experience having the desired effect, coalmining was taken off Paul's list of possible careers.

After Tanshelf primary school at Pontefract, Paul sat an examination known as the Eleven Plus that, together with an IQ test, determined whether one could go on to high school. If you did not succeed on those tests, your fate was to be a coalminer, bus driver or tradesman. Paul passed and went on to the state grammar Kings School at Pontefract.

From Kings School, Paul won a County Exhibition Scholarship to undertake a Bachelor of Arts in economics and geography with honours, graduating from Nottingham University in 1960. Following university, Paul became an apprentice manager at a Midland's chrome component factory for motor vehicles, which may well have been where he got his taste for fast cars!

The Careers and Appointments Board of Nottingham University had advised Paul that, as he had not been to Eton or Harrow, Cambridge or Oxford, any application of his for the civil service would not succeed. Paul went ahead and applied to become an administrative graduate trainee only to receive a rejection letter saying that he shouldn't bother to apply again in the future. Britain's loss was to turn out to be Australia's gain.

The son of the owner of an Australian company that was bought by Paul's employer was sent to the England to learn the ropes. Over a few sherbets one evening, he took Paul aside and asked why he was wasting his time working in the factory when he could come to Melbourne. Paul's response was that Australia was on the other side of the world and it was all desert.

At this point, serendipity played its role in Paul's future in the form him noticing an advertisement in a national newspaper calling for British subjects to join the Australian Commonwealth Public Service and offering a salary 50 per cent higher than Paul was being paid. He landed a job with the Department of Trade and, in return for a three-year bond, the Dibb family's relocation was paid for by the Australian Government.

Mr P. Dibb BA with Mrs Dibb and child left Tilbury Docks on 30 November 1961, a dreary, grey and foggy winter day, travelling first class on the SS *Orcades* with one suitcase and little money. Side trips to Gibraltar, Naples and Pompeii followed before transiting the Suez Canal, Aden and Colombo, arriving in Fremantle at the start of a blazing hot summer where the family were surprised to see local urchins running around in bare feet and shorts.

Paul can still remember his first encounter with the aroma of melting-hot road tar on the street outside the Adelaide railway station as they were on their way to Sydney, six weeks after their departure from England.

The family moved to Canberra to begin their new life in Hovell Street, Griffith, and in January 1962 Paul started as a Research Officer Grade 1 on the UK desk of the Department of Trade at a time when the imperial ties between Australia and the mother country were unravelling as Britain joined the Common Market. Paul worked with a number of Australian luminaries, including Max Moore-Wilton, during the period from 1962 to 1967.

In 1965, Paul joined Stuart Harris, the senior economist at the Bureau of Agricultural Economics (BAE), as a Class 8 to write a paper on the economics of the Soviet wheat industry. Coincidentally, I was also at the BAE at this time from November 1965 to March 1966, when I began my undergraduate degree at ANU. Paul's paper was published in 1966,[3] leading the US Department of Agriculture to observe that it was the best paper ever on the subject. This period continued Paul's long-term interest in the Soviet Union, which had been piqued during his university studies.

After a short stint in 1967 as a Class 9 working directly for George Warwick Smith, the Secretary of the Territories Department, on the independence negotiations for Nauru, Paul was enticed to ANU in 1968 to be a research fellow in the Research School of Social Sciences (RSSS) and to work with Harry Rigby, one of the top ten Soviet specialists in the world at that time. That led to Paul's book, *Siberia and the Pacific: A Study in Economic Development and Trade Prospects*.

---

3    Paul Dibb, *The Economics of the Soviet Wheat Industry: An Economic Study of the Structure, Trends and Problems from 1953 to 1965 with a Perspective to 1970* (Canberra: Bureau of Agricultural Economics, 1966).

From there, Paul went to work for Bob Furlonger in the Joint Intelligence Organisation (JIO) in Defence in 1970 in the Directorate of Economic Intelligence. In 1972, Paul moved to the National Assessments Staff (NAS) (the forerunner of Office of National Assessments (ONA)), becoming head of that office in 1974. Then, in 1980, Bill Pritchett, secretary of Defence, appointed Paul as senior assistant secretary of Strategic Policy.

In 1981, Bob O'Neill poached Paul back to ANU to write *The Soviet Union: The Incomplete Superpower*, for which he was awarded a PhD in 1988.[4] The first edition of the book on this subject was published in 1986, followed by a second edition in 1988.

Paul's status as Emeritus Professor of Strategic Studies at ANU is a fitting tribute to the continuing pre-eminence of his work. His Russian expertise is again at the fore, given recent developments in Russia and Vladimir Putin's ambitions, while his considered views on the rise of China are also increasingly important.

Indeed, another measure of the man lies in the nine years that he has spent as Australia's representative on the Association of Southeast Asian Nations (ASEAN) regional forum Experts and Eminent Persons Group, which he now co-chairs with Singapore.

It's no accident that ministers and parliamentarians of different political persuasions, ministerial staff, senior officials and think tanks (at home and abroad) have sought Paul's counsel (and continue to do so) on defence, foreign affairs and national security matters.

It's a particular privilege that I know Paul's adult children (a daughter and a son), and he has two grandsons, one of whom shares his passion for high performance cars in his work for the Red Bull Formula One racing team.

I'm proud to be a mate and very much appreciate the opportunity to provide this context on a modern-day giant — a, if not *the*, doyen of his field.

Current and future scholars who aspire to that honorific would do well to study and digest the lessons herein.

---

4    Paul Dibb, *The Soviet Union: The Incomplete Superpower* (London: International Institute for Strategic Studies and Macmillan, 1986).

# 2

# Introducing Paul Dibb (2): An Enriching Experience

Chris Barrie

I am very pleased to have been asked to provide an introductory note about Emeritus Professor Paul Dibb AM. However, even though I regard Paul as a close friend, I possess nothing like the detailed knowledge of Allan Hawke, who has worked with Paul over many years and shared many triumphs and a few disappointments with him as well. Also, I am not sure what to make of a geographer who, at one time in his early years, may have thought that Australia was 'all desert'!

I joined The Australian National University's (ANU) Strategic and Defence Studies Centre (SDSC) in 2003 as a visiting fellow. This was principally because Paul encouraged, and arranged, the needful for me to do so. Since that time we have worked together on a range of projects and that work, as well as a number of social engagements, has given me an insight into a wonderfully complex and interesting world that revolves around Paul's interests, of which there are many!

Before coming to SDSC, however, my first meeting with Paul occurred just before the delivery of his highly regarded *Review of Australia's Defence Capabilities* (Dibb Review). At that time, in 1985, I headed up the Royal Australian Navy's Tactical School (RANTACS) in Sydney. Paul had been seconded from his position at SDSC to undertake the review but, as a relatively junior Navy officer at the time, I certainly knew that Paul was an important person who was to be treated with proper respect. The Navy 'positioning' team, headed by Captain Adrian Cummins, had decided that the way to make an impression on Paul about the importance of the Navy's ambitions would be to get him to RANTACS where we could demonstrate all the wizardry of a modern navy and persuade him that his review should underscore the critical part a navy should play in the nation's strategic affairs, in peace and in war.

My strong recollection of that day was that Paul asked some hard questions of the Navy team (and I was not sure that we put our right foot forward). More positively, though, it seemed to me that, despite being a person of serious consequence, Paul was easy to get on with.

As history now records, the Dibb Review made a great deal of the critical importance of Australia's maritime approaches and the role a competent and properly structured navy and air force would play in providing the essential elements of the nation's defence.

Since that meeting I watched from the sidelines as Paul took on various other important responsibilities in the Defence organisation, including the preparation of the 1987 White Paper on *The Defence of Australia*. While I was unclear on the detailed responsibilities of these roles, I could not fail to observe that Paul was moving into increasingly more important positions as time went on ...

It was in the later years of my own career that I came to understand the nature and quality of the work in which Paul was engaged; it seemed he was successful in undertaking whatever task the government or secretary of the day wanted done! But, I knew very little about his work at the university.

In 2002 I retired to Oxford for just over 12 months after moving from being the Chief of the Defence Force, leaving Allan Hawke in charge of things at Defence. But, after 12 months of running down a sizeable portion of my pension lump sum in Oxford, I contacted Paul to see whether or not I could return to Canberra and perhaps work at SDSC. For me this would see a transition away from strategic leadership issues to taking a closer interest in strategic matters in Australia. It also goes without saying, I guess, that the events of 2003, which centred on the invasion of Saddam Hussein's Iraq, transformed many of our assumptions about the way in which we might manage our relationships with a wider world.

My proposal was taken on with considerable enthusiasm, which — as I came to learn over the following years — is typical of the Dibb approach to those things in which he is interested or that challenge him. So it came to be that I was able to take up a visiting fellowship with SDSC in December 2003.

What have I discerned about Paul from that time?

Well, first of all, how lucky have we been in Australia to have the talents of 'a lad from Yorkshire' working on strategic affairs and in our intelligence community? His achievements in Australia almost certainly could not have been matched by a similar career if he had remained in the United Kingdom. To put it bluntly, Paul was simply born on the wrong side of the tracks! We were also fortunate that he came to Australia early enough in his career to carve out a special niche for his skills and talents.

Having been recruited in the United Kingdom to work in the Department of Overseas Trade as a young man, it was not long before he began to leave his mark. In all this time he has worked assiduously to build a reputation of extraordinary significance: as an academic, as a strategist, and as an intelligence czar.

After becoming a highly qualified and effective public servant, Paul's impact on the making of public policy, especially in the defence field in the 1980s and 1990s, was superior, and yet he also carved out an outstanding career in academia through his work at SDSC, especially as head of Centre from 1991 to 2003.[1]

It was Paul's deep experience as a policy maker that I am sure underpinned his determination to fight to secure and maintain the critically important work of SDSC when there were forces at work seeking to undermine him, and the work of the Centre, inside the academic bureaucracy that was ANU at the time. What is highly

---

1    This aspect of Paul's career is spelled out in Meredith Thatcher and Desmond Ball's *A National Asset: Essays Commemorating the 40th Anniversary of the Strategic and Defence Studies Centre*, Canberra Paper No. 165 (Canberra: Strategic and Defence Studies Centre, 2006).

relevant to this part of the story was his steely offer to remove the SDSC from ANU campus and place it elsewhere if its position was seriously threatened by the forces of darkness.

In his recent history he has worked with the Association of Southeast Asian Nations (ASEAN) regional forum, served as adviser to the Defence SA Advisory Board, and been a consultant to ministers from both major parties, the departments of Defence and of Foreign Affairs and Trade (DFAT), companies and foreign missions.

Another aspect of Paul's deep commitment to his trade in the strategic studies field is underscored by his unwavering presence each year at The Australian National University's Kioloa Coastal Campus during which students in the Masters programs have an opportunity to bond together as a cohort and use this time to speak informally to the Centre's academic staff. Paul is admirably serious about this aspect of his academic life. On a lighthearted note, the coastal campus routine has been embellished by Paul's enthusiasm for a stop at the Nelligen pub, where a few dozen recently caught oysters are bought for later consumption, matched by fine wine and, if we are really lucky, Yorkshire chip butties! What I have seen indicates that Paul sees young people with potential as being worth his time in nurturing, encouraging and mentoring.

Finally, Paul speaks occasionally of dropping some of his workload. I appreciate that time pressures prompt this train of thought, but I have seen little evidence that he really means it. Instead, he continues to maintain a vigorous and punishing schedule of public lectures, advisory positions, and media publishing, either on his own cognisance or collaboratively.

Since coming to SDSC I have very much enjoyed sharing in Paul's love of good food and quality red wine, as well as hearing his perspectives on a raft of issues. As we mark Paul's long contribution to SDSC and the Australian defence discourse, highlighted in the articles in this collection, I believe we have all been enriched by the experience of working together in the company of such a fine intellect.

# 3

# Getting to Know Paul Dibb: An Overview of an Extraordinary Career

Desmond Ball

This chapter, which provides a brief overview of some of the major milestones in Paul Dibb's varied career interspersed with personal reminiscence, is intended to convey the extraordinary breadth of his achievements and contributions, and to better understand the character and personality that has provided the agency for these achievements.

My first recollections of Paul go back to the mid- to late 1970s, or around 40 years ago, when Paul was head of the National Assessments Staff (NAS), which was part of the Joint Intelligence Organisation (JIO) but serving the National Intelligence Committee (NIC) (and hence often called the NIC–NAS), and the forerunner to the Office of National Assessments (ONA). He became Deputy Director (Civilian) of the JIO in 1978. I first heard about him from three people who were important figures in the early stages of his career.

One was Harry Rigby, a professor at The Australian National University (ANU) and an internationally recognised scholar of the Soviet Union and especially the Communist Party of the Soviet Union (CPSU). Paul's work on the Soviet economy had impressed Rigby when Paul was a research fellow in the Department of Political Science in the Research

School of Social Sciences (RSSS) and then the Department of Human Geography in the Research School of Pacific Studies (RSPacS) at ANU in 1968–70. Paul's first major book, *Siberia and the Pacific: A Study in Economic Development and Trade Prospects*, published in 1972.[1]

The second was Bruce Miller, the head of the Department of International Relations at ANU. He participated as a member of a small group of academics in regular weekly meetings with Paul and other NAS staff during the preparation of the foundational study *The Environment of the 1980s*, completed in 1971. This was an exercise in forecasting in such areas as the global strategic balance, nuclear proliferation, developments in military and non-military (including transportation and communications) technologies, world energy requirements, and regional economic and political developments. It delineated the framework from within which strategic documentation over the next decade was derived.

The third was Bob Mathams, then the Director of Scientific and Technical Intelligence in JIO and a good friend of the Centre, later serving through the 1980s on the Centre's Advisory Board. In 1966, Mathams became the principal interlocutor with the CIA regarding selection of Pine Gap for the construction of the ground control station for the CIA's innovative new geostationary signals intelligence (SIGINT) satellites, then code-named 'Rhyolite', which were designed to intercept, inter alia, the telemetry generated in Soviet ballistic missile and other advanced weapons tests. Matham replaced E.L.D. White, the head of the Defence Science Division in the Department of Defence, as head of the site selection team. This program gave Australia a central role in maintenance of the global strategic balance and, at a personal level, forged connections between Australian defence and intelligence officials and the hierarchy of the CIA's Deputy Director, Science and Technology (DDS&T), the so-called 'wizards of Langley' — men such as Albert 'Bud' Wheelon, Carl Duckett and Leslie C. Dirks.[2]

I really got to know Paul in the early 1980s, when we both drank at the National Press Club, helping, through its bar takings, to establish the club as a national institution. Paul was usually there together

---

1    Paul Dibb, *Siberia and the Pacific: A Study in Economic Development and Trade Prospects* (New York: Praeger, 1972).

2    Jeffrey T. Richelson, *The Wizards of Langley: Inside the CIA's Directorate of Science and Technology* (Boulder, Colorado: Westview Press, 2001), p. 109.

with his great mate Jim Clapham, talking about cars, current political events (for Jim was an avid consumer of the daily media), car tyres, car engines, rpms, and other things about cars. He was also often joined by another good friend, Don Marshall, or 'the sheriff', then the head of the Australian Security Intelligence Organisation's (ASIO) Canberra regional office. Paul later brought Marshall over to Defence to head the Defence Security Branch and, in particular, to quietly abolish its malfunctioning Office of Special Clearances and Records (OSCAR).

In those days, Lev Sergeyevich Koshlyakov, the KGB resident in Canberra also used to drink at the Press Club with Paul, Clapham and Marshall, intermingling with journalists such as Brian Toohey, Bill Pinwill and Mungo MacCallum — every one of them more or less drunk as the evenings wore on. It was a fascinating scene and, while I never knew how much of it had been scripted by Paul and Marshall, I'm sure a lot of it had.

It was at the Press Club, later in the 1980s, that I first met Rhondda Nicholas; she and Paul had started to get to know each other when Rhondda was head of the Papua New Guinea and South Pacific Policy Section in Defence. Incidentally, they later wrote a book together, *Restructuring the Papua New Guinea Defence Force* (1996).[3]

Paul came back to ANU as a senior research fellow in the Department of International Relations in 1981, and then transferred to Strategic and Defence Studies Centre (SDSC) in 1984, becoming its deputy head. This was when he wrote his prescient study *The Soviet Union: The Incomplete Superpower*, first published in 1986,[4] which he regards as his single most important work.

In February 1985 he took leave from ANU to serve as a ministerial consultant to Kim Beazley, and completed his *Review of Australia's Defence Capabilities*, commonly known as the Dibb Review, in

---

3    Paul Dibb & Rhondda Nicholas, *Restructuring the Papua New Guinea Defence Force: Strategic Analysis and Force Structure Principles for a Small State*, report to the Minister for Defence of Papua New Guinea (Canberra: Strategic and Defence Studies Centre, 1996).
4    Paul Dibb, *The Soviet Union: The Incomplete Superpower* (London: International Institute for Strategic Studies and Macmillan, 1986).

June 1986.[5] He then returned to Defence, initially as Director of JIO (1986–88) and then as the Deputy Secretary (Strategy and Intelligence) from 1988 to 1991.

With regard to the strategy side of his portfolio, Paul's primary responsibility was to exercise oversight and direction of implementation of the 1987 White Paper *The Defence of Australia* with respect to force-structure acquisitions and operational concepts for controlling the sea–air gap and thus effecting the defence of Australia on a self-reliant basis. One of the responsibilities of the Deputy Secretary (Strategy and Intelligence) was to chair the Force Structure Committee, which approved new capital acquisitions. Paul regards this as having been his most powerful job, rather than either the strategic policy or intelligence dimensions. It was not easy to persuade the Services of the necessity of according new capability proposals with strategic guidance. The biggest fight was with the Navy, which wanted larger and more capable frigates than the ANZAC-class that Paul proposed. Paul won that fight, although he lost the argument about the size of the guns they would carry (five-inches rather than his recommended three-inches). Paul believes that the most important force-structure project he recommended to government was the *Jindalee* over-the-horizon radar system, about which the Royal Australian Air Force (RAAF) was unenthusiastic and that mired the Defence Science and Technology Organisation (DSTO) in technical matters.

On the intelligence side, he had considerable difficulties with the Defence Signals Directorate (DSD) hierarchy in Melbourne and, in particular, DSD's Director Tim James. In 1990, Paul, and thence the Secretary, Tony Ayres, learned that DSD maintained some SIGINT 'compartments' from which they and the Minister for Defence were excluded. As a result, they were persuaded that 'DSD's primary allegiance was to the UKUSA SIGINT community rather than Australia's policy priorities'. Ayres and Paul resolved that the DSD HQ should be moved to Canberra and, together with Allan Hawke, who was then the Deputy Director of DSD, they planned the construction of Building M in the Russell Hill complex in Canberra to which DSD's activities and records would be relocated. The move was strongly resisted by James, who argued that 'no-one would come from Melbourne', but who was

---

5    Paul Dibb, *Review of Australia's Defence Capabilities*, report to the Minister for Defence (Canberra: Australian Government Publishing Service, 1986).

really intent on preserving his operational autonomy. This is when Paul worked most closely with Hawke. (Hawke succeeded Dibb as Deputy Secretary (Strategy and Intelligence) in 1991.)

Paul also had important roles in the 'modernisation' of New Zealand's SIGINT capabilities. In the late 1970s, when he was Deputy Director of JIO (Civilian), he was involved in assisting the development of the NZ Government Communications Security Bureau (GCSB), which was established in 1977. He participated in discussions with GCSB about the establishment of a new SIGINT station at Tangimoana, equipped with a large *Pusher*-type circularly disposed antenna array (CDAA) for HF interception and direction-finding, which was to operate as part of the UKUSA naval ocean surveillance system. (Similar CDAAs were installed in the mid-1970s at DSD stations at the RAAF Base Pearce, near Perth; Cabarlah near Toowoomba; and Shoal Bay near Darwin.) In 1987–89, as Director of JIO and then Deputy Secretary (Strategy and Intelligence), he was directly involved with GCSB concerning the planning and development of the foreign satellite/communications satellite (FORNSAT/COMSAT) interception station at Waihopai, which has a close operational relationship with the Australian Defence Satellite Communications Station at Kojarena, near Geraldton.

Dibb also served during 1988–91 as the chief Australian interlocutor with the United States with respect to the joint facilities, including with the CIA and the National Reconnaissance Office (NRO) in the case of Pine Gap and the Rhyolite satellites and their successors. (Organisationally, CIA SIGINT and imaging satellites comprised the NRO's Program B). His prime responsibility was to ensure that all activities at Pine Gap were conducted with the 'full knowledge and concurrence' of the Defence Minister, which was to be guaranteed not only by the placement of Australians in all parts of the operations areas at the ground station but also the requirement that Australia approve all changes to the bore-sight of the intercept antennas, and hence the collection targets, of the satellites. He had been 'briefed into' (or 'indoctrinated into') the joint facilities in November 1974, when he became head of the NAS, a process directed by Mathams. One of the first matters with which he was involved was the preparation of draft advice for the Minister, in 1975, regarding a US proposal to target a Rhyolite satellite on the Soviet naval base and communications centre at Berbera, in north-west Somalia, on the Gulf of Aden. (Paul retained all his relevant clearances until 2004, a remarkable 30 years.) On the

US side, he dealt with Leslie Dirks, who succeeded Carl Duckett as DDS&T and head of Program B in 1976, and Richard Evans Hineman, who succeeded Dirks in 1982. He knew Milton Corley Wonus, the CIA Station Chief in Canberra in 1975–80. Wonus, who had joined DDS&T in 1963, later served as Director of the Office of SIGINT Operations in DDS&T, the office in charge of operating the Pine Gap ground station.[6]

In 1990–91, as shown in photos 7 and 8, Paul was recognised by the NRO for his 'outstanding support of US–Australian space cooperation' and, in particular, for his support of its Program B during his period as Deputy Secretary (Strategy and Intelligence) in 1988–91.

Paul is intensely loyal towards his adopted country. He is a nationalist and he loves Australia. As the geographic heart of his concepts for Australian strategic policy and defence planning, he found it natural to provide unequivocal representation of Australia's interests in the UK–USA intelligence cooperation councils. He was, despite his origins, in no sense beholden to his British counterparts. As Hawke relates in Chapter 1, he was quick to note during his last official visit to London in 1991 that he represented the Australian Government, and certainly not the British establishment, which had excluded him from its ranks.

I began sounding Paul out about possible interest in heading SDSC in mid-1989. I was frustrated with administration, which was undoubtedly less arduous than in more recent times, for which I was clearly unsuited. Somewhat to my surprise, for this involved a major career change and a commitment to academia rather than a temporary stay, Paul warmed to the idea. In July 1989 at the National Defence Seminar at Canungra, which was sponsored by Kim Beazley as Minister for Defence and General Peter Gration as Chief of the Defence Force (CDF), I asked the Minister what he thought about the proposition, and he gave it his blessing.

The references that the university solicited for Paul's appointment to a special professorship at ANU and headship of the centre were exceptional in their judgements. Sir Arthur Tange, commenting on Paul's 'rare versatility', said that as Deputy Director (Civilian) and later Director of JIO and Deputy Secretary (Strategy and Intelligence) he had 'done much to redirect the activities of the intelligence community

---

6   Richelson, *The Wizards of Langley* (2001), pp. 295–97.

to matters more closely related to the practical defence interests of the country'; and asserted that on defence policy issues 'there is none inside or outside the Defence Community better equipped at present to understand the issues in contention and the policy choices', and that Paul had exhibited remarkable 'courage in arguing with the Services about their own business [i.e. weapons acquisition]'. He also, I might add, could not resist using his reference for Paul to make some caustic remarks about myself, saying that I had evinced 'some imbalance in the choice of subjects of study', including the joint facilities 'which successive American and Australian Governments have deemed it a national interest' to keep secret, and expressing relief that I would no longer be heading the Centre. Gareth Evans said that 'Dr Dibb's intellectual capacities ... are among the most outstanding of the public servants I have encountered in this area of Government'. Gration commented on Paul's 'intellectual rigour', and noted that he had 'a unique blend of academic experience and real life strategic policy making, where theoretically attractive concepts have to be tempered with practical realities' and that he had 'a mature understanding of the capabilities, aspirations and limitations of the armed forces as instruments of national policy'. Admiral Ron Hays, who had just retired from the post of US Commander in Chief, Pacific, said he was 'by American standards, a national asset'. Michael MccGwire of the Brookings Institution in Washington said that he had 'earned a first class [international] reputation'. By this time, 1991, Paul had written two books, two major government reports, and more than 30 chapters and articles in scholarly books and journals.

Paul officially became head of the SDSC in October 1991, and went on to be its longest-serving head, passing Bob O'Neill's tenure in 1971–82 by a few months. He officially retired as head in February 2003, but went upstairs to chair the SDSC Advisory Board. The Centre took some hard knocks in the 1990s, as we suffered from the vicissitudes of dependence on funding from external sources and, more painfully felt, cuts in the Centre's university funding and a shift in school priorities, which decimated most of our work on Australian defence. It tested all of Paul's skills in academic diplomacy. But it did not diminish his productivity. He published an Adelphi Paper for the International Institute for Strategic Studies (IISS) on the emerging balance of power in Asia in 1995, and path-breaking articles on the revolution in military affairs in Asia, the US alliance, and Australian defence policy. He has also done substantial work, including studies of various sectors of Australian defence industry, that is not for publication.

Essential personal characteristics emerge from a review of Paul's career, apart from his high motivation and propensity for hard work. First, he places a high value on mateship, reinforced by regular eating and drinking sessions at restaurants in inner Canberra or at his farm at Robertson, with his closest mates (who include both current and former senior figures in the intelligence community). Second, he is proud to be an Australian and has, perhaps, even been thrilled that he could represent Australia's intelligence and defence interests so well. There are undoubtedly close connections between some aspects of his strong desire to preserve a high degree of personal privacy and his carriage of Australia's top intelligence secrets.

Third, like the Berlin–Ayson hedgehog, he can be very protective, even possessive, about his core ideas. As Ayson says, Paul can be 'intimidating to those unfortunate enough to get in his way'. Indeed, he can be blunt, even combative. I, for example, was the cause of his great displeasure when I openly disagreed with a couple of basic themes in the Dibb Review, and suggested that the policy of 'denial' needed to be complemented by capabilities for counter-offensive operations. I also stated that the review accorded insufficient attention to Australia's long-range strike requirements and under-valued the F-111s; I felt that the assumptions about 'warning time' were too sanguine.[7] I sometimes shudder when he characterises some of our academic colleagues, or the officials in a certain government department concerned with foreign affairs, or our allies across the sea to the south-east (notwithstanding his appreciation of the very close and mutually fruitful cooperation between DSD and GCSB in the SIGINT field).

How are these key characteristics of his personality — the mateship, the bluntness, the outspokenness, the combativeness — best explained? I think that there is still a fair dose of his upbringing in the Yorkshire coalmining villages in him.

---

7    Desmond Ball, 'Notes on Paul Dibb's *Review of Australia's Defence Capabilities*', notes prepared for an address at the Chief of the Defence Force's Exercise, Australian Defence Force Academy, Reference Paper No. 143, Strategic and Defence Studies Centre, The Australian National University, Canberra, 26–27 August 1986.

# 4

# Scholar, Spy, Passionate Realist

Geoffrey Barker

Paul Dibb understands the international concern over Islamist terrorism, but he retains a clear historical and strategic perspective on it: 'It's just plain nonsense to compare terrorism with the dangers of global nuclear war between the USSR and the US in the 1970s and 1980s, which would have wiped out 180 million people in the first 24 hours,' he says: 'That was not some theoretical threat, as those of us who had to live with it knew only too well. It was a very real global threat to the existence of the human race.'

Dibb is well qualified to rate and to compare the gravity of threats to Australia and the world. Throughout his distinguished career in Australia's defence, academic and intelligence establishments, he has been privy to the deepest anxieties of Western powers and to their darkest secrets in the Cold War years. Intellectually he is a balance-of-power realist whose approach to security issues essentially matches those of Hans Morgenthau, George Kennan and Henry Kissinger. He has engaged directly and personally with Australia's Soviet and Chinese communist adversaries and with Australia's Asian neighbours, friendly and hostile; he has studied the pathologies lurking in the international system, advising governments and teaching students how to understand and manage the threats to global peace and security.

Dibb is perhaps best known as the author of the 1986 *Review of Australia's Defence Capabilities* (Dibb Review), which fundamentally recast national defence policy by refocusing defence finance and force structure on the defence of Australia and on defence self-reliance. In the same year he published his groundbreaking study *The Soviet Union: The Incomplete Superpower*,[1] one of the first books to argue that the apparently awesome Soviet Union faced internal problems that could lead to instability and deepening crisis, although he also argued (perhaps too cautiously) that 'the Soviet system is not likely to collapse'. Formidably energetic and hardworking, Dibb still produces characteristically acerbic academic papers and newspaper articles. He continues to give lectures and seminars, to make media appearances, and to represent Australia at international forms including the Association of Southeast Asian Nations (ASEAN) regional forum (ARF) Experts and Eminent Persons (EEP) group.

His work with the Australian Security Intelligence Organisation (ASIO) in the dangerous world of Cold War counterespionage is less well-known. So is his personal and professional relationship with the late Don Marshall, ASIO's charismatic counterespionage chief. Some of that story can be told now. Born in 1939, Dibb was just 25 when he was introduced to the shadowy world of counterespionage. It was 1964 and, had he seen the future, he would have been astonished to see himself closely involved in counterespionage activities until the eve of the collapse of the Soviet Union in 1991.

In the mid-1960s, Dibb was a junior officer in the Bureau of Agricultural Economics (BAE) in Canberra researching prospects for wheat sales to the Soviet Union. A new recruit to the Australian public service from the United Kingdom, Dibb held a degree economics and geography, including Russian studies, from Nottingham University, spoke Russian, and admired Russian culture (especially music) as much as he abhorred Soviet communism. Australia was a place of infinite possibilities for a bright lad from the Yorkshire market town of Pontefract, which had been besieged three times by the Parliamentarians during the English civil war in the 17th century. The son of a coalminer, he had been rejected by the British foreign office because of his humble class origins and his Yorkshire accent, and because he had not been

---

1    Paul Dibb, *The Soviet Union: The Incomplete Superpower* (London: International Institute for Strategic Studies and Macmillan, 1986).

to Oxford or Cambridge universities. England's loss was Australia's gain when he arrived in Sydney in 1964 before heading for his job in Canberra.

His espionage career started innocently enough with an authorised visit to the Soviet Embassy to collect Soviet trade statistics publications for his research. Soon afterwards a supervisor told him that ASIO wanted to talk to him. Dibb guessed ASIO had observed his embassy visit and assumed the spy agency wanted his estimate of the Soviet wheat crop for the year. (This work brought Dibb to the notice of trade minister John 'Black Jack' McEwen: his correct estimate that Australia would be able to sell wheat to the Soviets, providing a major windfall for wheat farmers, pleased Black Jack very much indeed.)

But ASIO was not interested in Soviet wheat production figures. It wanted Dibb to do something infinitely more sensitive and potentially dangerous — to cultivate Moscow's diplomats in Australia with the view to obtaining information and, ultimately, persuading one of them to defect. The approach was made to him at a pub in north Canberra by the rising star in ASIO counterespionage, who was known throughout the organisation as DRM: Donald Ralph Marshall.

Marshall was a gregarious man of White Russian background born in China. He spoke with a serious stammer, which he told Dibb resulted from having seen a Japanese soldier bash out the brains of his baby sister against a brick wall in a Japanese internment camp. Marshall enjoyed the company of hard-drinking men and attractive women and had an hilarious, at times scatological, sense of humour.

Dibb says he might not have been persuaded to work with ASIO if anyone other than Marshall approached him: 'I couldn't resist the call of something that was so important to Australia and which also offered excitement and potential danger. It was dead-sexy stuff to be doing. And Don, although born a Russian, somehow exemplified the quintessential Australian larrikin. He had incredible strength of personality. If it had been anyone less charismatic I may have had second thoughts.'

Marshall was a man fated to work in Soviet counterespionage. His father Bill (Vladimir) fled from the Soviet Union to Australia in the 1920s, served in the Australian army and returned to Shanghai to serve in the police force. Don, the same age as Dibb, was born in

Shanghai in 1939 (his original name was Donal Mischenko) and he spent his childhood in the internment camp with his mother after the Japanese invasion. After the war, the family was reunited and Bill worked with the Hong Kong police before moving to Australia and joining ASIO, where he played a key role in the 1954 defection of the Soviet diplomats Vladimir Petrov and his wife Evdokia. Don attended the famous Fort Street High School in Sydney and studied philosophy at The Australian National University (ANU) before following his father into ASIO.

Dibb got to know Marshall slowly over a close 34-year friendship that endured until Marshall's death in 1999. Marshall's offer led Dibb into what has been called 'the wilderness of mirrors', the covert world of counterespionage where things are not always as they seem, where truth and trust are relative and where human weakness, greed and credulity are exploited in the service of national security. Ultimately, their relationship resulted in Dibb supporting ASIO's counterespionage efforts until the collapse of the Soviet Union in 1991.

Marshall told Dibb that ASIO wanted him to cultivate senior Soviet diplomats to get information on Soviet global strategy and its defence and intelligence targets in Australia, and to encourage defections. Although the Petrov defections had occurred 10 years earlier, Australia, as a US ally, remained a major target of Soviet espionage as Moscow sought to penetrate US secrets via Australia, including Australia's access to classified US satellite intelligence and electronic signals intercepts.

Soon after their first meeting, Marshall took Dibb to meet ASIO's legendary Deputy Ron Richards, who was a central figure in the Petrov affair and was the only man Dibb ever heard Marshall address as 'Sir'. Richards was direct: 'Will you work for us?' he asked Dibb. Dibb had only one condition, he recalls: 'I said I wanted my career protected.'

Marshall's influence on Dibb was deep and lasting: 'In my early years in Australia he taught me about Australian nationalism and Australian national interests. He taught me that what we were doing against the Soviet Union was of the utmost importance and that we were not to talk about it — not even to those in Australian intelligence or the US embassy who he did not trust. And he taught me that we did not always tell the Americans and the British everything — especially when they were being threatening in their demands. Don was a dynamic extrovert personality and he believed profoundly in the goodness of what we were doing despite the cynical views of others', Dibb says.

Dibb's disclosures of his ASIO activities throws new light on Australia's role in the Cold War — a role mostly remembered for the Petrov defections, the expulsion of the Soviet diplomat Ivan Skripov in 1963, the 1983 Combe–Ivanov affair,[2] and for the part played by the Pine Gap, Nurrungar and North West Cape bases in global US nuclear warning and targeting systems. Dibb had top-secret security clearances for these installations for more than 25 years and the first public hint of his ASIO involvement appeared in a collection of essays commemorating the 40th anniversary of The Australian National University's Strategic and Defence Studies Centre (SDSC), which Dibb headed from 1991 to 2003.

Des Ball revealed in that book that Dibb was tasked by Marshall to get the views of the Russians 'on issues concerning the central strategic balance and to discern the real interests and priorities, and perhaps persuade one or other of them to defect'.[3] Dibb did not succeed in 'turning' a Soviet diplomat. 'They were either too smart or they had a mole deep inside ASIO', he says.

A still highly secret hunt was mounted for a suspected ASIO mole, but none was found. Nevertheless, the Americans had their suspicions and, in 1981, the CIA Station Chief in Australia, Michael Sednaoui, told Dibb that his specific mission was to find out if there was a mole in ASIO. Sednaoui's posting was cut short by ill health (which he said he feared the Russians had caused) and he reached no conclusions, but he told Dibb he had some 'serious concerns' before he left Australia.

Soon after starting his secret ASIO work, Dibb left the BAE and took a research posting at ANU where he wrote a book on Siberia. He joined the Defence Department in 1970. From 1974–78 he headed the National Assessments Staff (NAS), which drafted national intelligence assessments for the National Intelligence Committee (NIC) and he was

2   See Shane Maloney & Chris Grosz, 'David Combe & Valery Ivanov', *The Monthly*, Aug. 2006, www.themonthly.com.au/encounters-shane-maloney-david-combe-valery-ivanov--274.
3   Desmond Ball, 'Reflections on the SDSC's Middle Decades', in Meredith Thatcher & Desmond Ball (eds), *A National Asset: Essays Commemorating the 40th Anniversary of the Strategic and Defence Studies Centre*, Canberra Paper No. 165 (Canberra: Strategic and Defence Studies Centre, 2006), p. 77.

the government's leading Soviet intelligence expert. From 1986–88 he was Director of the Joint Intelligence Organisation (JIO, now the Defence Intelligence Organisation (DIO)) and from 1988–91 he was Deputy Secretary (Strategy and Intelligence) in Defence.

Few would dispute that Dibb's most important public and personal contribution to defence policy was the Dibb Review. He was commissioned to produce the report by the then Defence Minister Kim Beazley, himself a formidable defence intellectual, when he was an external consultant to the government. The Dibb Review remains a seminal document in Australian defence policy: it put paid to the era of 'forward defence', which had been discredited by the Vietnam War. Instead it proposed a layered national defence of Australia to deny potential aggressors the possibility of successfully attacking the continent through its sea–air approaches to the north and north-west of the continent. It also proposed the policy of defence self-reliance at the heart of the 1987 and subsequent Defence white papers.

The Dibb Review was a controversial and contested document, widely praised and widely criticised. Dibb's views are still contested by those who support the creation of heavily armoured Australian expeditionary defence forces capable of deploying to distant theatres and aggressively supporting the United States in contingency planning for global war. The Dibb Review declared the joint US–Australia intelligence facilities at North West Cape, Pine Gap and Nurrungar, plus staging rights for US ships and aircraft, 'a sufficient tangible contribution to the [ANZUS] alliance'. Dibb at heart is a geographer and he takes pleasure in mocking the argument that geography and geographical proximity no longer matter in strategic policy. 'If that is true,' he asks, 'why are we more concerned with Papua New Guinea than we are with Guinea-Bissau?' He has yet to be answered.

The point is that the Dibb Review brought the key focus of defence policy home to the security of Australia and its regional neighbours. It is the strategic framework within which Australian Defence white papers are still shaped and the defence force structure is (imperfectly) decided. It is challenged primarily by contrarians, ideologues, and gung-ho military officers who oppose its essentially defensive attitude and note that Australia's major troop deployments still tend to be to distant theatres (which, of course, ignores the demonstrated flexibility of Dibb's defence of Australia doctrine).

As a frontline practitioner in security, it is perhaps inevitable that Dibb's approach is deeply realist: for him, national interest and *raison d'état* trump the moralistic and legalistic postures of the liberal internationalists. Dibb sees the international order of sovereign states as inherently anarchic and he believes the anarchy is best managed by balancing power through interlocking networks of treaties and alliances to ensure that no one aggressive power dare try to overwhelm others. Dibb accepts the reality of violence in international relations and the need for adequately funded and equipped armed forces. (His concerns over government inconsistency in the management of defence funding and policy, as well as the defence force structure and industrial support, have been major themes of his widely reported public statements.) For Australia, his support for regionally focused defence self-reliance acknowledges the overarching importance of the US alliance as the ultimate last-resort guarantor of Australian security. He admires American intellectual and technical innovation and he has powerful friends in Washington.

Yet Dibb is no reflexive hawk on social policy issues. The Yorkshire coalminer's son remains sensitive to the hardships and dangers endured by the blackened men he saw emerging from the pits and mills to live in meagre poverty in grim, terraced cottages without adequate hygiene or medical care (at least until Britain's postwar national health service was established). He remembers, as a child, hearing the thump of German bombs landing on Kingston upon Hull. He was aware of the sometimes violent industrial struggles between miners and mine owners, and he regrets the social and economic impact on parts of Yorkshire of mine closures from the 1970s. Even today, Dibb slips easily and amusingly into Yorkshire dialect to recite some long-remembered Yorkshire proverb, poem or prayer. His concern for the hard-pressed men and women of the Pontefract region may have been one of the deeper motivations driving his work in international security. His connoisseur's taste for high-performance sports cars may signal his determination to show that he has come a long way from the austerity of postwar Pontefract.

Dibb became the head of SDSC in 1991, a post he held until 2003. He remains Professor Emeritus, deeply engaged in the work of the centre and the national strategic policy debate. Dibb has always been part scholar/teacher/academic analyst and part advocate/activist/adviser. He does not shy away from the role of provocateur if he believes provocation is necessary to focus public and political attention. In his academic, defence and ASIO careers he has spent his life observing, analysing and, at times, engaging with the most intractable strategic policy issues in his life-long mission to reduce the threat of nuclear Armageddon.

The 1986 publication of *The Soviet Union: The Incomplete Superpower* caused controversy and some grief for Dibb in both the United States and Australia. Some in the CIA and in the Australian intelligence community thought it too soft on the Soviet Union. Dibb remembers that Robert Gates, former US Secretary of Defense, but then Deputy Director of the CIA and the agency's leading Soviet expert, did not recognise even in the mid-1980s that the Soviet Union had serious weaknesses. Neither did Australia's Office of National Assessments (ONA), the federal government's main intelligence analysis body. They were, in Dibb's view, unable to see the weaknesses because of an apparently deep psychological need to portray the Soviet Union as an expansionist and aggressive nuclear-armed power confident in its ability to fight and win against weak and beleaguered Western powers.

The Australian analysis of the Soviet threat at the time was greatly influenced by contacts between Australian intelligence analysts and their US counterparts. Its flavour is captured in the 1983 *Strategic Basis of Australian Defence Policy* prepared for Federal Cabinet by the top-level Defence Committee, chaired at the time by Bill Pritchett, the Defence Secretary, and with Michael Cook, then Director-General of the ONA, as an 'invited consultant'. The once-secret Australian Eyes Only document claims in part:

> The US sees the USSR as able to destroy virtually all US missiles on the ground using only a portion of Soviet forces, while the US cannot inflict similar damage on Soviet forces even using its entire ICBM force … US strategic planners must calculate that in a full nuclear exchange the USSR could have the final advantage in terms of survival at some level short of national extinction.

Dibb recognised the Soviet threat and argued that Soviet military power was 'great and constantly expanding'. He agreed with the Defence Committee report that nuclear conflict was 'improbable', but he disagreed profoundly with the overall thrust of committee report. He wrote of 'a narrow and distorted Western focus on implausible contingencies' that had led to 'an exaggeration of Soviet military strength'. In what amounted to a contemptuous dismissal of the report, Dibb added: 'It is the West that is proclaiming Soviet military superiority, not the USSR, but belief in our words could help to produce the timidity and lack of confidence that we are seeking to avoid.'

Dibb took a broad view of Soviet economic, social and technological progress and concluded that it was a global power 'only in the military dimension'. The country, he said, had a semi-developed economy with a poor standard of living, backward technology and a grossly inefficient system of central planning. He said it was facing serious challenges 'perhaps leading to instability and deepening crisis'. He did not predict the collapse of the Soviet Union, but the Berlin Wall came down only three years after publication of his book, heralding the collapse of the Soviet Union and its empire. Dibb's assessment of the Soviet threat had proved to be much more insightful and accurate than the Defence Committee's alarmist analysis.

The book also landed Dibb in a brutal bureaucratic conflict with Defence's internal Office of Special Clearances and Records, known as OSCAR. He had returned to Defence to be told by an aide that OSCAR, set up to oversee personnel security clearances, had decided without authority to take on a counterespionage role and was illegally tapping the telephones of some military officers. Outraged, Dibb reported the issue to the then department Secretary Tony Ayres who ordered him to task Don Marshall to shut down OSCAR and to quietly sack its staff. Marshall did so with ruthless and surgical bureaucratic skill, and OSCAR and its illegal activities vanished into the now only faintly remembered mists of internal defence politics.

Throughout the Cold War, Dibb remained closely involved with Marshall and with ASIO's efforts to cultivate and turn Soviet diplomats in Canberra. 'I enjoyed the cut and thrust', he recalls. 'You always remember the first person you try to cultivate.' Dibb's first person was Nikolai Poseliagin, the Third Secretary in the Russian embassy, who was to return to Australia as First Secretary in 1974 when Dibb headed the NAS. 'I had two goes at him', he recalls.

Dibb also sought to cultivate the Deputy Chief of Mission Yuri Pavlov and Minister–Counsellor Igor Saprykin. Dibb describes them as two of the most impressive Soviet representatives to serve in Australia. 'We knew the Soviets were sending very competent people here. Saprykin and Pavlov were sophisticated people', he says.

Marshall suggested that Dibb invite Saprykin home for dinner. 'We'll have the place wired for sound. Get the bastard drunk', he told Dibb. Dibb carried out Marshall's suggestion and after a heavy meal and many, many drinks, Saprykin unexpectedly remarked that he was aware of what was the big issue in Australian society in that summer of hard-fought Ashes cricket dominated by two lethal Australian fast bowlers. 'Paul,' he said, quoting a popular ditty, 'ashes to ashes, dust to dust, if Lillee don't get you, Thomson must.' 'Looking back,' Dibb recalls, 'I think that was when I realised he was a bit too smart for us.'

In 1968, one month after the Soviet invasion of Czechoslovakia, Dibb made his first visit to the Soviet Union. Marshall warned him that Britain's MI6 would ask him to do 'silly things'. Dibb, without elaborating, says he was approached 'in a rather cack-handed way, and I politely refused'. On his second trip to the Soviet Union in 1976 the then Secretary of Defence Sir Arthur Tange told him: 'I want an Australian view, not an American or British view. Stay with Jim Plimsoll (the Australian ambassador) and watch yourself.' In Moscow Dibb was not even allowed into the embassy courtyard without an Australian minder to protect him from Soviet provocations.

The top-secret report he delivered from Moscow in 1976 as head of the NAS created a stir in Australian intelligence circles. In talks with top-level officials of the Soviet Institute for the US and Canada Studies, Dibb established, among other things, that the Soviet Union had nuclear targeting priorities that included Australia. He also established the extent of a military base set up by the Soviets at Berbera on the coast of north-west Somalia to match the expanding US base at Diego Garcia in the Indian Ocean. Dibb's report, previously secret, said the Soviet officials had told him the USSR saw a potential threat from US missile-firing submarines in the Indian Ocean. They warned that 'if such an attack were directed from North West Cape [the communications station on the Western Australian coast] it could involve Australia in Soviet response considerations'. The officials also told Dibb that the USSR had installed a missile-handling facility, a communications station, an airfield, barracks, limited repair facilities and fuel tanks at Berbera. The Russian message was a frank warning to Australian defence planners that the US–Australia joint intelligence collection and communications facilities at North West Cape, Pine Gap and Nurrungar were potential nuclear targets. It also signalled the Soviet ambition to match the Diego Garcia installation.

Dibb's trips to the Soviet Union were obviously perilous given his secret counterespionage work in Australia. If the Soviets had learned that he was involved in cultivating and trying to 'turn' Russian diplomats, he might have spent a long time in a very cold part of the vast Russian tundra. As it was, he managed to supply an original Australian view of Russian policy in cables to defence planners in Canberra. Dibb also travelled regularly to the United States where he consulted with what he calls the covert side of the CIA. On one visit he met James Jesus Angleton, the CIA's legendary Soviet counterespionage chief. He recalls Angleton telling him that the Sino–Soviet split was a KGB set-up to fool the West.

Dibb's covert work with Marshall continued in Canberra, but their relationship was not just cloak-and-dagger business. They would drink together in the now-demolished Deakin Inn where Marshall enjoyed the company of the attractive young women who came into the bar. When they asked where he worked he would stutter: 'I … I … I'm a V … V … Victa l … lawnmower salesman.'

Marshall rose through ASIO's ranks to become Director of the Canberra regional office running counterespionage, and an Assistant Director-General. He spent his last working years as Director of Defence Security — a post that Tony Ayres directed Dibb to secure for him. The end of his life, after two failed marriages, was tragic.

'When the Soviet Union disappeared, Don's *raison d'état* disappeared', Dibb recalls. 'His world fell apart for personal reasons and he drank heavily.' Shortly before moving to Defence, Marshall was invited to visit ASIO's new Russell Hill offices. 'What are you doing here, Don?' a friend asked him. 'W … W … What are any of us doing here?' he replied gloomily. 'I will never forget telephoning him at home late in 1998 after Ron McLeod, the Inspector-General of Intelligence, rang me to say that Don's personal life was a real mess. I invited him for lunch with a group of old ASIS (Australian Secret Intelligence Service) friends. "N … no mate. I … I can't do it", Marshall replied, and hung up his telephone. A few weeks later he died.'

'I think he was determined never to see his 60th birthday,' Dibb says.

# 5

# The Power of Geography

Peter J. Rimmer and R. Gerard Ward[1]

Who rules East Europe commands the Heartland;
Who rules the Heartland commands the World-Island;
Who rules the World-Island commands the World.

— Sir Halford John Mackinder[2]

Paul Dibb follows a long line of geographers who have contributed to the evolution of contemporary geopolitics. Sir Halford J. Mackinder, because of his seminal paper 'The Geographical Pivot of History',[3] which was delivered at London's Royal Geographical Society in 1904, and his famous dictum, cited above, is considered to be one of the key progenitors of modern strategic geography.[4] Within Australia Thomas

---

1     The authors would like to thank the staff of ANU Archives, Dr Brendan Whyte of the National Library of Australia Maps collection, and Dr Marion Ward and Dr Sue Rimmer for their comments on the text.
2     Sir Halford J. Mackinder, *Democratic Ideals and Reality: A Study in the Politics of Reconstruction* (London: H. Holt, 1944 (1919)), p. 113.
3     See Halford J. Mackinder, 'The Geographical Pivot of History', *The Geographical Journal*, Vol. 23, No. 4 (1904), pp. 421–37. Mackinder's writing on land power from a global perspective is comparable to the influence exerted on sea power by Captain Alfred Thayer Mahan presented in his *Influence of Sea Power Upon History, 1660–1783* (1890), see E.W. Gilbert, 'Sir Halford Mackinder, 1861–1947: An Appreciation of his Life and Work', Mackinder Centenary Lecture given at the London School of Economics and Political Science (Bell and Sons Ltd, 1962), p. 28.
4     James D. Sidaway, Virginie Mamadouh & Marcus Power, 'Reappraising Geopolitical Traditions', in Klaus Dodds, Merje Kuus & Joanne Sharp (eds), *The Ashgate Research Companion to Critical Geopolitics* (Farnham & Burlington: Ashgate, 2013), pp. 165–88.

Griffith Taylor,[5] after the First World War, and Oskar Spate,[6] after the Second World War, drew attention to the country's isolated global position by centring their maps upon Canberra (see Fig. 1).[7] Since then, a legion of geographers in Australia and in other parts of the world have refined political geography's focus during the Cold War and post-Cold War eras, provided fresh concepts and contemplated how the future geopolitical map may be moulded.

This raises the issue of how Dibb's life work fits into the pantheon of geostrategists who have long recognised geography as a decisive factor in the fortunes of nation states? More specifically, how has his geographical training shaped his studies of the Soviet Union and his subsequent influence on reshaping Australia's defence policy? How have his contemporaries viewed his input into this arena, which recognises, like Mackinder, that the rise and fall of states, and prospects for war or peace have been heavily influenced by the balance of power between continental and maritime states? These are crucial issues, given the Australian Government has produced a new Defence white paper to guide the country's defence planning to 2035.

Before evaluating Dibb's role as a geographer in fashioning defence policy in Australia, it is pertinent to examine his early training at the Nottingham University that triggered his abiding interest in the geography of the Soviet Union and, after 1991, Russia, and more recently China. Then we are in a position to consider how his proposition that geography is a decisive factor in the fortunes of nation states has infused Australia's defence planning, adverse reactions to Dibb's views, and his vigorous counter response that reinforces the critical importance of possessing a geographical imagination in both regional and global affairs.

---

5    See T. Griffith Taylor, 'Air Routes to Australia', *Geographical Review*, No. 7 (Apr. 1919), pp. 84–115; and T. Griffith Taylor, *Australian Meteorology* (1920).
6    See O.H.K. Spate, 'The Nature of Political Geography', *Australian Geographer*, Vol. 6, No. 5 (1965), pp. 29–31; O.H.K. Spate, 'The Pacific: Some Strategic Considerations', in W. Gordon East & A.E. Moodie, *The Changing World: Studies in Political Geography* (London: George G. Harrap & Co. Ltd, 1965), pp. 518–33; and O.H.K. Spate, 'Australia and its Dependencies', in Gordon East & Moodie, *The Changing World* (1965), pp. 803–30.
7    Griffith Taylor gave the first presidential address to the Institute of Australian Geographers on 'geopacifics'. See T. Griffith Taylor, 'First Presidential Address: Geographers and World Peace: A Plea for Geopacifics', *Australian Geographical Studies*, Vol. 1, No. 1 (1963), pp. 3–17.

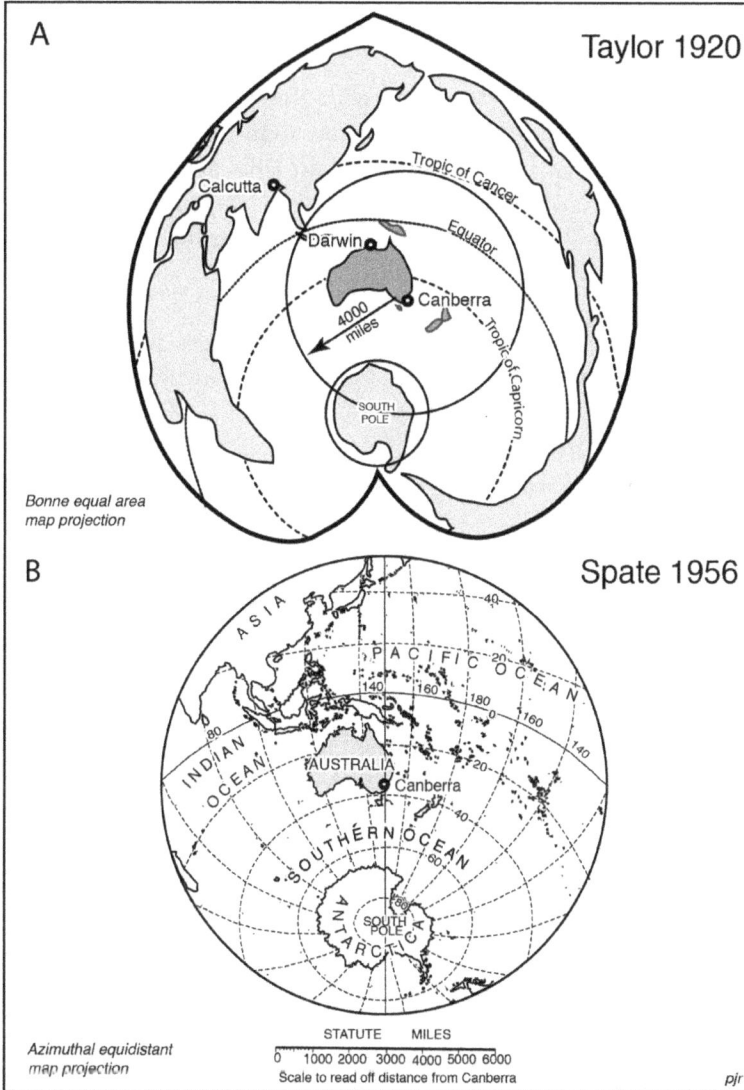

Figure 1A: The great ocean's isolation of Australia, with a radius of 4,000 miles from Canberra shown to pinpoint stepping stones through the Dutch East Indies for flights to England via Calcutta[8]

Figure 1B: The hemisphere around Australia centred on Canberra — all points on the map are at a proportionately correct distance from the centre point[9]

8    Based on T. Griffith Taylor, *Australian Meteorology: A Textbook including Sections on Aviation and Climatology* (Oxford: Clarendon Press, 1920), p. 274.
9    Based on Spate, 'Australia and its Dependencies' (1956), p. 804.

# Soviet Geography

How did Dibb's enduring concern with Soviet geography from an Australian perspective arise? As this may seem to be an uncommon focus for a Yorkshireman born Paul Leonard Dibb at the beginning of the Second World War in the coalmining settlement of Pontefract, which was dominated by the Prince of Wales Colliery, it is important to trace key stages in this process. Dibb's stepfather was a miner and he inherited his mother's ambition, which was nurtured further as a scholarship boy at the Kings School, Pontefract, where teachers interested him in the world of ideas.[10] Between 1957 and 1960 these ideas and their applications were refined at the Nottingham University when he was a student in the Department of Geography led by Professor K.C. Edwards who, coincidentally, had many connections with geographers in the Antipodes during the 1950s and early 1960s.[11] Although majoring in geography, Dibb also undertook a subsidiary in economics under Professor Brian Tew (formerly of the University of Adelaide) and was offered the opportunity of pursuing an honours degree in the subject. He decided that sticking to a geography degree, without neglecting his interest in economics, would better suit his future career.

His curiosity about the USSR stemmed from John Cole, his Sydney-born lecturer at Nottingham University, who was prominent among a bevy of postwar, British-based geographers studying the Soviet Union at the height of the Cold War.[12] After being force-fed during the immediate postwar era on G.D.B. Gray's *Soviet Land: The Country, Its People and Their Work*,[13] undergraduates, like Dibb, must have been captivated by Cole's fresh insights into the geography of the USSR from the 1950s.[14] These insights stemmed from Cole's training as a Russian linguist during his national service in 1951 at the British armed forces' Joint Services School for Linguists, where he had access

---

10   Bob Beale, 'We Can Defend Australia: Paul Dibb Is Just Sure of It', *Sydney Morning Herald*, 4 Jun. 1986, p. 17.

11   ANUA, '19/Box 278 8103855P ANU Staff Files: Paul Dibb', Canberra: The Australian National University Archives, 1967–2004.

12   D. Matless, J. Oldfield & A. Swain, 'Encountering Soviet Geography: Oral Histories of British Geographical Studies of the USSR and Eastern Europe 1945–1991', *Social & Cultural Geography*, Vol. 8, No. 3 (2007), pp. 353–72.

13   G.D.B. Gray, *Soviet Land: The Country, Its People and Their Work* (London: Adam and Charles Black, 1947).

14   J.P. Cole, *Geography of the USSR* (Hammondsworth: Penguin Books, 1967); and J.P. Cole & F.C. German, *A Geography of the USSR — The Background to a Planned Economy*, 2nd edn (London: Butterworth, 1970).

to the equivalent of an unpublished 'admiralty handbook' on the USSR.[15] Paradoxically, Cole undertook fieldwork not in the USSR, where he was wary of being enveloped in Soviet intrigue, but in Latin America, and first visited Russia on an Intourist guided tour in 1976; his major work after visiting the Soviet Union did not appear until the 1980s.[16] By then, Dibb had migrated to Australia and had made several visits to the USSR.

After a spell as a trainee manager in the British car industry and part-time lecturer in economics at the Northampton Technical College, Dibb arrived in Australia in December 1961 to take up a position in Canberra on the staff of the then Minister of Trade Sir John McEwen.[17] During his stint in the Department of Overseas Trade he was engaged initially in investigating the country's trade agreement with the United Kingdom in the light of the latter's proposed entry into the Common Market, before taking charge of Australia's trade with the Soviet Union and Eastern Europe. By 1963 he was also busy preparing reports on the country's secondary industries for the Committee of Economic Enquiry, which produced the Vernon Report.[18] While in the public service, Dibb was also conscious of the need to keep abreast of developments in geography, which was in the process of shifting from a qualitative perspective to a quantitative approach.[19]

In 1964 Dibb was awarded a part-time public service scholarship to study in the Department of Geography, School of General Studies at The Australian National University (ANU) under Professor Andrew Learmonth.[20] While there he was mentored by the political geographer Alfred James 'Jim' Rose, who had investigated the danger to Australia's security lying in its northern approaches, noting that 'the importance of New Guinea and Indonesia to Australia arises from their role as buffers or shields between us and the greater powers to the north ... India, China and Japan'.[21] Before Rose left for a Chair at Macquarie

15    Matless, Oldfield & Swain, 'Encountering Soviet Geography' (2007), p. 14.
16    J.P. Cole, *Geography of the Soviet Union* (London: Butterworth-Heinemann, 1984).
17    ANUA, '19/Box 277 8103855C ANU Staff Files: Paul Dibb', Canberra: The Australian National University Archives, 1969–99.
18    Commonwealth of Australia, *Committee of Economic Enquiry*, Sir James Vernon (Canberra: Australian Government Printing Service, 1965).
19    O.H.K. Spate, 'Quality and Quantity in Geography', *Annals of the Association of American Geographers*, Vol. 50, No. 4 (1960), pp. 377–94.
20    ANUA, '19/Box 278 8103855P ANU Staff Files: Paul Dibb'.
21    A. James Rose, 'Strategic Geography and the Northern Approaches', *Australian Outlook*, Vol. 13, No. 4 (1959), p. 314.

University he would have inculcated in Dibb the need for the greater use of statistics and model-building in geographical analysis within Dibb's study of the locational aspects of Australia's pulp, paper and paperboard industry.

In 1965 this additional geographical training came to the fore when Dibb was transferred from the Department of Overseas Trade to the Bureau of Agricultural Economics (BAE) under the direction of Stuart J. Harris.[22] Immediately he brought his new-found skills to bear on the postwar economics of the Soviet wheat industry, which had significant implications for Australia's trade policy.[23] By the end of 1966 Dibb had moved to the Department of Territories to work as a personal project officer for the Secretary on the economic, political and social development of Nauru and New Guinea. Although this interest in Pacific Island states persisted throughout his career, it was his study of the Soviet wheat industry's structure, trends and problems that attracted the interest of academia.

By 1968 this academic attention led to Dibb being recruited to a one-year appointment as a research fellow in the Department of Political Science within the then Research School of Social Sciences (RSSS) at ANU. Although its head, Professor Robert Parker, recognised that Dibb was an economic geographer, the accommodation was made to provide him with the opportunity for closer interaction with T.H. 'Harry' Rigby, the acknowledged doyen of Soviet (and later post-Soviet) studies in Australia.[24] While in the department he was able to undertake fieldwork in Britain, Japan and the USSR supported by the Ford Foundation, endorsed by the Australian Department of Trade and Industry, and facilitated by academic contacts from Parker and Spate, then head of Geography in the Research School of Pacific Studies (RSPacS). The project's purpose was to gauge economic development in Siberia and prospects for bilateral trade with Australia and Japan, including identifying commodities and assessing the quality of shipping services. Not only was Dibb able to have conversations with Soviet officials and academics in Moscow, Akademgorodok, Irkutsk, Bratsk

22   ANUA, '19/Box 278 8103855P ANU Staff Files: Paul Dibb'.
23   Paul Dibb, *The Economics of the Soviet Wheat Industry: An Economic Study of the Structure, Trends and Problems from 1953 to 1965 with a Perspective to 1970* (Canberra: Bureau of Agricultural Economics, 1966); and F.M. Collins & Paul Dibb, 'Wheat Production in the Soviet Union and the Five-Year Plan', *Quarterly Review of Agricultural Economics*, Vol. 20, No. 2 (1967), pp. 95–104.
24   ANUA, '19/Box 278 8103855P ANU Staff Files: Paul Dibb'.

and Khabarovsk, but also in Tokyo with businessmen from key Japanese trading companies and a struggling Australian firm, whose difficulties in trading through the Nakhodka port were taken up with a less than cooperative trade representative in the Soviet embassy (See Table 1).

Table 1: Paul Dibb's Soviet Union itinerary, 1968

| Date 1968 | Travel and stopovers | Mode | Stopover | Days | Activities |
|---|---|---|---|---|---|
| 24/8 | Canberra – Perth | Air | Perth | 1 | |
| 26/8 | Perth – London | Air | London | 14 | Foreign Office Central Asian Research Association Royal Institute for International Affairs |
| 11/9 | London – Harwich – Hook of Holland – Moscow | Sea/rail (via East Germany and Poland) | Moscow | 10 | Institute of the Peoples of Asia (18/9) State Planning Committee (Gosplan) officials responsible for central economic planning (19/9) |
| | Moscow – Nakhodka | Trans-Siberian Railway | | | Stopping over en route at Novosibirsk (for Akademgorodok), Irkutsk and Khabarovsk |
| 24/9 | Novosibirsk | | Novosibirsk | 3 | Economic Institute at Akademgorodok (academy town) |
| 27–28/9 | Bratsk | | | 3 | Dam and Power Station Wood-burning *kombinat* (permission not granted to visit aluminium *kombinat*) |
| 29/9 | Irkutsk | | Irkutsk | 1 | Irkutsk Oblast Gosplan |
| 30/9 1/10 | Khabarovsk | | Khabarovsk | 2 | Laboratory of Import–Export Specialization, Khabarovsk Research Institute, Siberian Branch of the USSR Academy of Sciences |
| 2–3/10 | Nakhodka – Yokohama – Tokyo | Sea (SS *Khaborovsk*) | | 1 | Meetings with Japanese businessmen on voyage |
| 7–9/10 | Tokyo | | | 3 | Meetings with Japanese trading companies (7–8/10) Soviet trade representative (9/10) |

| Date 1968 | Travel and stopovers | Mode | Stopover | Days | Activities |
|---|---|---|---|---|---|
| No date | Tokyo – Sydney – Canberra | | | 2 | |

Note: This schedule varied from the planned itinerary that had Dibb returning to Canberra on 17 October 1968

Source: Dibb (1968)

Of particular benefit from Dibb's initial visit to the USSR was the connection made in Khabarovsk with Professor Leon Vstovsky, Director of the Laboratory of Import–Export Specialization, Khabarovsk Research Institute, Siberian Branch of the USSR Academy of Sciences. Not only did he provide Dibb with books from regional publishing houses to deepen his knowledge of Siberia, but their interaction also led to a proposal for an exchange of publications between Australia and the Soviet Union. Nevertheless, this visit made Dibb aware of how conversations were partly standard interchanges of information between fellow academics and, on the Soviet side, partly deliberate propaganda statements along Communist Party political lines (including expressions of antipathy towards Australia's involvement in the Vietnam War). This awareness was important in his subsequent ability to interpret Soviet source materials and information from meetings.

In 1969 an opportunity arose for Dibb to extend his stay at ANU to analyse the material collected in the Soviet Union beyond the agreed one year plus short extension in the Department of Politics when the Department of Geography in the RSPacS was subdivided into the Department of Biogeography and Geomorphology, and the Department of Human Geography.[25] The latter, undermanned department wanted to extend its involvement beyond the Pacific and South-East Asia and recruited him as an economic geographer on a three-year appointment as a senior research fellow to provide a deeper Australian perspective on the USSR's geography; this appointment satisfied the long-standing interest of Spate, the school's new Director, in the Soviet Union's geographical theory and practice.[26]

---

25  O.H.K. Spate, 'Geography in the Research School of Pacific Studies', *Australian Geographical Studies*, Vol. 6, No. 1 (1968), p. 84.

26  O.H.K. Spate, 'Theory and Practice in Soviet Geography', *Australian Geographical Studies*, Vol. 1, No. 1 (1963), pp. 18–30.

Dibb's one-year stay in the Department of Human Geography at ANU advanced the skills that stood him in good stead for the rest of his career.[27] At the time, the visit to ANU by US geographer David Harvey, who elaborated the development of a scientific approach to geographical problems (i.e. the role of theory in scientific explanation), took the so-called quantitative revolution in geography beyond mere quantification.[28] The value of this experience in gaining an understanding through scientific explanation is apparent in Dibb's later explorations of the connections between international trade, the export base, and the location and health of Australia's rural industries — a shift from the preoccupation of economists with countries to the geographer's concern with the variable impact of policies on specific regions within countries.[29]

The main outcome of Dibb's time at ANU was the broad-gauge regional study of the East Asian half of the Soviet Union. At the time a focus on the economic development of Siberia, stretching from the Urals to the Pacific, was a relative rarity among geographers working on the USSR.[30] Drawing upon the well-honed skills developed by regional geographers, Dibb's study of 'Pacific Siberia' focused on the area from the Pacific seaboard inland to the Yenisey (Yenisei) River (See Fig. 2).[31] With a perceptive foreword by Rigby, this investigation evaluated what the Russians had accomplished, contemplated and projected within Siberia and their likely geopolitical reverberations on powerful neighbours, notably China and Japan, and more generally around the wider Pacific rim. The volume demonstrated his detailed understanding of the little-studied region, its particular geographical characteristics relating to permafrost, isolation, distance and transport costs on the Trans-Siberian Railway, and their consequences for human settlement and economic activities.

---

27  ANUA, '19/Box 278 8103855P ANU Staff Files: Paul Dibb'.
28  See David Harvey, *Explanation in Geography* (London: Edward Arnold, 1969).
29  Paul Dibb, 'International Trade, the Export Base and the Location of Rural Industries', in G.J.R. Linge & P.J. Rimmer (eds), *Government Influence and the Location of Economic Activity* (Canberra: Department of Human Geography, Research School of Pacific Studies, The Australian National University, 1971), pp. 115–40.
30  David J.M. Hooson, *A New Soviet Heartland?* (Princeton, NJ: Van Nostrand, 1964); and C.D. Harris, 'The USSR', in Stephen Goddard (ed.), *A Guide to Information Sources in the Geographical Sciences* (London: Croom Helm, 1983), pp. 179–88.
31  Paul Dibb, *Siberia and the Pacific, A Study in Economic Development and Trade Prospects* (New York: Praeger, 1972).

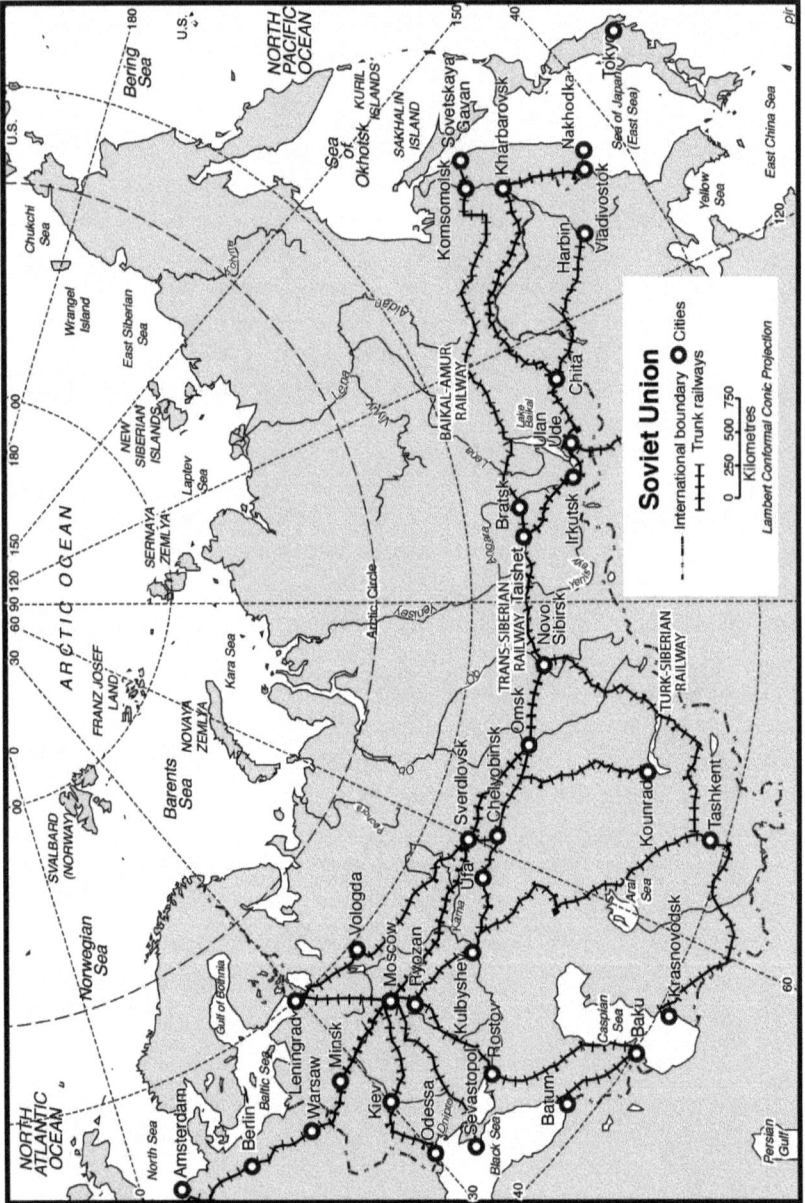

Figure 2: Soviet Union map showing the Trans-Siberian Railway c. 1990[32]

---

32    Based on Map G7000 1994 in the National Library of Australia's Maps collection.

By the time Dibb's book on Siberia was published in 1972, he had returned to the public service as an intelligence analyst in the Joint Intelligence Organisation (JIO) in the Department of Defence. This move did not diminish his continuing interest in the USSR's geography. During this period he also extended his purview to cover China's strategic interests and defence priorities in the 1980s.[33] His contribution showed that he had not lost touch with his geographical roots with his devising two maps showing: (a) a view of the world centred on Beijing with radiating circles at 5,000-kilometre intervals; and (b) the location of China's military regions and field armies, each with an estimated 43,000 men (See figs 3A and 3B). These maps, reflecting the importance of both distance and terrain, underlined 'the important contribution of geography … to China's strategy of protracted defence'.[34]

Dibb's twin focus on the USSR and China persisted when he returned from Defence to ANU in 1981, first to the Department of International Relations and then, two years later, to the Strategic and Defence Studies Centre (SDSC). In particular, he sought to continue this interest in examining: (a) the potential for global conflict over economic issues, notably oil; (b) the external relations of Pacific Island states; and (c) long-term threat assessments within Australia's strategic neighbourhood.[35] More specifically, the SDSC's Director, Bob O'Neill, encouraged him to produce a major book that sought to diminish the yawning void in accurate information on the USSR's military strength, economic capabilities and international relations; this topic provided a perfect foil to Desmond Ball's work on the United States. Although Dibb extended his reach beyond Siberia in *The Soviet Union: An Incomplete Superpower* to include the country's international relations with both Europe and the Middle East, he maintained a firm focus on the Pacific Ocean to provide a more integrated assessment of the USSR's strengths and weaknesses as a nation-state.[36] As this assessment, containing a critique of Mackinder's heartland theory, downplayed the threat

---

33 Paul Dibb, 'China's Strategic Situation and Defence Priorities in the 1980s', *Australian Journal of Chinese Affairs*, No. 5 (1981), pp. 97–115.
34 Dibb, 'China's Strategic Situation' (1981), p. 99.
35 ANUA, '19/Box 277 8103855C ANU Staff Files: Paul Dibb'.
36 Paul Dibb, *The Soviet Union: The Incomplete Superpower* (London: International Institute for Strategic Studies and Macmillan, 1986).

to Australia of the USSR's air power, the *Australian*'s reviewer Peter Samuel claimed that Dibb had dangerous illusions about Soviet *realpolitik*.[37] Nevertheless, the study's quality and originality shone through and resulted in the award of a doctorate by ANU in 1987 based on published work on the Soviet Union.[38]

Subsequently, Dibb remained focused upon the Soviet Union's international relations. In April 1991 he was present in Moscow with one of the authors of this chapter, R. Gerard Ward, at a meeting on Pacific regional affairs between representatives of The Australian National University's RSPacS and the Soviet Academy's Institute of International Relations and Economic Affairs. At a side gathering, a Soviet *apparatchik* sought to change the nature of the discussion from academic to intelligence matters — a move that Dibb immediately recognised from past experience and closed off! This suggested business as usual but, by the end of 1991, the Soviet Union had dissolved into independent republics, which also signalled the end of the Cold War. On reflection, Dibb thought that it was not possible to have foreseen the Soviet Union's impending dissolution because of the wide knowledge gap that existed on its economic, social and ideological base. Indeed, the Soviet Union's subsequent breakup impressed upon him the need to employ an interdisciplinary team to provide the broadest possible perspective in a continuing watching brief on both Russia's and China's prospects. Inevitably, in his view, given Australia's geopolitical situation, such a team would of necessity include a political geographer.

---

37   Peter Samuel, 'Dibb's Dangerous Illusions about Soviet *Realpolitik*', *Australian*, 23 Jan. 1987, pp. 9–10.
38   ANUA, '19/Box 278 8103855P ANU Staff Files: Paul Dibb'.

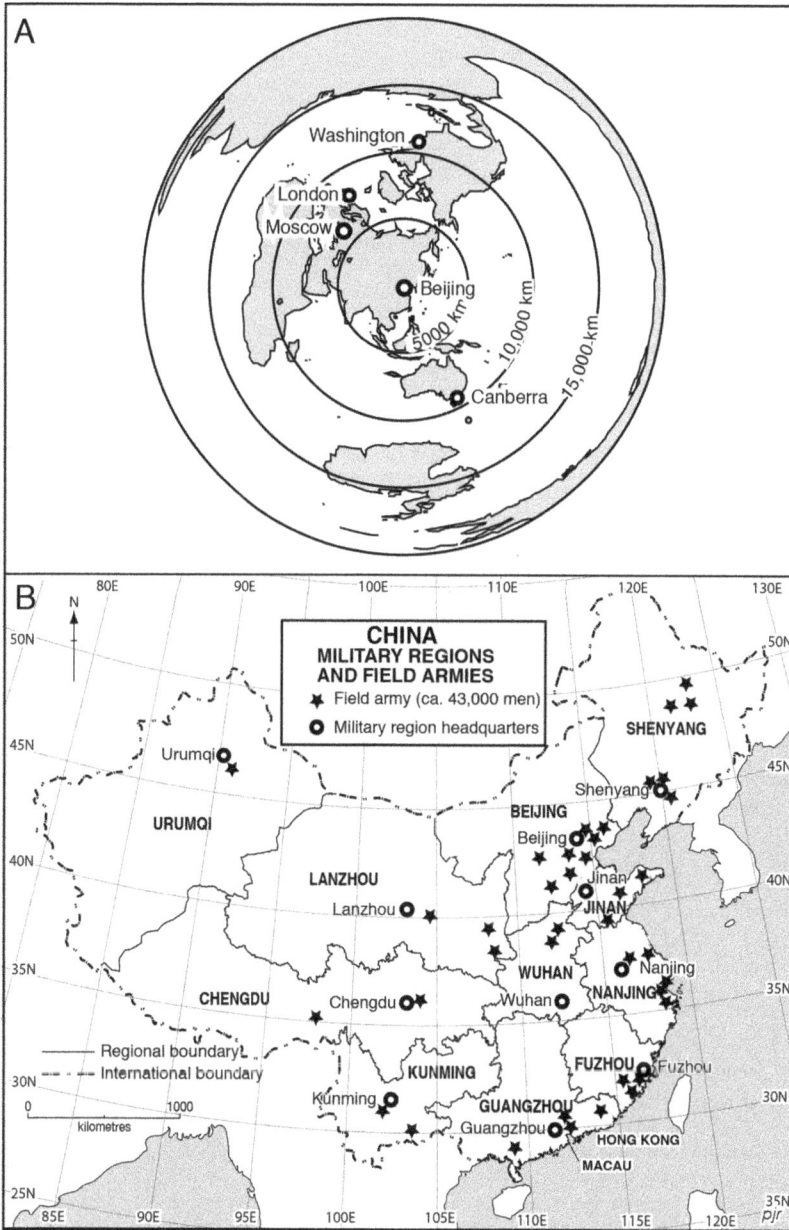

Figure 3A: A view of the world centred on Beijing

Figure 3B: Map of China's military regions and field armies, c. 1979[39]

39    Based on Dibb, 'China's Strategic Situation' (1981), pp. 97–115. Original figures are located between pp. 98 and 99.

# Australia's Strategic Geography

After returning to ANU in 1981 as a senior research fellow in arms control, disarmament and peace research, Dibb saw the need, following a review of Australia's external relations in the decade after the defeat of the United States in the Vietnam War,[40] to instil in Australians the belief that they could defend themselves.[41] He realised that this shift from a dependent to a self-reliant military strategy required the injection of a missing geographical perspective into Australia's defence policy to meet the request from the United States that its ally carry a greater burden of the security task.[42] In 1985 he was given the opportunity to elaborate his thesis that the fundamentals of Australia's *geographical location* should be key factors shaping military posture and force structure when was he was commissioned as a ministerial consultant to provide the first postwar review of the country's defence capabilities by the Minister for Defence Kim Beazley.[43] The resultant Dibb Review provided the springboard for Dibb again leaving ANU to become Director of the JIO (1986 to 1988) and then Deputy Secretary of Defence (1988 to 1991); he was also the primary author of the 1987 Defence White Paper.[44] In 1991 Dibb returned once again to ANU with a special appointment as professor and head of SDSC (1991–2003) to focus on the future balance of power in Asia.[45] Our interest, however, is not on his career movements between the intelligence community and academia, but on the way in which he has used his geographical skills to mutually benefit both spheres of activity. This double act is evident in Dibb's model for Australia's strategic geography that became known as the 'Defence of Australia' (DOA) paradigm.

40   Paul Dibb, 'Australia's External Relations: An Introduction', in Paul Dibb (ed.), *Australia's External Relations in the 1980s, The Interaction of Economic Political and Strategic Factors* (New York: Croom Helm Australia, 1983), pp. 11–16.
41   Richard Battley, 'War and Peace and Dibb', *Sydney Morning Herald*, 19 Apr. 1986, p. 25.
42   ANUA, '19/Box 277 8103855C ANU Staff Files: Paul Dibb'.
43   MFD, 'Media Release No. 20/84', Minister for Defence Kim Beazley MP, 13 Feb. 1985; and Paul Dibb, *Review of Australia's Defence Capabilities*, report to the Minister for Defence (Canberra: Australian Government Publishing Service, 1986), p. 3.
44   Commonwealth of Australia, *The Defence of Australia 1987*. Presented to Parliament by the Minister for Defence the Honourable Kim C. Beazley MP, Canberra: Australian Government Publishing Service, Mar. 1987.
45   ANUA, '19/Box 278 8103855P ANU Staff Files: Paul Dibb'.

# Defence of Australia

Dibb's conceptual base for the DOA paradigm, prioritising air and naval forces to defend the sea–air gap north of Australia, took its cue from Sir Arthur Tange's astute observation that 'a map of one's own country is the most fundamental of all defence documentation'.[46] Given Australia was a 'middle ranking power' with modest defence resources, Dibb proposed a layered geographical construct to guide defence planning (See Fig. 4):

1.  An area of direct military interest, accounting for 10 per cent of the globe, where attention should be concentrated upon securing the country from attack by another state by having a military technological advantage to defend the country's northern air and sea approaches through island or archipelagic states, and the inner arc of countries from or through which a threat could be mounted.

2.  A broader area of primary strategic interest, covering 25 per cent of the globe from the mid-Indian Ocean in the west to the mid-Pacific in the east and from South-East Asia and the China Sea in the north to Antarctica in the south.

3.  The rest of the world that afforded opportunities for coalitions but was not a primary determinant of force structure.

This concentric-ring model was designed to provide Australia's defence strategists with an ironclad discipline to shape strategy and force structure; it also provided a construct to distinguish between 'wars-of-necessity' and 'wars-of-choice' (i.e. the difference between interventions in the Solomon Islands and East Timor versus Somalia, Iraq and Afghanistan).

---

46   Arthur Tange, 'The Reorganization of the Defence Group of Departments: Reflections Ten Years On', address to CDF [Chief of Defence Force] conference, Canungra, Queensland, 26 Aug. 1986, in Arthur Tange, *Defence Policy Administration and Organization: Selected Lectures, 1971–1986* (Canberra: University College of New South Wales, 1986), p. 90.

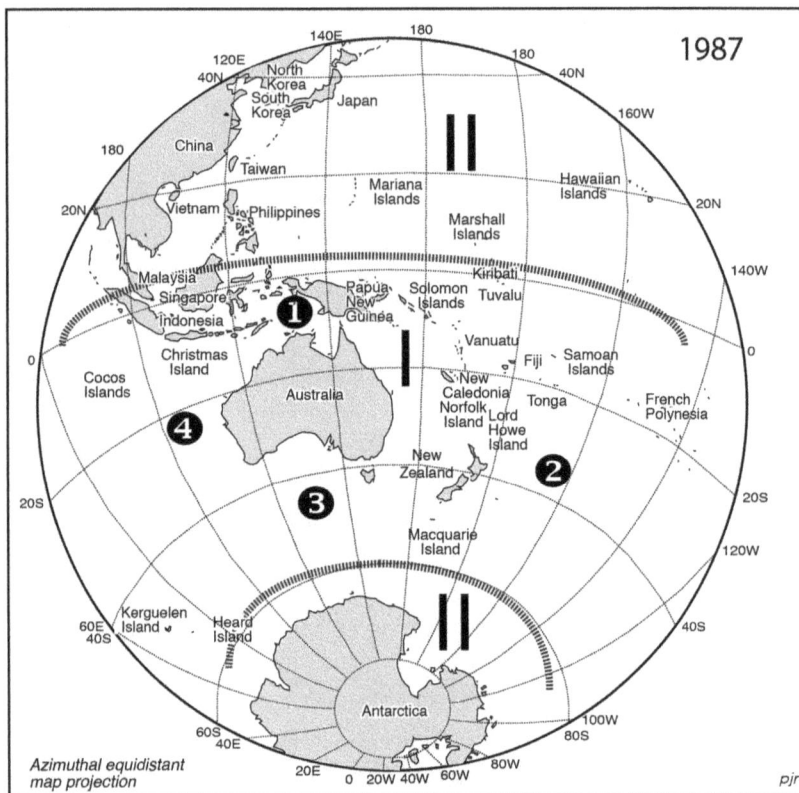

Figure 4: First and second regions (I and II) of Australian strategic interest established in the Defence White Paper, 1987.[47] Additional information has been added: (1) Cooperative Security Front, (2) Aid Front, (3) Environmental Security Front, and (4) Trade Front.[48]

After returning to ANU in 1991, Dibb was able to maintain the DOA credo. He criticised severely the Australian role in peacekeeping in Africa because it was deflecting the defence force from its primary task of defending Australia, but he also advised Defence on its 1994 White Paper, which flagged a deeper concern with security interests and perceptions of Indian Ocean countries.[49] Fostering the security of the

---

47   Based on Commonwealth of Australia, *The Defence of Australia 1987*, endpiece following p. 112.

48   Dennis Rumley, *The Geopolitics of Australia's Regional Relations* (Dordrecht, Boston, MA, and London: Kluwer Academic Publishers, 1998).

49   Cameron Stewart, 'Peacekeeping Deflects Defence Force — Dibb', *Australian*, 27 May 1993, pp. 1–2; and Commonwealth of Australia, *Defence White Paper 1994* (Canberra: Australian Government Publishing Service, 1994).

neighbourhood within Australia's immediate 'arc of instability' also led to him having direct involvement in the Association of Southeast Asian Nations (ASEAN) regional forum (ARF) and in determining the role and structure of Papua New Guinea's defence force.[50] Beyond Australia's region of prime military interest he argued that, given the cost of expeditionary forces, involvement supporting the United States should necessarily be limited to niche contributions. At the same time, soft diplomacy should be used to accommodate radical changes in Asian geopolitics following the economic crisis of 1997–98, which further exposed Japan's underlying economic weakness and catapulted China into the role of a leading East Asia power.[51]

The DOA paradigm prioritising 'proximity' held sway until after the United Nation's intervention in East Timor in 1999 and the 2000 Defence White Paper, which accommodated geopolitical changes with an additional concentric ring separating maritime South-East Asia from the rest of the Asia-Pacific region.[52] Although non-state actors, including international criminal elements and illegal immigrants, had been injected into the new millennium's post-Cold War strategic equation, Dibb cautioned at the time against restructuring Australia's military forces for constabulary actions.[53] As his position did not address the American challenge for Australia to play a greater role in the alliance, Paul Monk, a former Defence analyst, posed a dozen questions to Dibb.[54] Before these could be addressed, however, overseas events precipitated more fundamental criticisms of the DOA paradigm's underpinnings in strategic geography.

50   Gareth Evans & Paul Dibb, *Australian Paper on Practical Proposals for Security Cooperation in the Asia Pacific Region* (Canberra: Department of Foreign Affairs and Trade and the Strategic and Defence Studies Centre, 1994); and Paul Dibb & Rhondda Nicholas, *Restructuring the Papua New Guinea Defence Force: Strategic Analysis and Force Structure Principles for a Small State*, report to the Minister for Defence of Papua New Guinea (Canberra: Strategic and Defence Studies Centre, 1996).

51   Paul Dibb, *Towards a New Balance of Power in Asia*, Adelphi Paper No. 295 (London: International Institute for Strategic Studies, 1995); Paul Dibb, *The Remaking of Asia's Geopolitics*, Working Paper No. 324 (Canberra: Strategic and Defence Studies Centre, 1998); Paul Dibb, 'The Strategic Environment in the Asia Pacific Region', in Robert D. Blackwill & Paul Dibb (eds), *America's Asian Alliances* (Cambridge: MIT Press, 2000), pp. 1–17; and Rumley, *The Geopolitics of Australia's Regional Relations* (1998).

52   Commonwealth of Australia, *Defence 2000: Our Future Defence Force* (Canberra: Department of Defence, 2000).

53   Paul Dibb, 'A Trivial Strategic Age', *Quadrant*, Vol. 44, No. 7–8 (Jul./Aug. 2000), pp. 11–17.

54   Paul Monk, 'Twelve Questions for Paul Dibb', *Quadrant*, Vol. 45, No. 4 (2001), pp. 40–43.

## Adverse Reactions

The destruction of the World Trade Center on 11 September 2001 (9/11) and the Bali bombings of 2002 prompted a statement from the Minister of Defence, Senator Robert Hill, that 'it probably never made sense to conceptualise our security interests as a series of diminishing circles around our coastline, but certainly does not do so now' given the globalised nature of security concerns.[55] This view was reinforced by Alan Dupont's argument that the international security landscape had been transformed and a new strategy was required more in keeping with the 'post-modern era of Osama bin Laden' than 'the pre-modern world of Halford Mackinder' due to technological advances in airpower and the power of ideology.[56] Besides giving insufficient weight to transnational threats and recognition that modern defence forces had to win both the peace and the war, Dupont contended that the traditional emphasis on geostrategic imperatives not only ignored the globalised nature of modern conflict but also shaped the Australian Defence Force (ADF) for the wrong wars. Above all, 'in an age of globalisation and transnational threats', Dupont claimed that 'geography matters far less that it once did due to the compressions of space and time'.[57] This rejection of geopolitical considerations gained traction in updates of Australia's 2000 Defence White Paper, which gave greater support to expeditionary forces to operate in subordinate roles to support its US ally in distant theatres.

Dibb opposed 'tinkering' with the DOA policy, which was based firmly on the country's strategic geography; he also suggested a set of precepts to balance Australia's involvement with the United States after 9/11 that were weighted towards the specific defence needs of our region.[58] These precepts, prioritising the country's continental defence, prompted the winner of the Chief of Army Essay Competition, Major R.J. Worswick, to detail the mismatch between the defence of continental geography

---

55    Senator Robert Hill, 'Beyond the White Paper: Strategic Directions for Defence', address to the Australian Defence College, Canberra, 18 Jun. 2002.

56    Alan Dupont, 'Transformation or Stagnation? Rethinking Australia's Defence', *Australian Security in the 21st Century Seminar Series*, The Menzies Research Centre, Parliament House, Canberra, 13 Nov. 2003, p. 3.

57    Dupont, 'Transformation or Stagnation?' (2003).

58    Paul Dibb, 'Tinker with Defence and Risk Attack', *Australian*, 30 Oct. 2001; and Paul Dibb, *Australia's Alliance with America*, Melbourne Asia Policy Papers, Vol. 1, No. 1 (University of Melbourne, Mar. 2003), pp. 1–12.

and operational realities with overseas deployments in the Persian Gulf and the 'coalition of the willing' in Iraq.[59] This was followed by a contribution from the Chief of Army, Peter Leahy, which questioned 'how could the strategic reality of [offshore] operational commitments in support of interests be reconciled with a rigid strategic doctrine that upheld defence of geography?'[60] This counterview against the 'concentric circles theology' did not, as anticipated by Monk, result in a strategic changing of the guard.[61]

Instead the intervention of the ADF's Land Warfare Group led, as described by Major Stephanie Hodson, to the casting of Australia's strategic options in terms of 'regionalism versus globalisation'.[62] Not wanting to become entrapped in this dichotomy, Dupont nevertheless returned to the fray contending that 'geographical determinism is no substitute for sensible strategy'.[63] According to him, the ADF 'can no longer be configured solely for state on state conflicts or in the defence of the continent and immediate neighbourhood because of the compression of time and space that is the defining characteristic of a globalised world'.[64] It follows that 'our military forces must be versatile, smart, deployable over long distances and capable of protecting and sustaining themselves against all enemies, including the shadowy foes who will inhabit the urban battlefields of tomorrow'.[65]

## Counter Response

In response, Dibb was forced to reiterate the importance of strategic geography to Australia's defence policy to avoid being continually tarred with the geographical determinist brush that was so generously

---

59    R.J. Worswick, 'New Strategy for New Times: The Failings of "Defence of Australia"', *Australian Army Journal for the Profession of Arms*, Vol. 1, No. 1 (2003), pp. 147–56.

60    Peter Leahy, 'A Land Force for the Future: The Australian Army in the Early 21st Century', *Australian Army Journal for the Profession of Arms*, Vol. 1, No. 2 (2003), p. 22.

61    Paul Monk, 'A Strategic Changing of the Guard', *Australian*, 6 Jun. 2003, review section, pp. 6–7.

62    Stephanie Hodson, 'Regionalists Versus Globalists: Australia's Defence Strategy after 11 September 2001', *Australian Army Journal*, Vol. 11, No. 1 (2003), pp. 61–68.

63    Alan Dupont, *Grand Strategy, National Security and the Australian Defence Force* (Sydney: Lowy Institute, 2005), p. 4.

64    Dupont, *Grand Strategy* (2005), p. 6.

65    Dupont, *Grand Strategy* (2005), p. 6.

applied to Mackinder's ideas in the past.[66] While adhering to his overriding premise that geography is still a decisive factor in the fortunes of states, he has been careful to elaborate that a country's geographical environment does not absolutely dictate a state's defence policy.[67] Rather than imposing a geographical straitjacket on defence planners, he sees the use of geography as an 'independent variable' that can provide an important guide to the prudent structuring of Australia's air, naval and land force numbers.

Also, Dibb rebutted the argument that geography is less relevant in a globalised and spatially compressed world conjured up in such phrases that declare 'distance is dead' and the 'world is flat', which together presage the 'end of geography'.[68] Even in a flattening and shrinking world, geographical location is of prime importance, and distance remains to be modified, conquered and subjugated as Australia's isolation still accounted for two-fifths of its 20 per cent gap in productivity as compared with the United States.[69] Indeed Dibb's riposte was that geography is still relevant so long as Papua New Guinea is of more strategic importance to Australia than Guinea-Bissau in Africa! This stinging remark may have had some influence on defence

---

66    This was long after Spate (O.H.K. Spate, 'How Determined is Possibilism?', *Geographical Studies*, Vol. 4 (1957), pp. 2–12) had proposed 'probabilism' to end the interminable wrangle between 'determinism' and 'possibilism'. See Paul Dibb, 'Is Strategic Geography Relevant to Australia's Current Defence Policy?', *Australian Journal of International Affairs*, Vol. 60, No. 2 (2006), pp. 247–64; Paul Dibb, 'The Self-Reliant Defence of Australia: The History of an Idea', in Ron Huisken & Meredith Thatcher (eds), *History as Policy: Framing the Debate on the Future of Australia's Defence Policy*, Canberra Papers on Strategy and Defence No. 167 (Canberra: ANU E Press, 2007), pp. 11–26; and Paul Dibb, *Essays on Australian Defence*, Canberra Papers on Strategy and Defence No. 161 (Canberra: Strategic and Defence Studies Centre, 2006).

67    This sentiment echoes Nicholas Spykman's view that 'although the entire policy of a state does not derive from its geography, it cannot escape its geography'. See Nicholas J. Spykman, 'Geography and Foreign Policy, II', *The American Political Sciences Review*, Vol. 32, No. 2 (1938), p. 236.

68    Paul Dibb, 'The Self-reliant Defence of Australia: The History of an Idea', in Huisken & Thatcher, *History as Policy* (2007), pp. 11–26; and Paul Dibb, *The Future Balance of Power in East Asia: What are the Geopolitical Risks?*, Working Paper No. 406 (Canberra: Strategic and Defence Studies Centre, 2008).

69    Bryn Batterby, 'Does Distance Matter? The Effect of Geographic Isolation on Productivity Levels', *Treasury Working Paper 2006–03* (Canberra: The Treasury, Australian Government, Apr. 2006). Note Gerard Kelly and Gianni La Cava find evidence that Australia's average distance to final demand has *increased*, mainly during the 1990s. In 2011 Australia's trade costs were 17 per cent higher than the world average due to Australia's isolation, with goods and services being traded over longer distances, and resources being more costly to trade than manufactured goods. See Gerard Kelly & Gianni La Cava, 'International Trade Costs, Global Supply Chains and Value-added Trade in Australia', *Research Discussion Paper*, RDP–07 (Sydney: Economic Group, Reserve Bank of Australia, 2007).

planners shaping the 2009 Defence White Paper, *Force 2030*, which sought to reconcile the strategic geography and maritime approaches of Australia's inner arc, comprising Indonesia, the south-west Pacific, Timor-Leste and New Zealand, with an emphasis on terrorism, proliferation of weapons of mass destruction, and humanitarian and disaster responses, albeit in which Defence has a supportive rather than a leading role.[70] In the process, according to Hugh White, the concentric-rings model inherited from the 1987 and 2000 Defence white papers had, by 2009, become muddled with the removal of the ring separating maritime South-East Asia from the rest of the Asia.[71] Although the DOA rhetoric was maintained, Michael Arnold[72] has suggested that there has been a discernible shift towards a broader national security agenda espoused by Dupont and Paul Reckmeyer;[73] this prompted Dibb[74] to once again repeat the importance of the inner arc in Australian defence policy and planning. Even in a global virtual world, as noted by John Quelch and Katharine Jocz, place still matters![75] And given that troops on the ground must deal at first-hand with, and understand, the realities of local places (as in Afghanistan), local geography is of great importance at an operational level.

## Looking Ahead to 2035

By the 2013 Defence White Paper, there was a shift in strategy to reconceptualise a more expansive 'single strategic arc' by amalgamating Dibb's 'area of direct military interest' and his 'area of primary concern'. The resultant arc covers Indo-Pacific Asia, stretching from

70   Commonwealth of Australia, *Defending Australia in the Asia-Pacific Century: Force 2030, Defence White Paper* (Canberra: Department of Defence, 2009) pp. 46–47.
71   Hugh White, 'A Wobbly Bridge; Strategic Interests and Objectives in *Force 2009*', *Security Challenges*, Vol. 5, No. 2 (2009), pp. 21–29.
72   Michael Arnold, 'Australia's Defence Policy: A Market State Approach?', PhD thesis, Deakin University, 2012.
73   Alan Dupont & William J. Reckmeyer, 'Australia's National Security Priorities: Addressing Strategic Risk in a Globalised World', *Australian Journal of International Affairs*, Vol. 66, No. 1 (2012), pp. 34–51.
74   Paul Dibb, 'The Importance of the Inner Arc to Australian Defence Policy and Planning', *Security Challenges*, Vol. 8, No. 4 (2012), pp. 13–31.
75   John A. Quelch & Katherine E. Jocz, *All Business is Local: Why Place Matters More Than Ever in a Global Virtual World* (New York: Portfolio/Penguin, 2012).

the mid-Indian Ocean to the mid-Pacific Ocean.[76] Without reference to the influence of either Dibb or Dupont, Rory Medcalf casts this maritime super-region as 'Australia's new strategic map', encompassing the strategic interests of China, India, Japan, Indonesia and the United States.[77] However, Chengxin Pan[78] and Yang Yi and Zhao Qinghai[79] suggest that the intent of this new political space is to contain China rather than embrace it (See Fig. 5).

The sheer extent of this maritime environment centred upon South-East Asia, as highlighted by Dibb and Richard Brabin-Smith,[80] raises the issue of the Australian Government's ability to provide and operationalise the necessary force structure and budget to defend the country's lines of communication and contribute to military contingencies.[81] Given this dilemma, it is hoped that a new generation of geographers will be brought into interdisciplinary teams of analysts and thinkers to evaluate the validity of this meta-geographical concept.[82] Such an intergenerational change, foreshadowed by Alex Burns and Ben Eltham,[83] would bring about Dibb's plea[84] to return geography to its proper place in defence planning in the post-Afghanistan era so as to focus on the country's northern and north-

---

76   Commonwealth of Australia, *Defence White Paper 2013* (Canberra: Department of Defence, 3 May), p. 2; Cameron Hill, 'Australia in the "Indo-Pacific" Century: Rewards, Risks, Relationship', Parliament of Australia, (Canberra: Parliamentary Library, 2014); and Mohan Malik, 'The Indo-Pacific Domain: Challenges and Opportunities', in Mohan Malik (ed.), *Maritime Security in the Indo-Pacific: Perspectives from China, India and the United States* (Lanhan, MA, and London: Rowman & Littlefield, 2014), pp. 1–44.

77   Rory Medcalf, 'In Defence of the Indo-Pacific: Australia's New Strategic Map', *Australian Journal of International Affairs*, Vol. 68, No. 4 (2014), pp. 470–83.

78   Chengxin Pan, 'The "Indo-Pacific" and Geopolitical Anxieties about China's Rise in the Asian Regional Order', *Australian Journal of International Affairs*, Vol. 68, No. 4 (2014), pp. 453–69.

79   Yang Yi & Zhao Qinghai, 'The "Indo-Pacific" Concept: Implications for China', in Malik, *Maritime Security* (2014), pp. 61–83.

80   Paul Dibb & Richard Brabin-Smith, 'Challenges for Defence (And Do We Really Need 12 Submarines?)', *ASPI: The Strategist*, 12 Dec. 2013.

81   Andrew Phillips, 'Australia and the Challenges of Order-Building in the Indian Ocean Region', *Australian Journal of International Affairs*, Vol. 67, No. 2 (2013), pp. 125–40; and Rory Medcalf & James Brown, *Defence Challenges 2035: Securing Australia's Lifelines* (Sydney: Lowy Institute for International Policy, 2014).

82   See Dennis Rumley, Timothy Doyle & Sanjay Chaturvedi, '"Securing" the Indian Ocean? Competing Regional Security Constructions', *Journal of the Indian Ocean Region*, Vol. 8, No. 1 (2012), pp. 1–20; and Dennis Rumley, 'Western Australia: Peripheral State and Indian Ocean Orientation', *The Otemon Gakuin Journal of Australian Studies*, Vol. 39 (2013), pp. 7–30.

83   Alex Burns & Ben Eltham, 'Australia's Strategic Culture: Constraints and Opportunities in Security Policy Making', *Contemporary Security Policy*, Vol. 35, No. 2 (2014), pp. 187–210.

84   Paul Dibb, 'Strategy Must Shift Back to Asia-Pacific', *Australian*, 31 May 2014.

western approaches, its immediate neighbours and South-East Asia. Indeed the time may be ripe for a new-style Dibb Review offering a long-term vision that defines strategic risks, approach and the role of Australia's armed forces to 2035.

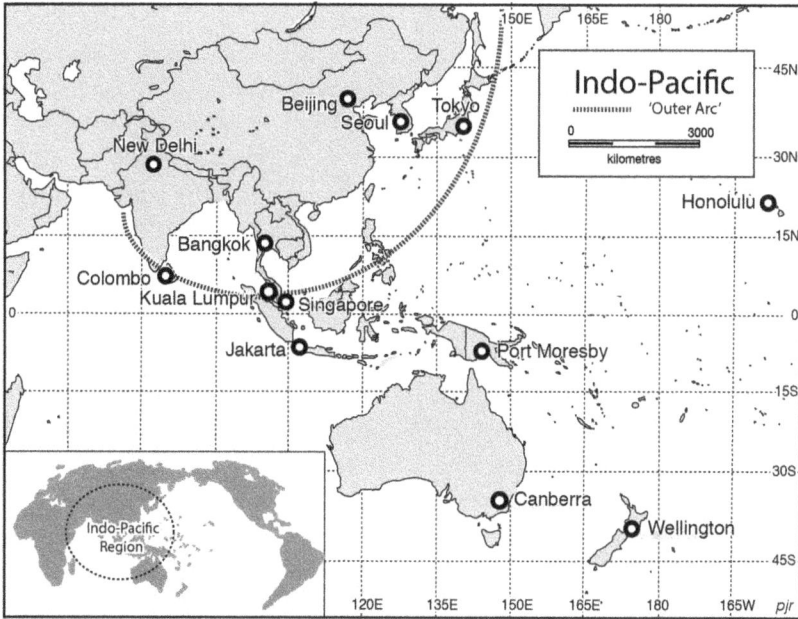

Figure 5: The new Indo-Pacific strategic arc construct connects the Indian and Pacific oceans through South-East Asia.[85] Not only does the construct cover East Asia and the west Pacific regions but also includes the hitherto neglected regions of south and west Asia. As illustrated by the inset showing the Indo-Pacific region centred on India, the definition of the Indo-Pacific concept varies according to the particular country concerned[86]

## Conclusions

Fellow geographers are keenly aware that Dibb's influence on Australia's defence policy in the aftermath of the Vietnam War reprises that exercised by the geographers Griffith Taylor and Spate after the

85    Commonwealth of Australia, *Defence White Paper 2013*, p. 7; EGP, 'Australia Places itself at the Center of Things', *EnerGeoPolitics*, 15 May 2013, energeopolitics.com/tag/indo-pacific/.
86    Atul Kumar, 'Indo-Pacific Security', 2 May 2014, www.indopacificsecurity.com/2014/05/about.html.

First and Second World Wars. Indeed his direct impact as a strategic planner on defence policy has outstripped even these luminaries. His signal contribution has been in highlighting geographical location as a key factor in reshaping the country's defence policy. Incorporating this factor into a set of principles to guide policy has enabled him to make his mark in the wider community almost in the same league as that exerted in another era by the leading American geographer Isaiah Bowman,[87] who accompanied US President Woodrow Wilson to the Paris Peace Conference held after the First World War in Versailles.[88] An added bonus has been his watching brief as Australia's leading academic specialist on Russian geography in which he has presciently noted the 'bear is back' and its willingness to contemplate disruption in order to expand its strategic space. This style of analysis has also been extended to commentary on China's economic, political and military affairs.[89]

All political geographers from Mackinder to Dibb have emphasised the important role of 'the map' (though often one is not provided!). Neglect of the map's value has led Robert Kaplan to refer to the 'revenge of geography' from ignoring what the map tells us about coming conflicts and battles.[90] Contemporary political geographers, represented by Gerard Toal, want to go beyond this style of analysis by arguing that the resultant geographies 'cannot be considered without, at the same time, examining how economies are organized, states are governed, technological systems deployed and power distributed across the earth'.[91] This observation coincides with Dibb's plea for having political geographers as members of interdisciplinary teams

---

87    Isaiah Bowman, *The New World: Problems in Political Geography* (Yonkers-on-Hudson: New York World Book Company, 1921).

88    John K. Wright & George F. Carter, *Isaiah Bowman, 1878–1950: Biographical Memoir* (Washington, D.C.: National Academy of Sciences, 1959); Griffith Taylor, 'First Presidential Address' (1963); and Dibb, 'A Trivial Strategic Age?' (2000).

89    Paul Dibb, 'The Bear is Back (A Resurgent Russia?)', *The American Interest*, Vol. 2, No. 2 (Nov./Dec. 2006), pp. 78–85; Paul Dibb, 'Why I Disagree with Hugh White on China's Rise', *Australian*, 13 Aug. 2012; and Paul Dibb, 'Why did Putin Decide to Invade Ukraine?', *ASPI: The Strategist*, 24 Mar. 2014.

90    Robert E. Kaplan, 'The Revenge of Geography', *Foreign Policy* (May/Jun. 2009), pp. 1–9; · and Robert E. Kaplan, *The Revenge of Geography: What the Map Tells Us About Coming Conflicts and the Battle Against Fate* (New York: Random House, 2012).

91    Gerard Toal, 'Movie Geopolitics: Response to Robert Kaplan's "The Revenge of Geography" essay', *Human Geography*, Vol. 2, No. 2 (2001), p. 51.

to reflect upon the strategic implications of Australia's cul-de-sac position in relation to the 'Main Street' connection linking Europe, Asia and North America.[92]

Geography, and geopolitics in particular, have sought to reinvent themselves in the years since Dibb was a member of the Department of Human Geography in RSPacS at ANU in 1969.[93] In the process, geography's disciplinary clout has been lost in some Australian academic centres due to amalgamations of departments with cognate disciplines and the suffusion of its identity in omnibus titles. This experience is contrary to that of their thriving counterparts, with multiple professors of geography in other centres within Australia, Hong Kong, Singapore, the United Kingdom and the United States, many of whom are well versed in geopolitics. These vibrant departments have been buoyed by the use of geographical information systems, the need to address the logistical and local implications of climate change, and explorations of such contemporary topics as terror and territory.[94] Not only their output but also Dibb's life work as a political geographer in Australia should remind both governments and university decision-makers of the power of geography in public policy and discourse, and the need to ensure that it is front and centre in both teaching and research programs.

---

92  Commonwealth of Australia, *Defence White Paper 2013*, p. 13; and Peter J. Rimmer, *Asian-Pacific Rim Logistics: Global Context and Local Policies* (Cheltenham and Northampton, MA: Edward Elgar, 2014), pp. 35–36.

93  Gearóid Ó Tuathail & Simon Darby, 'Introduction: Rethinking Geopolitics: Towards a Critical Geopolitics', in Gearóid Ó Tuathail & Simon Darby (eds), *Rethinking Geopolitics* (London and New York: Routledge, 1998), pp. 1–15; David Harvey, 'Reinventing Geography', *New Left Review*, Vol. 4 (Jul.–Aug. 2000, pp. 75–97; and Klaus Dodds, Merje Kuus & Joanne Sharp, 'Introduction: Geopolitics and its Critics', in Klaus Dodds, Merje Kuus & Joanne Sharp (eds), *The Ashgate Research Companion to Critical Geopolitics* (Farnham and Burlington, VT: Ashgate, 2013), pp. 1–14.

94  Stuart Ebden, *The Birth of Territory* (Minneapolis: University of Minnesota Press, 2013).

# 6

# The Importance of Geography

Robert Ayson

At the end of an article in which he explains why geography should matter in Australian defence policymaking, Paul Dibb resumed a long-standing duel. Citing Alan Dupont's argument that the confines of Australia's location should matter less and its wider interests and values rather more, Dibb's assessment is typically caustic: 'explain to me', he demands, 'just how we are going to defend our values in Myanmar and the People's Republic of China or our trade interests in such far-flung parts of the world as Nigeria or Argentina?'[1]

But in the several years over which I was a colleague of Dibb's at The Australian National University (ANU) I was struck by the energy and consistency of his criticism of another counterpart in the Australian strategic debate. This unlucky person was Senator Robert Hill who, from 2001 to 2006, was Defence Minister under Prime Minister John Howard. Clearly holding Hill personally and principally responsible for what he saw as a confusion and refutation of the geographical logic that had underpinned Australian strategy since the early 1970s, Dibb's attacks were frequent and severe (and the vocabularly was even more colourful in hallway conversations at ANU than it was in print).

---

1    Paul Dibb, 'Is Strategic Geography Relevant to Australia's Current Defence Policy', *Australian Journal of International Affairs*, Vol. 60, No. 2 (Jun. 2006), p. 262.

By the time he was writing the article just cited, Hill had resigned from the Senate, an event that was undoubtedly a cause for celebration in the Dibb household. For all we know it may even have been the occasion for the purchase of another in a long list of German motorcars. Even once that change had occurred, however, Dibb showed little mercy in his assessment of Hill's legacy, stating that, during his time in office, Hill 'presided over a force structure development that lacked rigorous intellectual prioritization'[2] — one of the deadly sins in Dibb's universe of strategic thinking. In Dibb's view, Hill consistently confused 'our broader strategic interests with our vital defence interests'.[3] Elsewhere he recounted another apparent transgression: Hill 'seemed to be more interested in the foreign policy aspects of the Defence portfolio'.[4] So much, then, for diplomacy, which appears much less important to Dibb for the protection of Australia's vital interests than intelligence assessment (his own original area of work) and defence capability (which would become an increasing focus as his career blossomed).

The basis of Dibb's criticism is not difficult to locate. Hill was 'responsible ... for seriously undermining the logical strategic priorities of our force structure' because he had ignored the importance of Australia's geography.[5] In fact Hill had done even worse; in Dibb's view he had deliberately argued that in an age of global security threats, exemplified by the World Trade Center attacks of September 2001 (9/11), geography was essentially irrelevant. By unpicking the carefully honed logic of geography, which had served Australia well since the end of the days of forward defence, ad hoc policymaking in this crucial part of the Howard era gave rise to such dangerous notions that Australia could even have vital interests in the Middle East. That was far too far from Australia's neighbourhood for Dibb.

It is difficult to exaggerate the importance of geographical considerations in Dibb's approach to strategy and defence policy decision-making, especially, but not only, in the case of Australia.

---

2    Dibb, 'Strategic Geography' (2006), p. 248.

3    Dibb, 'Strategic Geography' (2006), p. 252.

4    Paul Dibb, 'The Self-Reliant Defence of Australia: The History of an Idea', in Ron Huisken & Meredith Thatcher (eds), *History as Policy: Framing the Debate on the Future of Australia's Defence Policy*, Canberra Papers on Strategy and Defence No. 167 (Canberra: ANU E Press, 2007), p. 22.

5    Dibb, 'The Self-Reliant Defence of Australia' (2007), p. 22.

In later writing he anticipates the concerns of some about his analysis by protesting that '[n]ation states do not find themselves in a geographical straitjacket'.[6] Just two pages later, however, Dibb insists that 'the consistent application of strategic geography should be an iron discipline for a country with Australia's modest size[d] defence force'.[7] Little room for choice is left for determining the sort of capabilities that Australia requires: 'The characteristics of the archipelago to our north ... demand', he writes, 'that we be able to deploy air, naval and land forces there.'[8] Elsewhere he writes that for Australia:

> Concepts of operations have to be assessed on the contribution they can make to the unique problems in defending a large continent with extensive maritime surrounds and flanked by the archipelagic chain to the north.[9]

There is more than a hint of material determinism in these passages. The overriding message appears to be that if the straitjacket of strategic geography fits, Australia needs to be wearing it.

According to Dibb, Australia's straitjacket is not a one-size-fits-all garment but, rather, is a specially crafted piece of clothing that offers permanent restraint to its singular wearer: 'Our unique strategic geography will not disappear.' Dibb's view of the importance of strategic geography is connected to one of the main organising concepts for Australian thinking in the late 1990s, which he helped popularise:

> What I have called the 'arc of instability' to our north ... promises to confront us with even more challenging contingencies than those we have experienced recently in East Timor and Solomon Islands. These are abiding strategic interests for Australia.[10]

---

6    Paul Dibb, 'The Importance of the Inner Arc to Australian Defence Policy and Planning', *Security Challenges*, Vol. 8, No. 4 (2012), p. 14.

7    Dibb, 'The Importance of the Inner Arc' (2012), p. 16.

8    Dibb, 'The Importance of the Inner Arc' (2012), p. 255.

9    Paul Dibb, *The Conceptual Basis of Australia's Defence Planning and Force Structure Development*, Canberra Papers on Strategy and Defence No. 88 (Canberra: The Australian National University, 1992), p. 23.

10   Dibb, 'The Self-Reliant Defence of Australia' (2007), p. 24. Dibb's influential depictions of that arc of instability in the wake of the collapse of the Suharto regime in Indonesia included one special piece of geopolitical hyperbolae that 'a balkanised Indonesia, a broken-backed Papua New Guinea and a weak New Zealand are very real prospects'. Paul Dibb, David D. Hale & Peter Prince, 'Asia's Insecurity', *Survival*, Vol. 41, No. 3 (Autumn 1999), p. 18.

That last sentence, and the logic which informs it, is crucial. If Australia's strategic geography is unique, and if that same strategic geography shapes Australia's abiding (and truly vital) interests, then it follows that Australia's abiding interests are also unique.[11] One finds in Dibb's work few references to that frequent reference point of liberal thinkers: the common interests that can unite countries in common endeavour. Dibb finds reassurance not in the possibility of concerts of power or effective regional security mechanisms for a changing Asia, but in what he regards as the consistent pursuit of their interests by self-regarding nation-states. Nothing more and nothing less should be expected or required from Australia.[12]

This also means that even the closest of allies, who presumably have their own unique geographies and interests, may be limited in the extent to which they are ready to come to anyone else's assistance. Indeed, as Dibb observes in citing the work of T.B. Millar (the founding Director of The Australian National University's Strategic and Defence Studies Centre (SDSC)), Canberra's recognition of the limits of likely American support in a tricky immediate neighbourhood helped give rise to Australia's enthusiasm for a defence force that was able to operate independently closer to home. In the 1960s this meant recognising 'the possibility of Australian forces being required to act without the assistance of the United States against any future Indonesian threats to Papua New Guinea'.[13]

It must be remarked here that Dibb does see major powers as belonging to a different category in terms of their willingness and drive to exert their much stronger military power globally, and in some of the

---

11   To continue that theme of uniqueness, Dibb has also argued that 'In the absence of a threat, the Australian defence community has developed a unique conceptual basis for defence planning and force-structure development which reflects Australia's geography, the nature of the sea and air approaches to the continent, and the characteristics of regional military capabilities and potentialities.' Dibb, *The Conceptual Basis* (1992), p. xv.

12   In a possible and somewhat unexpected exception, Dibb argued in the early 1980s that Australia needed to be more aware of the concerns of developing countries in its neighbourhood, which included calls for justice. He chided Australia for ignoring these and other demands, not for some altruistic purpose but instead because to do so would be in 'Australia's long term interests'. Paul Dibb, 'Introduction', in Paul Dibb (ed.), *Australia's External Relations in the 1980s, The Interaction of Economic, Political and Strategic Factors* (New York: Croom Helm Australia and St Martin's Press, 1983), pp. 12–13.

13   Dibb, 'The Importance of the Inner Arc' (2012), p. 17.

capabilities (including nuclear weapons) that they possessed.[14] His long-standing study of Russia (about which more will be said later) was part of the inspiration, and this helped bring Australia into consideration. Geography meant that Russia's main interests were also concentrated closer to home, 'on the main land mass of continental Asia, particularly with those countries that are near to Soviet territory or which are capable of mounting (or supporting) military strikes against the Russian homeland', he wrote less than half a decade before the Soviet Union collapsed. But, at the same time, he observed '[t]he USSR is a global power with world-wide interests',[15] which meant an interest in events far away, including in Australia and New Zealand, two allies of Moscow's main Cold War foe.

Anyone who has listened to Dibb speaking will have heard him referring to the real threat analysis of those Cold War years, when the West was faced with the awesome strikepower of the formidable Soviet nuclear arsenal. Dibb treated nuclear weapons as special partly because, unlike so many other factors in the strategic environment, these systems were genuinely able to transcend geography when mated to long-range delivery systems. They therefore preceded (and trumped) the exaggerations about security in a world of globalisation that had so beguiled what he regarded as lesser Australian minds.

Dibb did recognise the immediate impact of the attacks on the World Trade Center twin towers in New York and the Pentagon, Washington, in September 2001.[16] He noted the effect that these events had on American thinking as Washington contemplated 'the threat from a small group of individuals, without a major power behind them, which has proved capable of inflicting death and damage on a horrendous scale'.[17] But he was less worried about the damage that the terrorists could do to the West in material terms than he was about America's willingness to be distracted from its main purpose as a great power:

---

14    The principal outworking of this logic is a superb monograph that, in my opinion, is his best piece of published writing. See Paul Dibb, *Towards a New Balance of Power in Asia*, Adelphi Paper No. 295 (London: International Institute for Strategic Studies, 1995).

15    Paul Dibb, 'Soviet Strategy Towards Australia, New Zealand and the Southwest Pacific', *Australian Outlook*, Aug. 1985, p. 69.

16    See Paul Dibb, 'The Future of International Coalitions', *The Washington Quarterly*, Vol. 25, No. 2 (2002), pp. 129–44.

17    Paul Dibb, *The Future Balance of Power in East Asia: What are the Geopolitical Risks?*, Working Paper No. 406 (Canberra: Strategic and Defence Studies Centre, 2008), p. 7.

> We saw in the Cold War how one-eyed America's policies could be: the United States brooked no other subject of national security warranting serious attention. There is a risk that we are not in a similar period of US preoccupation, just when serious geopolitical challenges are set to emerge in East Asia.[18]

There was a message here not just for thinkers in Washington, but for anyone in Canberra who Dibb felt had become dangerously obsessed by the war on terror. And, unlike the great powers, Australia did not have the sheer material base to spend too much time on matters away from its own neighbourhood. Instead, the iron discipline of geography mattered even more to Australia because of its inherent limitations, which in comparison to the few major players he had no hesitation in depicting as a one of the region's 'smaller powers'.[19]

## The Dibb Review and All That

The idea that geography bequeathed Australia a unique position in the world in general, and in Asia more particularly, and that it put particular and unquestioning demands on Australia's defence requirements is most famously conveyed in the review Dibb wrote for Labor Prime Minister Bob Hawke's Defence Minister, Kim Beazley.[20] Its author is a little shy about the publicity that is still often given to that work, but I do not think he minds people mentioning it as much as he sometimes indicates. I think his concern is that they may think it is the only thing he has done. Dibb is rightly respected for constructing such a cogent and influential document that crystallised the tone of the past decade or more of Australian strategic thinking.

The review is of Australia's defence capability requirements. And, like the 1987 Australian Defence White Paper that it helped to inspire, the capability question is always the $64 million — or, closer to the point, the multi-billion dollar — one for defence planning. But Dibb's review would simply not hold together without the geographical logic that

---

18  Dibb, *The Future Balance of Power in East Asia* (2008), p. 11.

19  For that depiction, see Paul Dibb, 'The Strategic Inter-relations of the US, the USSR and China in the East Asia-Pacific Area', *Australian Outlook* (Aug. 1978), p. 181.

20  Paul Dibb, *Review of Australia's Defence Capabilities*, report to the Minister for Defence (Canberra: Australian Government Publishing Service, 1986).

underpins so much of the reasoning. If Australia wanted to get serious about the question of strategic guidance, then there was one main answer. 'There is a requirement', Dibb writes:

> To study more seriously the effect of our geography on force development. Because of its proximity, the archipelago to our north is the area from which a conventional military threat to the security of Australian territory could most easily be posed. A thorough understanding of the air and sea gap to our north, and of Australia's northern hinterland, will enable us to take account of the limitations and risks that geography places on any attacking force.[21]

In this sense, at least, geography was the Australian defence planner's friend, and that defence planner should exploit that friendship for the advantages it offered. 'The sea gap to our north', the review continues, 'is a formidable barrier to any enemy, and the problems of crossing it need to be assessed thoroughly.'[22] In combination with other geographical constraints (for adversaries rather than for Australia at this point), this was a crucial explanation for Dibb's advice that Australia focus on lower level challenges to its sovereign interests: 'There are few nations', he observes, 'that could undertake such hazardous and exposed operations.'[23]

But some of the very same material factors were complications for Australia in its ability to project military power, and they were complications that could not be ignored. In the preceding section Dibb takes this point on directly. Raging against the machine, he cries out that '[m]uch of what are presented as national security interests are basically current political perceptions of what is favourable and unfavourable'.[24] Instead, the formula should lie in the political aims stemming from material authority:

> Definition of our national security interests should begin with the statement that the exercise of authority over our land territory, territorial sea and airspace is fundamental to our sovereignty and security. The size of our continent and the location of some external island territories makes this a formidable task.[25]

---

21   Dibb, *Review of Australia's Defence Capabilities* (1986), p. 38.
22   Dibb, *Review of Australia's Defence Capabilities* (1986), p. 38.
23   Dibb, *Review of Australia's Defence Capabilities* (1986), p. 38.
24   Dibb, *Review of Australia's Defence Capabilities* (1986), p. 36.
25   Dibb, *Review of Australia's Defence Capabilities* (1986), pp. 36–37.

Dibb returns to this point as an enduring theme for the determination of an appropriate defence force posture for Australia:

> An important and recurring theme of this Review is the need to concentrate force structure priorities on our area of direct military interest. This area stretches over 4000 nautical miles from the Cocos Islands in the west to New Zealand and the islands of the South West Pacific in the east and over 3000 nautical miles from the archipelago and island chain in the north to the Southern Ocean. Defending such a large area is a formidable task.[26]

## The Russia Expert

An interesting common theme in Dibb's thinking, which goes beyond the 1986 review, is his application of the idea of an area of primary strategic interest defined by one's immediate geography to his depiction of Russia's priorities. This is unsurprising, given that the work of which Dibb is most proud, his study of the Soviet Union, was published in the same year as the Dibb Review.[27] But the research underpinning that book stretched back further than the concentrated period of one year that he had to work on his review. Thus, it is not unreasonable to argue that the roots of Dibb's assessment of Australia's strategic geography lie somewhere much further away than the archipelagic screen.

In fact, while economic and political problems are one of the central reasons for Dibb's assessment of the Soviet Union as an *incomplete* superpower, geographical challenges also loom prominently in his explanation. Having both cited and challenged Sir Halford J. Mackinder's prescription of the control of Eurasia as a sure basis for world power, Dibb argues that the location and expanse of Soviet Russian territory is as much a curse as it is a blessing:

> The great geographical spread of the USSR — from Europe in the west and the Middle East in the south to China and Japan in the east — makes the USSR a primary factor in the security considerations of many neighbouring countries. Sometimes this proximity works to the

---

26   Dibb, *Review of Australia's Defence Capabilities* (1986), p. 57.
27   Paul Dibb, *The Soviet Union: The Incomplete Superpower* (London: International Institute for Strategic Studies and Macmillan, 1986).

advantage of the USSR (as in the case of Eastern Europe, Mongolia and even Finland), but it can also cause suspicion and hostility (as with China, Japan, Pakistan, Iran and Turkey).[28]

Unlike Australia, it was not the politics of other governments (i.e. the one in Jakarta) that was most likely to cause that antagonism in the neighbourhood. It was Russia's policies themselves that were causing many of the problems. Soviet Russia gets a backhanded compliment: 'Geopolitically the USSR has succeeded in realizing its worst fears by ensuring that it is surrounded with enemies on virtually every side.'[29] Moscow's political choices mattered. But, again, geography was the necessary (if not the sufficient) condition for these problems. Dibb argued earlier that: 'The very vastness of the Russian land mass allows for the existence of powerful and almost inevitably unsympathetic nations around the Soviet periphery.'[30] In a play on Mackinder, which turned Eurasia from an asset into a liability, geography was very nearly the Soviet Union's destiny.

But this was not unchanging, as if what had limited (and advantaged) Russia yesterday would always limit it (and advantage it) tomorrow. Geography always matters, but the parts of a country's geography that matter most can shift. Here Dibb pointed to the increasingly important role of Siberia in Russia's strategic geography. This was partly due to that area's energy and resource wealth and what this would mean for the Soviet Union's economic future. It was also due to Siberia's proximity to China, which for Dibb is an almost perpetual strategic competitor for Russia. And, with Siberia, the mix of strategic geographical pros and cons, which would become a pattern in Dibb's thinking more generally, come through loud and clear:

> Seen from the Kremlin, Siberia is a distant possession flanked by hostile states. There is a keen awareness that Siberia is a large and resource-rich domain, but that it is sparsely populated and has poorly developed and vulnerable transport links with the European USSR. Moreover, it shares a very long border with 1 billion Chinese and is close to Japan, the major ally of the US in the Pacific.[31]

---

28  Dibb, *The Soviet Union* (1988), p. 22.
29  Dibb, *The Soviet Union* (1988), p. 133–34.
30  Dibb, *The Soviet Union* (1988), p. 22.
31  Dibb, *The Soviet Union* (1988), p. 55.

The parallels should be clear by now. With its vast expanses, its huge distance from the most populated areas of the country and its own sparse demography (and a hostile climate to boot), and abutting the maritime areas where putative adversaries exist, the north of the island continent of Australia is to Canberra what Siberia is to Moscow. Just as Siberia 'abuts on the populous Asian civilizations of China and Japan',[32] the same might be said of the northern reaches of Australia in relation to the populous Indonesia (where a Javanese civilisation is part of its make-up). *The Incomplete Superpower* is, in this sense, the model for the Dibb Review. Dibb's assertion that '[t]here is a certain unease in Moscow about the longterm security of Siberia',[33] is not far from what he wished Canberra to feel about Australia's northern stretches and approaches. Maybe Australia's strategic geography wasn't quite so unique after all.[34]

In favour of the hypothesis that there was something Russian in the water when Dibb was thinking about Australia is the fact that Russia, and Siberia in particular, have not been passing enthusiasms.[35] Not only was Siberia the *future* for the concentration of Russian strategic effort (just as he wanted Australia to shift more of the focus of its defence force towards the far north, where it could sit close to the sea–air gap), Russia, and Siberia in particular, also formed the *past* for much of Dibb's published research effort.

The earliest of Dibb's publications that can be readily found is an ANU occasional paper on Soviet agriculture from 1969, which features tables on such glamorous subjects as sugar beet, potato and

---

32   Dibb, *The Soviet Union* (1988), p. 56.
33   Dibb, *The Soviet Union* (1988), p. 55.
34   There may have been triplets. In the early 1980s, writing while Deputy Director of Australia's Joint Intelligence Organisation, Dibb observed that 'China's vast territory and huge population offer both strategic advantages and disadvantages to its leaders … Beijing must feel confident that the natural barrier provided by the sea in the east, couple with the extensive presence of military and paramilitary forces in the coastal areas, makes a major assault from this direction remote … Also, the nearly impenetrable Himalayas opposite India free China from major concern over threats to its heartland from that direction. Only in the north and north-east does geography complicate Beijing's defence planning, with major areas susceptible to Soviet air and ground attack. Even there, however, the mountainous nature of the terrain narrows the avenues of approach available to an invader and allows Chinese forces to be prepositioned to block historical attack routes'. Paul Dibb, 'China's Strategic Situation and Defence Priorities in the 1980s', *Australian Journal of Chinese Affairs*, No. 5 (1981), p. 99.
35   Of course Russia has been nothing less than a continuing passion. For a return to his favourite subject but under a title which was not of the author's choosing, see Paul Dibb, 'The Bear is Back', *American Interest*, Vol. 2, No. 2 (2006), pp. 78–85.

wheat production.[36] But, three years later, Dibb published his first book, a sector by sector study of Siberia that, early on, displays the hallmarks of its author's geographical emphasis, even to the point of putting the most advanced of military capabilities in context. 'The lack of compactness of the USSR, its great longitudinal extent, and the disparate location of population and industry in Siberia are positive strategic assets', writes Dibb. And yet, in the very next sentence we again catch that glimpse of the yin and yang of strategic geography. 'The dangers of a conventional invasion across permeable land frontiers from neighbouring China, which ironically the USSR itself helped to industrialize in the 1960s,' he continues, 'may thus be of more real concern to Moscow than the theoretical implications of nuclear attack.'[37] Moreover, right at the front of this early volume comes a hint that there is something to one of the parallels suggested above when Dibb compares the spread of human habitation of Siberia with a more local example. In Eastern Siberia, he writes: 'The distribution of population is about 3.3 persons per square mile, which may be compared with a sparsely populated country such as Australia with over 4 persons per square mile.'[38]

## Conclusion

To resort to Isaiah Berlin's typology, Paul Dibb is more of a hedgehog (a thinker who focuses on one big idea) and less of a fox (who knows many).[39] Dibb's big idea is that material factors are the things that matter for understanding a country's outlook on security and for determining its defence posture. Principal among these material factors is a country's geography. Most of Dibb's career has been spent pondering the impact of the unique strategic geographies of two countries: his adopted home in Australia and the vast country he was so drawn to in Russia. Readers of *The Incomplete Superpower* may be surprised that someone who is often assumed to be focused on questions of defence

---

36    See Paul Dibb, *Soviet Agriculture since Khruschev*, Occasional Paper No. 4, Department of Political Science, Research School of Social Sciences (Canberra: The Australian National University, 1969), p. 8.

37    Paul Dibb, *Siberia and the Pacific, a Study in Economic Development and Trade Prospects* (New York: Praeger, 1972), p. 17.

38    Dibb, *Siberia and the Pacific* (1972), p. 5.

39    Isaiah Berlin, *The Hedgehog and the Fox: An Essay on Tolstoy's View of History* (London: Weidenfeld and Nicolson, 1953), p. 1.

capability should spend so much time on the non-military material bases of power: geography, economics and demography. The first of these factors was needed to show what sort of defence capabilities it made sense for a country to develop. The second and third shaped what scale of that defence undertaking would be possible.

If there was a calculation of threats it began with these material factors. Politics was then the variable which came on top of these to determine whether friendship or enmity would result. Indonesia was important to Australia, Dibb argued, because of inescapable material factors: 'simple prudence suggests', he wrote in the early 1980s, 'that Indonesia is the only country with the size, the proximity and the potential in the longer term for significant assault against Australia.'[40] But it would be its politics that would decide whether these material factors turned it into a friend or foe. Dibb wrote recently:

> We have got used to the fact that Indonesia's military forces have little in the way of strategic reach. Over the next two or three decades that may change if there are sustained high rates of economic growth and higher defence budgets ... A well armed, unfriendly Indonesia would be a first order strategic challenge for Australia and would preoccupy us to the exclusion of practically every other defence planning issue. On the other hand, a well-armed friendly Indonesia would be a security asset for Australia and the region.[41]

Politics matter. Yet, without economic strength, and the military power it affords, Indonesia cannot be a great power. This continues to be relevant to Canberra because of Indonesia's unique place in Australia's unique strategic geography.

As a hedgehog, and a very able one, Dibb's single-minded focus has been intimidating to those unfortunate enough to get in his way. He has little patience for those who, in his view, have failed to give a rigorous accounting of a country's vital interests grounded in a crystal-clear assessment of material factors (hence the importance of intelligence analysis). This makes Dibb something of a determinist, and someone who takes an approach to the relationship between material factors and force structure the way a Marxist sees the relationship between material economic factors and politics. Power matters, and the material

---

40    Paul Dibb, 'Issues in Australian Defence', *Australian Outlook* (Dec. 1983), p. 162.
41    Dibb, 'The Importance of the Inner Arc' (2012), p. 28.

sources of power matter most. Hence the instructions given by Dibb
to one of the SDSC's longest-serving administrators that he should not
be bothered by invitations to converse with representatives of 'PACs'
(piss-ant countries). But that rigour also meant that he had a clear
sense of how much was enough. A country's defence posture was not
only energised by geography, demography and economics, it should
be controlled by these factors as well.

Two examples serve to illustrate this logic. The first is from the subject
of his original and primary affection. 'The Soviet presence in East Asia
and her status as a world power are inextricably combined', he wrote
for the International Institute for Strategic Studies (IISS) in the early
1980s. 'Unlike the US, the USSR cannot even consider withdrawing
from a part of the world where nearly 30 million of her people live in
a territory vital to her economy.'[42] The second comes in the conclusion
to what Dibb has described as 'an historic document',[43] the Dibb
Review begins its close with these surprisingly upbeat lines:

> Australia is one of the most secure countries in the world. It is
> distant from the main centres of global military confrontation, and
> it is surrounded by large expanses of water which make it difficult to
> attack. Australia shares no land borders with any other nation, it does
> not stand astride any vital international sea lanes, nor does it control
> crucial maritime choke points.[44]

Is Australia's relative security a reality in Dibb's view because of the
extent of its defence force? The answer is no. Is it secure because
of its alliance with the United States? The answer again is no. Does
Australia's security come to it by virtue of its stable democratic
politics? No. Because of the strength of its economy and the size of its
population (other material factors)? No and no. The solitary answer is
quite clear. That answer is geography.

---

42   Paul Dibb, 'Soviet Capabilities, Interests and Strategies in East Asia in the 1980s', *Survival*,
Jul./Aug. 1982, pp. 155–62, p. 156.
43   Dibb, 'The Self-Reliant Defence of Australia' (2007), p. 18.
44   Dibb, *Review of Australia's Defence Capabilities* (1986), p. 174.

# 7

# Paul Dibb's Impact on Australian Defence Policy

Former Ambassador Kim Beazley

Paul Dibb is indelibly badged in Australian political debate as the creative spirit behind the 1980s Labor Government's defence strategy, which prioritised the defence of Australia. He is guilty as charged. His review of Australian defence capabilities, published in March 1986, and his leadership of the writing team for the 1987 Defence White Paper, *The Defence of Australia*, are the founding documents. The concept of self-reliance and the geographical priority assigned to Australia's approaches, predated him — these were ideas circulating in the Australian bureaucracy in the 1960s. They emerged as the underpinning of the defence policy of Gough Whitlam's government over 1972–75. Weighed down by the complexities of merging multiple departments into a single Defence Department, and distracted by the tumult around a cataclysmic reforming agenda, Whitlam and his ministers did not, however, have the capacity to put flesh on the bones of the doctrine.

Malcolm Fraser's conservative successor government, in its 1976 White Paper, *Australian Defence*, encapsulated the thinking in a systematic reading of Australia's changing strategic environment. It produced a paradigm which contemplated 'self-reliance' as a priority, focusing on Australia's approaches geographically.

Strategic thinking in the previous two decades reflected an approach that was 'outside-in'. Rehearsing the changing strategic environment was almost more important than defining what self-reliance meant. Dibb's approach was 'inside-out', in a sense that was dictated to him by the assumptions given him for his study. The strategic settings were a given and his job was to articulate a capability plan that responded to the exigencies of those assumptions. Taken together, those two documents for the first and, arguably, only time in government presentation, put our force structure in its complete strategic and military context.

He defined the concepts underpinning defence planning — the wars most likely and possible to occur, and the relevance of warning time in analysing the burdens these would place on our defenders. A disciplined relationship between national strategy, 'self-reliance'; military strategy, 'defence in depth, layered defence and denial'; geographical dimension, 'our approaches'; force-structure determinants prioritising the most likely threat for the force in being, least likely but plausible, for an expansion base; and resources, industry policy and realistic financial requirements.

The remorseless, detailed, systematic argument for a concrete structure from a distilling of the valid elements of an often politically charged analysis of our strategic circumstances has never been bettered. Dibb is loathed not so much for his plan, but for disagreement with the distillation of the day. New circumstances have changed some previously valid strategic assumptions and rejected, invalid components of the 1980s strategic arguments are devotedly held largely for ideological reasons. Shooting Dibb is shooting the messenger. It was the government of the day that adopted his views and detailed his strategic assumptions. Critics do not delve too deeply into the disciplined linkages that he forged between national strategy, military strategy, geography and force structure. To do so leaves a critic essentially saying that defence of our approaches does not matter. This is not saleable in an environment where defending those approaches has become harder rather than easier due to the exponential growth of military capabilities in our region. To dismiss his argument with a wave of the hand is politically possible. To confront it in detail risks appearing a fool. Upon appearing a fool, a threat emerges to one's political saliency. Australians, when they turn their attention to defence, perceive a threatening environment at least long term. When they consider a response, they start with what will guarantee our approaches. They approve our alliances but none think that we are a better partner if we are not making a devoted attempt at defending ourselves.

We have been at war or in heavy peace-enforcing/keeping operations for most of the time since Dibb reported and, for most of that, outside our areas of direct military interest (ADMI) and primary strategic interest (APSI). With few exceptions, none of that, however, has invalidated the argument that was first presented by the Fraser Government but then detailed by Dibb that we can contribute to operations broader afield than the 10 per cent (military interest)/25 per cent (strategic interest) of the earth's surface, with the forces recommended for that closer zone. Few can identify in their writings the prescience of the example attached to the claim in the 1987 White Paper: 'For example, our guided missile frigates equipped with Seahawk helicopters are capable of effective participation in a US carrier battle group well distant from Australia's shores.' Read the Kuwait War. The Timor commitment certainly tested the assumptions, but didn't defeat them (just).

Nevertheless, some aspects of experience have undermined the exclusive focus on the priorities to which Dibb responded. Firstly and importantly, finances. In Dibb's day, defence enjoyed about 2.3 to 2.5 per cent of Australia's GDP and around 9 per cent of the budget. Dibb was clear that the force structure he recommended required that allocation and a routine 3 per cent real growth. That was obtained through the 1980s with the massive reforms of government defence industries and restructuring of Defence. Defence obtained the 3 per cent as production was closed and privatised and the savings kept by the department. Government assumptions that industrial employment would be sustained as the private sector established export standard in production and foreign primes moved in were validated.

Underlying expenditure, however, was not sustained. Defence took a massive 'peace dividend' at the end of the Cold War and, in the last 15 years, defence expenditure has rarely hit the 2 per cent mark and is closer to 6 per cent of the budget. At 2.3 per cent we would routinely be spending AU$5–7 billion per annum more on defence now. Consider our force structure if that was the case. The most obvious large reduction in response was in Dibb's recommended navy. We have got nowhere near his 17 tier-one and tier-two ships. The size of the force was based on calculations about anti-submarine warfare (ASW) requirements at the choke points to Australia's approaches. An at-the-time non-existent but projected submarine capability in the region has emerged, but the platforms don't deal with it. For a time, neither were the ASW-capable helicopters prioritised, but that is being addressed. Overall, the task for Australia's forces in our area of direct strategic interest has become more difficult, and the impact of purchases that are not based on serious prioritisation is becoming much more damaging to achieving the objectives of the core effort.

A second factor has been the emerging priority of stabilisation arrangements in our region and wars in the Middle East. The latter have had less impact, but soldiers in the field now require kit that was not anticipated in Dibb's time. That expenditure, however, has been small compared with the cost of the amphibious capabilities that are required for stabilisation arrangements in our region. This was a weakness in 1980s policy. That was not Dibb's fault. Though the contemporaneous response to the coup in Fiji demonstrated the need for an amphibious capability it was not until the 1994 White Paper that the government addressed it. The issue identified was picked up in equipment terms by subsequent governments. None of this would have been problematic in better financial circumstances.

The major contribution our service personnel have made in the various conflicts and operations (substantially so in current efforts in Iraq and Afghanistan with allies and in the South Pacific on our own) has embellished their long-standing record. As the issue of the day, however, it attracts, on the surface, greater public attention than the older Defence of Australia (DOA) requirement.

However, that is only on the surface. One of the assumptions of the 1970s and 1980s was that self-reliance was to be defined in an alliance context. This was a verity to which Dibb always paid obeisance. Part of the motive was that we were members of the Western alliance and should pay our dues. Just as important was the understanding that even if we needed to respond ourselves to our challenges, access to American intelligence, first-class equipment and exercises and training was vital to any successful defence of Australia.

In contemporary terms, the value of this can be seen in the air defence of Australia's approaches we are developing. We have comprehensive satellite surveillance of our region, a product directly of the American relationship. We have the world's best over-the-horizon radar, a product in its early phases of scientific collaboration with the US. From Boeing we have an excellent airborne early warning capability. Our P–3 *Orion* maritime surveillance and ASW aircraft are being replaced by P–8 *Poseidons*, also from an American source. Our frontline Hornets, Super Hornets, Growlers, and the coming F–35s are as good as anything in the region and further afield. We get the best variants. What keeps a defence minister up at night is the thought, 'what if all our calculations are wrong and a threat appears overnight. What can we do from a standing start?' This air defence answers the question.

Much of the Navy is not US sourced in terms of platforms. What makes the platforms work however has a lot of the United States in it. That is even so with our submarines. The *Collins* owes much to help from the US Navy. They get something in return. We have been experimented on. When I visited the US submarine construction facility in Connecticut I had a tour of the USS *Missouri*, a new *Virginia*-class SSN. The captain asked me in the control room if I recognised anything. I said, 'Yes it is a *Collins*-class'. Exactly, he said. He had been an exchange officer in a *Collins*-class submarine. In his view it was the best conventional boat around. Whatever we do with our replacement submarine has to have the approval of the Americans if the platform is to succeed as well. Interestingly as our frontline aircraft are naval aircraft, when added to our ASW helicopters and other American kit, we are the largest foreign-military-sales partner that the US Navy has.

Apparently outside the Dibb realm, our biggest contemporary purchase is the landing helicopter dock (LHD) amphibious assault ship. They are potentially capable ships. If they are ever to be developed, however, in our increasingly submarine-infested environment, they cannot be put to sea unless our ASW defences improve. No likely escort capability can provide sufficient ASW support. Our old carriers were ASW carriers. These LHDs will need organic ASW capabilities as well. To do the job properly they will need onboard sonars and four to six of the new Romeo helicopters as well. They can carry 24 aircraft so their inclusion will not interfere with the Army's lift. Dibb might not have prioritised them, but in extremes perhaps we might get closer to the 1980s choke point objective. But perhaps not. On our own we might not go looking for trouble with platforms so valuable. In conjunction with the Americans, maybe.

I was a lucky defence minister; I was one of the few who had a 'defence afterlife' in politics. I had the job in an era when the government was forced to take defence very seriously. The self-reliance within alliances formula was perfect for the Australian Labor Party (ALP) where significant elements were highly sceptical, after the Vietnam War, of alliance commitments. In the day national security was a forefront issue in party conclaves enhanced by the relationship between defence industry and reform of Australian industry overall.

Dibb was critical to the settling of dissention within the ALP on the value of the American alliance commitment. His colleague Des Ball, whose writing shone a light on the US–Australian joint facilities, enhanced to some extent the strength of the arguments of alliance sceptics. He also, however, demonstrated the value of the facilities and the alliance to the avoidance of nuclear war and the effectiveness of confidence-building and arms control. Dibb made clear that self-reliance with its foreign policy-liberating, security-guaranteeing, industry-enhancing value, would not be affordable without the American alliance. The pair laid down a clear path that settled the minds of sceptics with the empirically based intellectual power of their argument.

Those circumstances have altered the picture post-Cold War, the power of these positions has transitioned to a new distribution of global power in a more complex international system. In terms of bipartisanship in alliance policy in Australia this has been crucial. Dibb was part of this luck. I was deeply shocked when my departmental Secretary told me that were the department to produce a white paper it would irrevocably destroy the always tense relationship between civilian and military sides. I would need to find a consultant. He and the Chief of the Defence Force had agreed to give him all the support necessary for the study and the ultimate white paper. There were several who might have done the job. Dibb was the only one who could have been security cleared quickly enough to do it. His reputation was embellished by the job he did for the country. It also made him a target. Unfairly, the strategic calculations were the government's not his. As strategic calculations have changed over time and political debate has from time to time been brutal, he has become a lightning rod.

Nevertheless as his legacy has been examined he has come up pretty well. A new term is likely to come into use in alliance relationships. It is not 'expeditionary'. That is still there. It is 'integration'. As the US shifts the weight of its capability to the Asia-Pacific region it will look to allies to make up for shortfalls in its capabilities. The US Marine Corps, for example, will look with fascination on our LHDs.

Still, all things considered, any Australian government will want to be able to answer the question ordinary Australians always ask. Can we defend our approaches? If an enemy gets ashore can our Army deal with it before it seizes a bargaining chip? We know the answers on layered defence. We have thought about it in detail. We understand the essence of our strategic geography. We are nearly 30 years on from the time of Dibb's most significant contribution to our national defence. His legacy remains real. It endures.

# 8

# Concepts for Defence Planning

Richard Brabin-Smith

Paul Dibb's main contribution to the development of concepts for defence planning came through his *Review of Australia's Defence Capabilities*, and it is for this review that he is best known.[1] The public prominence that this work gave Paul is well-deserved, for it provided a much-needed rationale and direction to the development of defence capabilities that Defence itself had been unable to agree on. The principal conclusions and recommendations of the review were accepted by the Minister for Defence Kim Beazley, Defence Secretary Sir William Cole and Chief of the Defence Force General Sir Phillip Bennett. A few years later, Dibb was appointed to the position of Deputy Secretary B in Defence, giving him the authority to help ensure that the further development of defence capabilities was consistent with the concepts and principles set out in his review.

---

1     Paul Dibb, *Review of Australia's Defence Capabilities*, report to the Minister for Defence (Canberra: Australian Government Publishing Service, 1986), henceforward referred to as the Dibb Review. The original classified version of the review, on which the public version is based, is held by the National Archives of Australia. Since the writing of this essay, it has become available for public access, with excision of material still considered sensitive (see National Archives of Australia: K967, 8, barcode 12581224).

# The Background to the Review

The roots of the disagreement that the review was commissioned to resolve went back a long way. Some readers will recall the hostile incredulity that greeted the initial articulation of its defence policy by Gough Whitlam's Labor Government in the early 1970s. But in spite of the storm that the new policy created, the government stuck to its position, and the policy was developed further, both under Whitlam and by the subsequent Coalition Government of Malcolm Fraser, making it in effect bipartisan. The policy was set out formally in Australia's first Defence White Paper, published by the Coalition in 1976.[2] In brief, it gave priority to self-reliance in the defence of Australia and in operations closer to home. Small-scale contingencies might arise with little warning but these would not put at risk Australia's sovereignty or independence. More serious contingencies might arise but only after many years of warning, during which Australia's armed forces would be expanded. The prospect that Australia might contribute to operations further afield would have only limited influence on the capabilities and preparedness of the Australian Defence Force (ADF).

This policy became the framework for Australia's maritime strategy, giving prominence to the importance of capable naval and air forces but giving less importance to equivalent levels of capability for the Army. It was the context for the government's decision to choose the more capable F/A-18 fighter aircraft over the F-16 to replace the Royal Australian Air Force's (RAAF) Mirage fleet, and to set the demanding parameters for the capabilities of what became the *Collins*-class submarines. Other decisions at that time on maritime capabilities included the replacement of the 10 P-3B Orion long-range maritime patrol aircraft with the same number of new P-3Cs, the upgrading of the F-111C fleet with precision-guided munitions (including the Harpoon anti-ship missile), the modernisation of the three guided missile destroyers (DDG), and the acquisition of the fifth and sixth *Adelaide*-class guided missile frigates (FFG). In practical terms and

2    Commonwealth of Australia, *Australian Defence* (Canberra: Australian Government Publishing Service, 1976), henceforward referred to as the 1976 Defence White Paper.

given the constraints of the defence budget, the champions for Australia's maritime and strike capabilities did not have too much to grumble about.[3]

Interpreting strategic guidance for priorities for the development of the Australian Army was, however, proving more problematic. With little or no priority for major expeditionary warfare, least of all outside our own region, with a priority for strong maritime forces (expanded if and when necessary) that would deter or defeat any attempt at major attack on Australia, and with a confident expectation of many years of warning of any such major attack, how were we to approach the question of the size and shape of the Army? Would a consensus on these difficult issues emerge? Would it prove possible to reconcile the Army's ambitions with views on priorities derived from a top-down analysis of Australia's strategic circumstances by the civilian policy areas? It is fair to say that matters came to a head once General Sir Phillip Bennett became the Chief of the Defence Force Staff on the retirement of Air Chief Marshal Sir Neville McNamara in April 1984.[4]

The issue on which the civilian policy staff, led by Cole as Secretary, and the headquarters of the ADF (HQ ADF), led by General Bennett, disagreed was quite fundamental: how should the various levels of contingency that strategic guidance set out, together with the associated warning times, determine priorities for the force structure? HQ ADF preferred to emphasise higher level contingencies; the policy civilians gave greater emphasis to shorter term needs and force expansion. While the issue in principle concerned the whole of the ADF (and for that matter other elements of Australia's defence capacity, such as intelligence, science and industry), it was more contentious for the Army for, as we have seen, the capabilities being acquired for the Royal Australian Navy (RAN) and RAAF did not leave much room for

---

3    This policy was also the framework for the lengthy debate about whether to continue with an aircraft carrier and embarked fighter aircraft once the former carrier HMAS *Melbourne* had paid off. The civilian policy areas of Defence argued that such an acquisition did not command priority and, with the promotion of Air Chief Marshal Sir Neville McNamara to Chief of the Defence Force Staff on the retirement of Admiral Sir Anthony Synnot RAN, the official position of the headquarters of the Defence Force became very similar. In the event, the election of Bob Hawke's Labor Government in March 1983 put an end to the matter, with the government's early decision not to take the proposal any further. The Navy was disappointed by this decision of course.
4    The position of Chief of the Defence Force Staff was retitled Chief of the Defence Force in October of that year.

complaint. As Dibb commented, the disagreement became so intense and the parties so intransigent that they could not even agree on what the disagreement was.

This situation was hardly tolerable and, to help resolve it, Beazley turned to outside assistance, appointing an adviser to prepare a report on Australia's defence capabilities. Dibb was the ideal appointment for this, possessing a fearlessly independent mind and advanced analytical and conceptual skills (to use words favoured by the public service), having a solid defence background from his time in the Defence Intelligence Organisation (DIO) (to use its current name) and the former Strategic and International Policy Division, and having institutional independence by virtue of his position at The Australian National University (ANU). In February 1985 the work got underway.

We must remember that the terms of reference for the review were wide-ranging but, also, set some important constraints. In particular, the review was to be conducted 'in the light of the strategic and financial planning guidance endorsed by the Government'.[5] The former meant that the *Strategic Basis of Australian Defence Policy 1983* (*SB83*) would be a central point of reference.[6] The latter would help the review from falling into the trap of concluding merely that 'more is better', a failing to which far too many defence studies are prone.

In essence, *SB83* continued with the policies set out in previous documents in the series and in the 1976 Defence White Paper. In so doing, it reinforced what might be called the new orthodoxy that emerged with increasing cogency from the late 1960s: it found 'a substantial measure of continuity with the recent past'.[7] So, for example, *SB83* endorsed the priority to be given to self-reliance in the defence of Australia and operations in our region, noting inter alia: 'In sum, the basic strategic features of our own neighbourhood

---

5    Dibb, *Review of Australia's Defence Capabilities* (1986), p. xv.

6    *The Strategic Basis of Australian Defence Policy 1983*, formerly *Secret Austeo*, National Archives of Australia A13977, henceforward referred to as *SB83*. In September 1983, Cabinet endorsed *SB83* inter alia 'as guidance for the forthcoming review of defence planning [by the Minister for Defence, Gordon Scholes] and for the development of Australian defence policies'. This followed its endorsement in May 1983 by the Defence Committee. The latter was a standing inter-departmental body, chaired by the Defence Secretary, with membership comprising the Chief of the Defence Force Staff, the three Service Chiefs of Staff, and the Secretaries of Prime Minister and Cabinet, the Treasury, and Foreign Affairs. Its equivalent today (with changed membership) is the Secretaries' Committee on National Security.

7    *SB83* (1983), p. 72.

have potential to absorb our total defence effort.'[8] With respect to the central importance of self-reliance, it commented that '[t]he defence policies of Australian Governments have already recognised that we cannot rely upon US support in a defence emergency arising within our own neighbourhood but must develop our capacities to defend our interests by ourselves'.[9] And it continued to endorse 'an approach to defence planning which is based on insurance against future uncertainty'.[10]

It summarised the requirements of this approach as being intelligence collection and assessment, military planning, and a force-in-being capable of dealing with 'the kinds of defence contingencies that are credible in the shorter term, including deterrence of such escalation as an enemy might be capable of; and capable of providing a basis for timely expansion to counter deteriorating strategic circumstances'.[11] A major conventional attack on Australia remained 'only a remote and improbable contingency'.[12] *SB83* also reiterated the important policy conclusion that forces developed for operations relevant to neighbourhood contingencies 'will generally provide government with practical options for use of elements of the force in tasks beyond the neighbourhood in support of friends and allies'.[13] In brief, therefore, the policy context that the terms of reference set for the review focused on low-level contingencies that were credible in the shorter term, including the need to deter the possibility of escalation, and a defence force capable of expanding to meet the challenges of deterioration in Australia's strategic environment. The latter would require 'the careful and informed weighing of lead time [for force expansion] and warning time'.[14]

---

8    *SB83* (1983), p. 62.
9    *SB83* (1983), p. 61. See also, for example, p. 10 of the 1976 Defence White Paper: 'Indeed it is possible to envisage a range of situations in which the threshold of direct US combat involvement could be quite high.'
10   *SB83* (1983), p. 64.
11   *SB83* (1983), p. 64.
12   *SB83* (1983), p. 60.
13   *SB83* (1983), p. 62.
14   *SB83* (1983), p. 65.

# The Review's Concepts

The review acknowledged this continuity in policy development:

> strategic guidance developed ... over the last decade or more may thus be regarded as a continuum. Although certain thoughts and strategic concepts have been developed in more detail, there is substantial continuity of thinking. Successive Defence Committees (and some 20 different Service Chiefs and Secretaries of Departments) have endorsed the *Strategic Basis* series of documents which have, in turn, been agreed to by governments of various political persuasions.[15]

This was an important point, which Dibb frequently emphasised: not only had a wide range of ministers adopted the policies set out in the *Strategic Basis* series, but a large number of public service officials and ADF officers at the most senior levels had also endorsed them.

Nevertheless, given the central importance of *SB83*'s analysis of Australia's strategic circumstances for the development of defence concepts and capability priorities, Paul sought to reassure himself that its conclusions were sound. In brief, the review examined and accepted the fundamental premise of different levels of warning time for different levels of contingency: only lesser contingencies were credible in the shorter term, even with escalation, while the warning time for more serious levels of contingency would be many years. With the theme of this festschrift being 'geography and power', it is appropriate to include the review's observation that '[a]bove all else, our geographic position provides assurance that we would have considerable warning of the possibility of substantial threat ...'.[16] The review goes on to reaffirm that '[i]t would take at least 10 years and massive external support for the development of a regional capacity to threaten us with substantial assault'.[17] This is, of course, the critical point.

The review observes also that these judgements were not universally accepted within the Australian defence community, even though they were government policy. Related to acceptance of the concept of warning time was Dibb's conclusion that, although the concept of the core force was not sufficient for force-structure planning,

---

15   Dibb, *Review of Australia's Defence Capabilities* (1986), p. 26.
16   Dibb, *Review of Australia's Defence Capabilities* (1986), p. 33.
17   Dibb, *Review of Australia's Defence Capabilities* (1986).

'its approach to expansion base planning needs to be retained'.[18] Further, '[a]n expansion base, which plans on timely force expansion to meet higher levels of threat, is confirmed as an important defence planning concept'.[19]

Not surprisingly, the theme of geography occurs in many places in the review. The many examples include 'There is a requirement to study more seriously the effect of geography on force development'; 'geography is an unchanging factor in our strategic calculations'; 'What is needed … is a strategic concept focused rather more deliberately on our geographical circumstances …'; and 'We take into account the effects of the enduring features of geography on the forces of an attacker and on our own forces'.[20]

Perhaps critically with respect to drawing conclusions about capability priorities and thus meeting its terms of reference, the review 'dismissed the prospect of invasion as a determinant of Australia's force structure needs'.[21] Further, in terms of priorities for military capability, 'any tendency to prepare for unrealistically high levels of threat, such as preparing to meet an invasion force, must be resisted …'.[22] Such conclusions, reached independently from Defence's and the government's official position, were nevertheless strongly consistent with it.

The review drew some important conclusions about different levels of conflict, contrasting those that are 'credible now and for the foreseeable future, and the time that would be available to develop our defences in response to possibilities for higher levels of conflict'. It drew a careful distinction, therefore, between, on the one hand,

---

18  Dibb, *Review of Australia's Defence Capabilities* (1986), p. 49. The term 'core force' was a convenient defence policy shorthand for describing an ADF 'capable of dealing effectively with the kinds of defence contingencies that are credible in the shorter term, while providing a basis for timely expansion to counter deteriorating strategic circumstances should these arise.' Dibb, *Review of Australia's Defence Capabilities* (1986), p. 34.

19  Dibb, *Review of Australia's Defence Capabilities* (1986), p. 50.

20  Dibb, *Review of Australia's Defence Capabilities* (1986), pp. 38, 40, 49, 59 respectively. It is only fair to add that Dibb was not alone in recognising the profound influence that geography should have on Australia's defence planning; to give just one example, the 1972 *Australian Defence Review* comments that '[g]eography has a compelling influence on Australian security'. See Commonwealth of Australia, *Australian Defence Review* (Canberra: Australian Government Publishing Service, Mar. 1972), p 3.

21  Dibb, *Review of Australia's Defence Capabilities* (1986), p. 52.

22  Dibb, *Review of Australia's Defence Capabilities* (1986), p. 55.

contingencies that might be credible in the shorter term — low-level conflict and escalated low-level conflict, in which the enemy's objectives would be political rather than expansionist — and, on the other hand, more substantial conflict, credible only in the longer term, in which the adversary would seek to achieve significant military victories. The extent of any escalation that might be encountered in escalated low-level contingencies would be limited by the military capacity of the aggressor.[23]

Such considerations led to the articulation of the review's 'strategy of denial', which would ultimately rest 'on a capability to defeat an opponent in defined areas of our own vital national interest'.[24] Integral to this strategy was the concept of layered defence, 'a series of interlocking barriers to an attack on Australia', comprising: extremely high quality intelligence and surveillance; capable air and naval forces with the capacity to destroy enemy forces in the sea–air gap to Australia's north; defensive capabilities to prevent enemy operations closer to our shores; and ground forces capable of denying the enemy our vital population centres and military infrastructure.[25]

# The Review in Practice

Let me now give examples of how this conceptual framework led to specific recommendations and consequent development of the force structure.

## The Navy

For the RAN, the central issue was the fleet of new destroyers and their level of capability. The concept emerged in the review of at least eight 'light patrol frigates', which would 'primarily be for ocean patrol and sovereignty tasks'. Their most valuable characteristics 'would be range, sea-keeping, good surveillance and local command,

---

23   Dibb, *Review of Australia's Defence Capabilities* (1986), pp. 53, 54. Page 25 of the 1987 Defence White Paper made the important further point that there would also be practical constraints on the extent to which an aggressor could apply military force in escalated conflict. See Commonwealth of Australia, *The Defence of Australia* (Canberra: Australian Government Publishing Service, 1987).

24   Dibb, *Review of Australia's Defence Capabilities* (1986), p. 50.

25   Dibb, *Review of Australia's Defence Capabilities* (1986), p. 51.

control and communications capabilities, rather than advanced or complex weapons and high speed'. They would have a gun and an air defence system for self-protection and a hangar for a reconnaissance helicopter.[26]

As a matter of course, Dibb agreed to discuss his draft chapters, as they were written, with the Chiefs of Staff Committee. The chapter proposing frigates with less ambitious capabilities than the RAN had hoped for met heavy weather when it was thus discussed — so much so that the draft minutes bore only passing resemblance to what had actually been spoken and agreed. Dibb's strong representations led to an extensive revision of the draft minutes and a private meeting between him and Vice Admiral Mike Hudson RAN, the Chief of Naval Staff (CNS), at which they reached a broad agreement about the concepts behind these ships and the level of capability to be proposed.[27] This agreement did not stop the Navy subsequently arguing vigorously at the Force Structure Committee and the Defence Force Development Committee for more capable vessels.[28]

In brief, however, the ideas set out in the review prevailed and led to the government's decision to build the eight ANZAC-class frigates at the former Williamstown Naval Dockyard (by then in private hands), at more or less the level of capability that the review had proposed.[29] The only difference of significance was that the Navy won the argument for a five-inch gun, rather than the three-inch gun that the review had proposed.[30]

---

26   Dibb, *Review of Australia's Defence Capabilities* (1986), p. 129.
27   Dibb, *Review of Australia's Defence Capabilities* (1986), p. 130, esp. fn. 19. See also p. 44 of the 1987 Defence White Paper.
28   The Defence Force Development Committee, chaired by the Secretary, was the equivalent of today's Defence Committee. The Force Structure Committee was a subordinate group chaired by the Deputy Secretary.
29   There were, in addition, two ANZAC-class ships built for the Royal New Zealand Navy. There was also a subsequent midlife program to upgrade the ANZACs.
30   Force Development and Analysis Division argued that if there were a priority for a greater capacity for surface engagement than that which the three-inch gun would provide, then the best way ahead would be to fit the ANZAC frigates with the Harpoon anti-ship missile. The CNS, however, preferred the five-inch gun, saying that he would not want to be outgunned by any regional navy.

The review also supported the priority of surface-towed acoustic arrays for the protection of shipping in focal areas from attack by submarine.[31] The importance of this program emerged from analysis of the way ahead for anti-submarine warfare in the wake of the government's decision not to continue with an aircraft carrier. Nevertheless, the Navy's interest in this was at best only lukewarm, in spite of support for it in the 1987 Defence White Paper,[32] and the 1991 *Force Structure Review* in effect ended it.[33] To this day, the anti-submarine capacity of the surface fleet against a capable adversary remains equivocal.

## The Army

The part of the review addressing the Army proved a challenge to write, largely because this was the core issue that had led to the review, and because Defence's processes of review, analysis and priority-setting had tended to sidestep Army-related matters. As the review pointed out, the most recent consideration of the Army as a whole by the Defence Force Development Committee had been in 1973, when the ideas of the Defence of Australia (DOA), the core force and expansion base were at a relatively early stage. For example, the consideration in 1973 had looked at scenarios that were 'based on strategic assumptions quite different from those which dominate today's Australian Defence analysis', including the 'implications for the expansion base were there to be a need to expand to a million-man army for the defence of Australia against major attack'.[34] This was a polite way of saying that the conceptual foundations of arguments for the Army's size, shape and development were fragile and unconvincing. The review was similarly dismissive of the then contemporary *Army Development Guide*, having 'substantial reservations' about its conceptual framework, especially for more substantial levels of conflict.[35] Absent from Army's arguments

---

31 Dibb, *Review of Australia's Defence Capabilities* (1986), p. 119.
32 1987 Defence White Paper, p. 38.
33 Commonwealth of Australia, *Force Structure Review*, report to the Minister for Defence (Canberra, May 1991), p 11.
34 Dibb, *Review of Australia's Defence Capabilities* (1986), p. 78.
35 Dibb, *Review of Australia's Defence Capabilities* (1986), p. 84. The *Army Development Guide* included a scenario where a major power lodged a four-brigade divisional group on mainland Australia, requiring a Australian field-force element of some 135,000 personnel and a total army of some 270,000 to counter it.

was acknowledgement that operations in the defence of Australia would be joint-force in nature and that the Navy and Air Force would have decisive roles.

In brief, and building on its earlier analysis of priorities derived from Australia's strategic geography, the review dismissed the Army's arguments that gave priority to more substantial conflict and the force-structure judgements that flowed from this. In particular, it dismissed Army's plans for mechanisation: it regarded 'Army's case as resting on premises that are at variance with Australia's strategic circumstances'.[36] It concluded that capabilities most relevant to that level of conflict should be included in the force structure only in limited quantity, 'having due regard to lead times for capability development and expansion, for both ourselves and other countries in the region'.[37]

In contrast, the review gave priority to an Army capable of countering a protracted campaign of dispersed raids across the north of Australia, in which the enemy could deploy armed forces of up to company size. Australian forces would be needed to protect potential military and civilian targets and to react quickly to incidents before the raiding forces could achieve their objectives. The demands of such responsibilities would be formidable, and would require forces that were lightly but adequately armed, tactically mobile, and with good communications and good surveillance and reconnaissance capabilities. The logistic support for these forces would be demanding.[38]

Just as the review was dismissive of the Army's case for a focus on higher levels of conflict, so too did it reject the arguments from some in the civilian policy areas that low-level contingencies would involve only terrorist-type activities, leading to a situation where the role of the Army would be 'little more than that of an armed police force'.[39] It chose also not to argue against the retention of a 'divisional' structure for the Army. In the context of potentially high levels of disputation on the central issue of how levels of contingency should influence priorities for the Army's development, proposing to get rid of 'the division' would have risked an unnecessary distraction.

---

36  Dibb, *Review of Australia's Defence Capabilities* (1986), p 138.
37  Dibb, *Review of Australia's Defence Capabilities* (1986), p. 84. See also p. 89.
38  Dibb, *Review of Australia's Defence Capabilities* (1986), p. 88. See also pp. 81, 82.
39  Dibb, *Review of Australia's Defence Capabilities* (1986), p. 81.

And besides, if done properly, inherent to the division would be the flexibility needed for command and control, the allocation of resources and administration.[40]

The geostrategic foundations of the review gave rise to its proposal to base elements of the Regular Army in the north of the country, to facilitate exercising there and to gain greater familiarity with the area. It quotes the Army as saying 'the environment itself is neutral and those forces which are best trained and equipped to operate and be supported in it will have the greatest chance of success'. The review's preference was for 'at least a Regular infantry battalion, with perhaps a brigade headquarters ...', while the preference of HQ ADF was for a reconnaissance unit based on 2nd Cavalry Regiment, with an intention of establishing a brigade group in the longer term.[41] It is appropriate here to acknowledge the enthusiasm of the Chief of the General Staff Lieutenant General Peter Gration (later Chief of the Defence Force) for such an initiative (he had already been thinking along such lines), and the Army's initiative in setting up the Reserve-based regional surveillance units across the north of the country, such as NORFORCE.

As the 1991 *Force Structure Review* subsequently set out, planning proceeded on the basis that the 2nd Cavalry Regiment would deploy to Darwin in 1993, followed by an armoured regiment and an aviation squadron in 1995, and an infantry battalion in 1998.[42] This led to the position today where the 1st Brigade, one of the Army's three multi-role combat brigades, is based at Robertson Barracks, south of Darwin.[43] An associated suggestion was to establish a Northern Command (NORCOM). This was on the basis that, in an extended contingency in the north, there would likely be a need to establish a local joint-force headquarters.[44] Such a command was set up at Larrakeyah Barracks in Darwin, and continues there to this day.

---

40   Dibb, *Review of Australia's Defence Capabilities* (1986), p. 82.
41   Dibb, *Review of Australia's Defence Capabilities* (1986), p. 144.
42   Commonwealth of Australia, *Force Structure Review* (1991), pp. 23, 24.
43   For details about the 1st Brigade, see '1st Brigade', *Army*, 3 Jun. 2015, at www.army.gov.au/Our-people/Units/Forces-Command/1st-Brigade.
44   Dibb, *Review of Australia's Defence Capabilities* (1986), pp. 92, 93.

# The Air Force

An issue for the RAAF was how best to achieve broad-area surveillance. Again, the problem was driven by geography: the huge areas of Australia's north and proximate waters did not lend themselves to surveillance by conventional radars, either on the ground or in the air. To meet these challenges, the Defence Science and Technology Organisation (DSTO, now the Defence Science and Technology Group (DSTG)), with strong support from Defence's policy areas but with only lukewarm interest from the Air Force, had been exploring the possibility of using high-frequency (HF) over-the-horizon radar (OTHR) — the experimental program known as *Jindalee*. This had started in the early 1970s and, by the time of the review, was showing great promise: 'there can be no doubt of OTHR's ability to provide valuable wide-area surveillance, although with some technical limitations.'[45] The review gave high priority to its continued development (not just for air surveillance but also in the technically more demanding area of sea-surface surveillance) and to planning for an operational network.[46]

By happy coincidence, Dibb was Deputy Secretary at the time that a decision was needed on the siting of the radars of the Jindalee Operational Radar Network (JORN), thus helping to ensure that its coverage would be consistent with strategic priorities.[47] Although the contractual arrangements for the construction of JORN were problematic (with the contract being novated after a few years), the operational network is said be an outstanding success. It is a pity that security considerations do not allow more to be said publicly.

The review was more equivocal on the related issue of the priority to be given to airborne early warning and control (AEW&C) aircraft. While there was no doubt that they would improve Australia's air defence capabilities, '[c]urrent circumstances do not demand AEW&C aircraft',

---

45    Dibb, *Review of Australia's Defence Capabilities* (1986), p. 62.

46    Dibb, *Review of Australia's Defence Capabilities* (1986), pp. 117, 118, 148, 149.

47    This was less straightforward than might be imagined, with an unseemly brawl breaking out between DSTO and Force Development and Analysis Division on how technical considerations might affect siting decisions. As might be imagined, Dibb was not amused by having to worry about differing views on the conductivity of black soil in central Queensland in wet conditions! There was also the occasion when, bombarded by claims of 'scientific fact', he retorted that 'cold fusion' was claimed to be a scientific fact too.

and '[t]he position should be reviewed after data on the operational performance of OTHR is assessed'.[48] In the event, it was not until 2000 that the government agreed to the acquisition of the six E–7A *Wedgetail* AEW&C aircraft, by which time technological solutions more suited to Australia's needs were becoming available and Australia's strategic circumstances were being seen in some respects from a different angle. This project, too, had some difficulties in execution but the capabilities now in service are said to be outstanding.

The issue closest to Air Force's heart was the future of the F–111C strike-reconnaissance aircraft, and the review was equivocal in some respects here, too. As the review commented, 'given the long warning times for contingencies that would call for the substantial use of strike capabilities, we need to exercise discrimination in determining the types and numbers of these forces'.[49] In brief, strike aircraft would have limited use in low-level contingencies and, while they would be more valuable in escalated contingencies, there would still be constraints on their use, with maritime strike being favoured over land strike. They would come into their own only in more substantial contingencies that the review and strategic guidance judged remote and improbable. At issue was whether the costs of upgrading them and keeping them in service would be commensurate with their operational and strategic value, or whether alternatives should be explored, such as an F/A–18-based option.

In summary, the review came down in favour of retaining the F–111, but with a 'minimum update program designed to sustain rather than enhance the aircraft in service until around the mid-1990s',[50] after which further options should be considered. Again, Dibb was Deputy Secretary when the Force Structure Committee (which he chaired) and then the Defence Force Development Committee agreed to recommend to government that the F–111s undergo a major upgrade.[51] The 1991 *Force Structure Review* expected that they would remain in service

48  Dibb, *Review of Australia's Defence Capabilities* (1986), p. 132.
49  Dibb, *Review of Australia's Defence Capabilities* (1986), p. 65.
50  Dibb, *Review of Australia's Defence Capabilities* (1986), p. 122.
51  The level of upgrade was probably more than the review had envisaged, but the proposal had been thoroughly examined by, and subsequently supported by, Force Development and Analysis Division.

until around 2010,[52] and the 2000 Defence White Paper imagined their retention in service until between 2015 and 2020,[53] but, in the event, they were out of service by the end of 2010.

## The Review Team

The review was a serious piece of work, of course, but there were some diversions along the way. For example, drafts of the review's chapters would sometimes draw the response from HQ ADF that the arguments 'were simplistic and naïve and lacking in professional military judgement'. At first, we worried about such comments but, after a while, came to realise that they signified merely that the HQ had run out of substantive argument against what we were proposing. Being old Defence hands, we turned 'professional military judgement' into an acronym — and allegations of lacking PMJ became a badge of honour.

The five full-time members of the Dibb team also met the criteria for entering a team in the annual Defence fun run: military/civilian, male/female, SES/non-SES. I can't now recall how well the team did, but we did all finish. There was also the multi-hour 'FISHEX' maritime surveillance flight in a P–3C from Edinburgh via Learmonth to Darwin, at the end of which a diligent air force NCO plus guard dog tried to stop Dibb taking a photograph of the airbase. There were endless references to and sometimes inspections of the standby emergency generators at many of the bases we visited, so much so that they became something of a review joke. There was the failure just after take-off of one of the Caribou's two engines when we were flying out from the *Jindalee* transmitter site at Hart's Range near Alice Springs. And the Air Force gave Dibb a flight in an F–111, including a phase in terrain-following mode, about which he never stopped talking.

When the review was over, we all went our separate ways. Dibb's personal assistant, Ferol Beazley, became personal assistant to Deputy Secretary B and then to the head of Australian Defence Staff in Washington; Colonel Bill Crews was later promoted to Major General

---

52 Commonwealth of Australia, *Force Structure Review* (1991), p. 28.
53 Commonwealth of Australia, *Defence 2000, Our Future Defence Force* (Canberra: Australian Government Publishing Service, 2000), p. 93.

and became Director of the DIO; Martin Brady returned to the policy area and later became Director of the Defence Signals Directorate and, after that, Chair of the Defence Intelligence Board; and I, too, returned to policy work, later becoming the Chief Defence Scientist and then Deputy Secretary for Strategic Policy.

As for Dibb, he completed the edited version of his review for public release and worked on the drafting of the first half of the 1987 Defence White Paper.[54] He was then appointed Director of the DIO and, after two years, was promoted to the position of Deputy Secretary B, the principal senior policy position in Defence. Dibb was the last person to hold this position with the responsibilities allocated to it under Sir Arthur Tange's reorganisation: force development and analysis, strategic and international policy, and programs and budgets. This combination of responsibilities was demanding but it recognised that the allocation of resources within Defence was primarily a *strategic* function, not an exercise in accounting. There were good reasons for removing programs and budgets from the control of Deputy Secretary B and replacing it with responsibilities for the oversight of intelligence, but it did weaken the mechanisms for ensuring that the allocation of resources within Defence, changing as necessary over time, was consistent with strategic priorities — a weakness that has continued to this day. More recently, the Peever Review has recommended that the responsibilities of the Deputy Secretary for Policy include once again oversight of intelligence and 'a strong and credible internal contestability function', for which read a modern version of the former Force Development and Analysis Division.[55] These responsibilities will be very similar to Dibb's in the early 1990s but which subsequently became much diminished. Then, in October 1991, he returned to ANU to become professor of strategic studies and

---

54  He was supported in this by Steve Merchant, later the Director of the Defence Signals Directorate and then Deputy Secretary for Intelligence and Security.

55  Department of Defence, *First Principles Review, Creating One Defence* (the 'Peever Review'), 2015, p. 25. The government has agreed, or agreed in principle, to this and all but one of the review's other recommendations. However, the review has recommended that Defence's Chief Finance Officer have formal accounting qualifications (*First Principles Review*, p. 26), thus allowing room to question whether it has sufficiently recognised the strategic nature of decisions on resource allocation.

head of the SDSC, making him one of the relatively few examples in Australia of someone who was equally distinguished at senior levels in both the public service and academia.[56]

## The Review's Legacy

For the decade or more following its publication, the review was strongly influential. Perhaps most importantly, it resolved the impasse of disagreement between Secretary and Chief of Defence Force, with both of them signing up to the review's proposals. The importance of this cannot be overstated. While the review put forward an orthodox interpretation of Australia's geostrategic circumstances and government-endorsed strategic guidance, it served to give significant momentum to the development of capabilities that were unequivocally consistent with this guidance. This influence was reflected in the concepts, priorities and programs set out in the 1987 Defence White Paper and in the 1991 *Force Structure Review*, with Dibb being closely involved in the drafting of both of these important papers. It heightened the recognition of the influence of geography on the development of the ADF and its basing, especially with respect to operations in and to the north of the country. At least until the end of the century, it served to guide the Army's perspectives and ambitions. It played an important part in encouraging a joint-force perspective from the ADF, rather than one that focused more on the separateness of the three services.

But the passage of time has changed in some respects the prism through which Australia's strategic circumstances are seen. The idea of the core force and expansion base had been developed at an earlier time as a concept with which to argue for levels of defence funding when, otherwise, funding levels would have gone much lower. Those times have passed, and with them the need for that kind of argument, although the logic of needing to plan for force expansion remains compelling even if neglected. Further, and to be blunt, with Dibb's

---

56   An early publication on Dibb's return to ANU was his monograph *The Conceptual Basis of Australia's Defence Planning and Force Structure Development*, Canberra Papers on Strategy and Defence No. 88 (Canberra: Strategic and Defence Studies Centre, The Australian National University, 1992), drawing inter alia on the ideas set out in his review, the 1987 Defence White Paper, and the 1991 *Force Structure Review*.

departure the ranks of those comfortable with such sophisticated concepts became too thin to win the arguments, with most other players preferring simpler ideas.

A characteristic of Australian strategic thinking in the 1970s and 1980s was concern about the nature and commitment of American leadership and the judgements behind it. This followed the outcome of the war in Vietnam and the US enunciation of the 'Guam doctrine' (also known as the 'Nixon doctrine'), which made it clear that the United States would expect its allies to become more responsible for their own security. Such reservations are less in evidence today, and Australia has followed the American lead in the first and second Gulf wars (Kuwait and Iraq), Afghanistan, and currently in operations against Jihadist extremism in the Middle East.

Additionally, Australia's prosperity and security depend critically on the stability of the current world order, to the preservation of which America's commitment and armed forces are vital. This is especially relevant in the Asia-Pacific region, with uncertainty about whether China, in seeking to advance its own interests, will attempt to make radical changes to at least the regional order. Australia, so the argument runs, should therefore plan to make a more significant military contribution to US-led operations than we did in the Cold War, where the locus of potential conflict was more distant from us.[57] This would argue that expeditionary warfare should become more influential in the planning of Australia's military capabilities than in recent decades. Some would argue that Australia is so naturally secure and its neighbourhood so benign that the defence of Australia is no longer an adequate foundation for Australia's defence policies, thus amplifying the case for an expeditionary focus. And others argue that modern threats of terrorism and cyber attack are so little constrained by geography that the geographic focus of Australia's defence policies should be correspondingly broadened. Whether those who put forward such arguments are always being impartial deserves serious reflection.

---

57   It should be remembered, nevertheless, that, even in the Cold War, Australia made an important contribution to the Western cause, for example by hosting the Australian–US Joint Facilities (thus making Australia a nuclear target (see p. 12 of the 1987 Defence White Paper)) and by conducting maritime surveillance against Soviet nuclear submarines.

Dibb addresses many of these observations in a set of essays published in 2006.[58] In brief, he argues for the continued relevance of the then current 2000 Defence White Paper. He notes that there are many potential flashpoints for major interstate conflict in the Asia-Pacific and that there continue to be instabilities closer to the Australian homeland. He accepts — and argues for — the need for some adjustments at the margins of defence planning in response to the threats of terrorism (at home and abroad), in readiness and, for example, in interoperability with the United States. But he rebuts those who argue that the risks of terrorism require radical changes to Australian defence priorities. And he dismisses as 'strategically indefensible' arguments that would focus Australia's defence efforts on what would only ever be a small expeditionary Army, capable of little effect against a serious adversary yet requiring most of the Navy and Air Force to protect it.

At the time of writing, with the 2016 Defence White Paper still in preparation, we can only speculate on the changes that Malcolm Turnbull's Coalition Government will make to Australia's defence policies. It would, however, be a brave government that stepped away to any significant degree from policies that retained a strong focus on the defence of Australia. And besides, the country's economic situation will constrain any more ambitious approaches to defence planning for the foreseeable future. But to the extent that defence policy moves on from what it was when Dibb conducted his review, so the influence of the review will fade.

Yet many of the ideas that Paul has promoted have enduring value. It is Australia's geography that leads us towards a maritime strategy, with capable naval and air forces. It is Australia's geography that leads us to differentiate carefully between priorities for maritime capabilities and those for the Army. And the nature of Australia's geostrategic circumstances allows us to avoid the expense of large standing forces at high levels of preparedness, at least for now. In summary, the imperatives of Australia's strategic geography need to remain the foundation upon which Australian defence planning continues to build.

---

58   Paul Dibb, *Essays on Australian Defence*, Canberra Papers on Strategy and Defence No. 161 (Canberra: Strategic and Defence Studies Centre, 2006).

# 9

# The Politics and Practicalities of Designing Australia's Force Structure

Peter Jennings

In the cover letter to his 1986 *Review of Australia's Defence Capabilities*,[1] Paul Dibb set out for then Defence Minister Kim Beazley the key challenges for his study:

> The Review could obtain no material centrally endorsed by the higher Defence structure which explained, for example, the strategic rationale for a 12-destroyer Navy, three fighter squadrons, six Regular Army battalions and an Army Reserve target of 30,000. Few of the documents made available to the Review examine, in any rigorous, analytical way, the size of forces we should have for credible contingencies and as a contribution to the expansion base. Most focus on justifying the present force structure rather than estimating what our strategic circumstances require. The key difficulty here is that the Department and the ADF do not agree on the appropriate level of conflict against which we should structure the Defence Force.

It has almost been 30 years since these words were written. Arguably Australian defence policy still suffers from the first of Dibb's identified problems: an inadequate way of framing the strategic rationale behind

---

1    Paul Dibb, *Review of Australia's Defence Capabilities*, report to the Minister for Defence (Canberra: Australian Government Publishing Service, 1986).

capability acquisitions. In 2016 we might ask what the rationale is for a 12-submarine navy, or an air force with 100 fighter aircraft and an army with three regular brigades. In fact, the shape of the Australian Defence Force (ADF) remains similar to that of the mid-1980s, albeit with more capability based on significant technological advances. By contrast, the modern Australian Defence Organisation seems largely to have overcome — or at least hides more effectively — deep conceptual divisions over key force-structuring concepts.

Have Australia's defence policymakers got better at designing the conceptual basis for force-structure decisions? To answer that question, it is necessary to understand how defence policymaking interacts with politics. It must be remembered that the locus of defence decision-making resides around the Cabinet room and ministerial suites in Parliament House, not at the Defence headquarters at Russell, which is just a few kilometres away. This chapter argues that Dibb's 1986 review set the model for how political decision-making intersects with defence force development thinking. Some important benefits flowed from continuing the 'Dibb model', including achieving relatively high levels of political bipartisanship around force-structure decisions and establishing a cross-party consensus on the importance of the US alliance. As governments have articulated their evolving strategic orientations for defence it seems almost incidental that the structure of the ADF remains remarkably unchanging. Looking to the future we need to ask if Dibb's approach to taking force-structure options to government will continue to shape how Australian policymaking is done.

## The Theatre of Defence White Papers

A curious artefact of Australian defence policymaking is the attention lavished on Defence white papers. While other countries may write these policy statements more often (Japan has an annual white paper), none vest in them such talismanic power as Australia. Since the end of the Vietnam War, Australian governments have prepared a white paper in 1976, 1987, 1994, 2000, 2009, 2013 and 2016. Each is more elaborate in terms of the effort invested in developing them and the political and public attention devoted to their release. In the case of the last four white papers, it took large teams more than 12 months' work to develop policy material for government. In 2000 and 2009 a deputy secretary worked full time on policy work. In those years, and in 2015–2016, extensive public consultation processes were established to support the white paper; many Cabinet submissions were prepared to help steer policy direction; and extensive supporting work was done internally to inform force-structure design, estate, science, industry, personnel and equipment costing.

There is no doubt that politics plays a critical role in motivating governments and oppositions of the day to commit to develop these documents.[2] The 2000 White Paper was prompted by the need for the government under John Howard to be seen to respond to the strategic shock of East Timor's violent transition to independence from Indonesian sovereignty. The 2009, 2013 and 2016 white papers were all initiated by pledges to deliver these policy statements either after an election or just before one.

It is hardly surprising in a competitive and open electoral system that political parties would want to use policy statements to seek partisan political advantage, even though this advantage is often pursued through a veil of pledges of bipartisanship on national security. Defence white papers have become the principal vehicle for Australian governments to align their political interests with a credible strategic plan for the country's defence. A successfully concluded white paper confers a degree of credibility on a government and a hoped-for public view that the government in question is strong on national security. White papers create the opportunity to address challenging and divisive policy issues.

Given their political value, Defence white papers will always have a measure of theatre about them — the 2009 document, for example, was launched from the deck of a warship in Sydney Harbour and the 2013 statement was released at the Royal Australian Air Force (RAAF) Base Fairbairn in Canberra, with an array of military equipment flown in to act as background props. So intense has the focus become on the development and release of these documents that one wonders if white papers are not at risk, like the largest of the dinosaurs, of sinking into the mire under their own ponderous weight. But one should not

---

2     I chart the intersection of politics and policy in Defence white papers up to 2013 in 'The Politics of Defence White Papers', *Security Challenges*, Vol. 9, No. 2 (2013), pp. 1–14.

underestimate the seriousness of the policy intent in these documents. Given the scale and duration of the military-capability investments involved, as well as the seriousness of the strategic challenges at issue, white papers will likely persist as key vehicles driving the politics and policy of Australia's defence.

## A Critical Precursor to the Review of Defence Capabilities

At 58 pages, the 1976 White Paper is the shortest of the seven Defence statements since that time, and the one with the clearest authorial voice — that of the formidable Secretary of Defence, Sir Arthur Tange. Almost 40 years after it was released, the 1976 Defence White Paper remarkably echoes many of today's defence and security preoccupations. For example, it uses the term 'Indo-Pacific' to describe Australia's broad strategic canvas, within which South-East Asia and the south-west Pacific are 'areas of Australia's primary strategic concern'. The paper worries about prospects for the Australia–Indonesia relationship, noting that it has 'successfully weathered occasional sharp differences'.[3] Critically, the document sets out the beginnings of the idea of 'self-reliance' in defence planning in the context of Australia's close alliance with the United States.

On force structure, Tange's document would not require much editing to pass muster as a description of the current status. It puts a premium on maritime capabilities for intelligence, surveillance and reconnaissance, proposes to expand the size of the surface fleet 'preferably for construction in Australia' and has a helpfully clear and direct statement on the role of submarines:

> Submarines are a potent deterrent with important functions in anti-shipping and anti-submarine warfare, covert reconnaissance/ surveillance and patrol, clandestine operations, and mine warfare.

On land forces, the focus is on deployability and sustainability over long distances using a divisional structure as recognisable today as it was on the Western Front in 1918. The biggest structural difference

---

3 Commonwealth of Australia, *Australian Defence*, presented to Parliament by the Minister for Defence the Hon. D.J. Killen (Canberra: Australian Government Publishing Service, Nov. 1976).

between the ADF of 1976 and 2016 is the contemporary absence of carrier-borne fixed-wing aircraft. The 1976 document foreshadows that this capability was in decline — it was phased out half a decade later. A briefly revived interest in the short take-off and vertical landing (STOVL) version of the F–35B in 2014 and 2015 shows how doggedly force-structure ideas persist.[4]

For all of its intellectual promise, the 1976 Defence White Paper failed — as quite a number have — because of a lack of follow-through on budget and force-structure implementation. In the aftermath of the Vietnam conflict, defence spending levels declined. The then Prime Minister Malcolm Fraser had a prickly relationship with the military based on his unhappy experiences as Defence Minister in John Gorton's government at the end of the 1960s. Tange criticised Fraser for his 'overly distrustful' and unreasonable demands on the department, which was not well equipped to meet Fraser's requests for short-notice briefing material. The Defence Department, Sir Arthur observed, 'had, with few outstanding exceptions, a mediocre intellectual level in 1969 when Fraser became minister'.[5] Fraser's own Minister for Defence, Jim Killen, was held in great affection by many but was not regarded as a strong driver of departmental policy. As such the policy plans articulated in the 1976 White Paper languished for want of a sponsor.

## Defence Dysfunction: Dibb Does his Duty

When Labor was elected to office in 1983, Prime Minister Bob Hawke faced a series of dilemmas on defence and national security policy. His predecessor as leader of the Australian Labor Party in opposition, Bill Hayden, had taken the party to the left on nuclear and US-alliance issues. Anti-nuclear support in Australia was growing at the same time as Hawke faced pressure from the United States to support testing of the MX missile. Vocal campaigns against Australia–US joint facilities and the visits of potentially nuclear-armed warships were generating

---

4    Richard Brabin-Smith & Benjamin Schreer, 'Jump Jets for the ADF?', *ASPI Strategic Insights*, No. 78 (Barton: Australian Strategic Policy Institute, 17 Nov. 2014).
5    Sir Arthur Tange, quoted from an interview with Philip Ayres, *Malcolm Fraser: A Biography* (Melbourne: William Heinemann Australia, 1987), p. 163.

popular support. In New Zealand, David Lange was articulating an unambiguously anti-nuclear policy that saw trilateral Australia–New Zealand–United States (ANZUS) cooperation suspended in 1984.[6]

Hawke's challenge was to set out an approach to the US alliance, the joint facilities and Australian defence policy more broadly that could become the basis of Labor policy. Against this difficult background, the government directed Defence to develop a full-scale review of Australia's defence policy options. The Secretary of Defence at the time was Sir William 'Bill' Cole. Writing a few years after these events, Cole reflected on the experience:

> For well over a year, the Department, under successive Secretaries, and ADF Headquarters, under Successive Chiefs of the Defence Force, made absolutely no progress with that review — to which all concerned knew Government attached great importance — because the various protagonists could not agree on how the review should be approached. Let alone not getting the task finished, despite considerable efforts, Defence could not get it started.[7]

Cole added rather archly in a footnote: 'If the issue here was which of the contending parties was responsible for the stalemate or what the Minister should have done, I would have more to say.' The lack of communication between the ADF and defence civilians became legendary. Dibb's 1985 appointment by the newly promoted Defence Minister, Kim Beazley, to conduct the review of Australia's defence capabilities was the government's solution to break this impasse.

It's always the case that well-designed processes give rise to better policy outcomes. The processes put in place for the Dibb Review directly contributed to what was a successful Defence White Paper for Labor in 1987. First, Dibb was given powerful and unambiguous terms of reference, most particularly to review 'the content, priorities and rationale of defence forward planning in the light of the strategic and financial planning guidance endorsed by the Government', and 'to advise on present and future force capabilities'.[8] In effect there was no hiding from the government's intent as to what it wanted.

---

6   Bob Hawke, *The Hawke Memoirs* (Melbourne: William Heinemann Australia, 1994), p. 228.
7   Bill Cole, 'A New Approach to Defence: The Wrigley Report and After', *Australian Institute for Public Policy (AIPP) Policy Paper*, No. 19 (1990), p. 24.
8   Dibb, *Review of Australia's Defence Capabilities* (1986), p. xv.

A second process strength was that Dibb was to report directly to Beazley, so Defence was unable to filter his advice. Third, Dibb's report was to reflect his views only, it was not to be a statement of government policy or departmental preference. This produced a fourth process advantage, which was that the government gave itself an option not to follow all of Dibb's recommendations. On tabling the report, Beazley told parliament: 'The Dibb review will now become a basic input to the development of a government white paper on Defence policy.'[9] The government could, and indeed did, change elements of Dibb's recommendations to take account of some of the critiques of the review.

Dibb's proposed force structure was built around what he called a 'strategy of denial', a layered defensive concept that put a premium on air and maritime capabilities protecting the approaches to Australia, and an Army primarily designed around vehicle-mounted infantry able to respond to low-level and 'escalated low-level' contingencies on Australian territory. Dibb's focus was strongly based on strategic geography and the assessment that 'the archipelago to our north is the area from or through which a military threat to Australia could most easily be posed.[10] While the review's focus was on force structure, not regional security, a good deal of Dibb's capability proposals flowed from that single sentence.

One of the most difficult issues tackled in the review was to set an appropriate balance between the low likelihood of high-intensity conflict against a Service interest to sustain forces able to operate in the most demanding combat scenarios. Dibb concluded Defence should 'emphasise the weight to be given to credible contingencies — but not at as low a level as the department supports'. The report set out the benefits of the US alliance but stressed 'there is no requirement for Australia to become involved in United States contingency planning for global war'.

The critique of the review began in earnest even as Beazley tabled it in parliament. The leader of the Opposition, Andrew Peacock, snapped at Beazley: 'It is a policy of retreat — right into a shell'. To which the

---

9    Kim Beazley, 'Ministerial Statement: Review of Australia's Defence Capabilities', *House of Representatives Hansard*, 3 Jun. 1986.
10   Dibb, *Review of Australia's Defence Capabilities* (1986), p. 4.

Minister replied: 'It is a shell which covers 25 per cent of the entire globe.' (Watching the show from the House of Representatives visitors' gallery helped inspire me into a Defence career.) Ian Sinclair, then leader of the National Party and Shadow Minister for Defence, cannily positioned the Coalition voice for the debate. He agreed with some equipment proposals, moving an Army presence to Darwin and also supported creating a Vice Chief of the Defence Force (VCDF) to boost more joint capability development across the Services. But Sinclair worried that the Association of Southeast Asian Nations (ASEAN) would see the report as 'isolationist', that it did not encompass the 'wider role' Australia should play in the US alliance and was concerned that the report could be seen as 'restricting Australia's defence capability, not expanding it'.[11]

Media commentary on the review was extensive and broadly favourable — remarkably all the major newspapers editorialised on it, something very unlikely to occur today. Tange, then approaching 72 years of age, wrote for the *Age*:

> It is inconceivable that the services, or the outside critics of the bureaucracy, would tolerate a senior departmental officer drafting a report on military capabilities for the minister. Dibb was presumably accepted because of his abundant abilities, and because he was no precedent for the future.[12]

In fact the review set a precedent, followed many times by subsequent governments, for ministers to appoint external advisers to review defence functions.

The 1987 Defence White Paper (actually titled a 'Policy Information Paper') made some subtle changes of emphasis — promoting a 'defence self-reliance' concept rather than Dibb's strategy of denial. The White Paper placed significantly more emphasis on regional engagement.

---

11  Ian Sinclair, 'Speech in Reply to the Ministerial Statement', *House of Representatives Hansard*, 3 Jun. 1986.

12  Sir Arthur Tange, 'The Dibb Report: After the Excitement of Heroes and Villains ...', *Age*, 5 Jun. 1986. Press clippings on the review were collected by the Current Information Service of the Department of the Parliamentary Library, 'Editorials and Selected Press Comment on the Dibb Report', 10 Jun. 1986. This compilation includes a biographical piece on Dibb by John Moses, writing in the *Australian* of 4 June 1986. Titled 'Bright light in the bureaucratic murk', Moses writes: 'Paul Dibb has been now, for more than 10 years in Australia, a quiet but formidable strategist and intelligence expert. The kind of person who might appear in a BBC television series (but not as principal actor) about the hidden world of global information gathering.'

On South-East Asia, for example, Dibb stressed the importance of Indonesia but said that '[i]n defence terms, other ASEAN states do not have the geographical proximity to involve our military interests so closely. The Five Power Defence Arrangements (FPDA), including our presence at Butterworth, reflect the concerns of a previous era.' By contrast the White Paper stressed that FPDA 'formalised' Australia's 'regional responsibilities' and anticipated 'scope for increased emphasis on logistic arrangements in regional military co-operation' with the FPDA countries. There was also a strong statement of Australian obligations to the security of Papua New Guinea, which was not mentioned in the public Dibb review.[13]

The Hawke Government used the 1987 Defence White Paper to address a US concern that it was tending to be too isolationist. Hawke observed in his memoirs: 'Dibb addressed only the issue of capabilities. Then in 1987, in the Defence White Paper, the government configured the self-reliance concept with our alliance arrangements.'[14] It's important to remember that the tenor of the times was shaped by New Zealand's defection from ANZUS. In September of 1986 — that is after the Dibb Review's publication but before the 1987 Defence White Paper — the United States suspended its ANZUS-treaty obligations towards New Zealand over Wellington's anti-nuclear policy. Beazley noted: 'Basically the Americans were not worried about the New Zealanders. They were worried about us ...'[15] The White Paper set out to remove any possible basis for US concern about its alliance with Australia.

As a policy exercise, the combination of the Dibb Review and the 1987 White Paper met a number of important objectives. It helped Labor establish a basis for its continued support of the US alliance — something that was critically important in electoral terms, given the strong public attachment to the relationship. For the Liberal and National coalition the reviews helped to crystallise their own approach to defence policy, by stressing a more outward-looking, expeditionary

---

13  Dibb, *Review of Australia's Defence Capabilities* (1986). The ASEAN and PNG references are at p. 48 (Commonwealth of Australia, *The Defence Of Australia 1987: A Policy Information Paper* (Canberra: Australia Government Publishing Service, 1987)). References to FPDA and PNG are on pp. 6–7.

14  Hawke, *The Hawke Memoirs* (1994), p. 229.

15  Kim Beazley, quoted in a discussion on the New Zealand relationship, Parliament of the Commonwealth of Australia, *ANZUS After 45 Years: Seminar Proceedings 11–12 August 1997*, Joint Standing Committee on Foreign Affairs, Defence and Trade, House of Representatives, Canberra, 1997, p. 56.

bias for the ADF. This contrasted with Labor's more constrained approach to using the ADF based on geography. These were important shades of difference, but still enabled the parties to claim that large parts of defence policy had bipartisan support.

The 1986 and 1987 statements established an enduring set of criteria for evaluating force-structure proposals. The statements broke an impasse in Defence preventing proper joint-capability development. Elements of this approach have been used by subsequent governments in defence policy development right up to the 2016 White Paper. Regrettably, the 1987 policy set another pattern for subsequent white papers: its release was quickly followed by a reduction in the growth of defence spending. To date only the 2000 White Paper has not followed this trend and it remains to be seen once the 2016 statement is issued if there will continue to be bipartisan support to lift defence spending to 2 per cent of GDP.

## The 1990s and a Strong Australia

The politics of defence force structure development has remained remarkably consistent in the quarter of a century that has followed Dibb and Beazley's work, but Australian policy settings have changed in reaction to the shifting global and Asia-Pacific strategic outlook. Three broad strategic changes in particular led to a dramatic increase in the use of the ADF: first, the end of the Cold War unlocked a frozen strategic balance in the Middle East, giving rise to the first cycle of Gulf Wars, the Soviet invasion of Afghanistan and the rise of Islamist extremism, which ultimately led to the 11 September 2001 Al-Qaeda attacks in the United States.

Closer to home, the second strategic change was the marked decline of political and social stability in Indonesia, East Timor and the Pacific Island states. Indonesia's difficult transition from a kleptocratic dictatorship to an at times uncertain democracy gave rise to Australia's East Timor intervention in 1999 and, separately, to a substantial threat from homegrown Islamist terrorism. In the Pacific Islands, internal instability fuelled by crumbling social structures, political incompetence and economic stagnation provided the fuel for a series of violent eruptions forcing Australia to lead costly Defence and police stabilisation missions. In contrast to the 1980s and most of the

1990s, from 1998 until the present the ADF has been on continuous operations, at times simultaneously in two or more areas. The surprise is that this has had such minimal impact on ADF force-structure design.

The third strategic change was the rapidly emerging growth of Asia, fuelling expanding military capabilities. China's economic reform juggernaut started with Deng Xiaoping's reforms in December 1978. From a slightly earlier start, a number of South-East Asian countries were emerging as the 'Tiger economies' and enjoying rapid growth. Australia was increasingly engaging the region in trade and investment and the case for deepening military engagement was becoming stronger. While the core element of Australian Defence white papers focused on long-term military capability development, there was also a need to address defence *posture* — that is how the current force engaged with regional counterparts. Shaping the behaviour of key countries in ways that promoted Australian interests could make an important peacetime contribution to stability.

The curse of policy statements is that they start to date as soon as they are released and governments are forced to decide how long to stick with a policy line or to make a break with the past and accept the inevitability of strategic change. Labor's *Defending Australia: Defence White Paper 1994* reflected an awkward compromise between continuity and change, in particular how far to acknowledge that the end of the Cold War and the fall of the Berlin Wall was recasting Australia's broader strategic outlook. Tabling the White Paper in parliament, then Prime Minister Paul Keating hinted at the underlying challenge:

> Some commentators have seen a tension in the two objectives of defence self-reliance and greater strategic engagement with the countries around us, but I believe no such tension exists. In defence policy no less than in other areas of Australia's engagement with Asia, our efforts to improve our own capacities as a nation and our ability to operate successfully in the region are two sides of the same coin.[16]

---

16  Prime Minister Paul Keating, 'Ministerial Statement: Defending Australia: Defence White Paper 1994', *House of Representatives Hansard*, 8 Dec. 1994.

In his brief tenure as Leader of the Opposition, Alexander Downer replied that the 1987 White Paper was 'outdated and superseded' and that the 1994 statement 'comes several years too late':

> May I refer the government to ... the Coalition's 1992 defence policy, *A Strong Australia*. Those opposite will find there a rational and detailed blueprint for what we called then 'a policy of cooperative regional defence'. No doubt those who wrote the white paper are well acquainted with those pages, because the ideas in them have been extensively adopted.[17]

*A Strong Australia* (a document that I was closely involved in writing) sought to differentiate the Coalition's defence offering by promoting a stepped-up policy of practical military-to-military cooperation in the Asia-Pacific. It argued:

> central to Australia's own security is the security of the immediate region. It is almost axiomatic that a direct threat to territorial Australia will only emerge if there is initially a collapse in the region's security environment. Australian defence planning should, therefore, be at least partially directed towards enhancing the security of the region.[18]

The Coalition lost the 1993 election and so never had the opportunity to implement *A Strong Australia*. Three more years of Opposition saw the Coalition continuing to chew on the issue of how to articulate a defence policy setting that wasn't constrained to a narrow approach to the Defence of Australia (DOA). In part this was about product differentiation — seeking a convincing political explanation for a different approach — but just as important was an emerging view that strategic changes were forcing Australia to take a more outward-looking approach to defence. *Australia's Defence*, the Coalition's defence policy statement issued in February 1996 a few weeks before the March election, set out a sharply different approach to that of the 1987 White Paper:

> The Coalition believes that the best way to ensure the security of Australia is to maintain a capable Defence Force and to take actions that support a favourable strategic environment in Southeast and

---

17    Alexander Downer, Leader of the Opposition, 'Ministerial Statement: Defending Australia: Defence White Paper 1994', *House of Representatives Hansard*, 8 Dec. 1994.

18    The Coalition, *A Strong Australia: Rebuilding Australia's Defence: Defence Policy of the Federal Liberal Party/National Party Coalition* (Oct. 1992), p. 25.

Northeast Asia and the South Pacific. Close military, economic and political ties with the region are an effective way of providing for Australia's security.[19]

In its discussion of ADF capabilities, the policy statement prudently said it would wait for Defence advice before being too prescriptive about future acquisitions, but the document set out some guiding priorities, which included:

- Capacity for control and surveillance of the sea-air gap …
- And the capacity to undertake strategic strike against an adversaries' operational and support infrastructure and to interdict proximate sea lanes of communication.[20]

In effect, this was taking DOA into the archipelago to Australia's north. The flurry of election campaigning often means that pre-polling day policy announcements are ignored, as was *Australia's Defence*. But in its focus on the wider Asia-Pacific and with a forward interpretation of DOA, the document articulated a distinct Coalition approach to defence.

In his speeches as the first Defence Minister in the Howard Government, Ian McLachlan searched for the right language to capture the Coalition approach.[21] In a May 1996 speech delivered at The Australian National University's Strategic and Defence Studies Centre (SDSC), McLachlan said:

Our key defence policy aim is to develop military forces able to defeat any attack against Australia. No country has the interest or capacity to launch a full-scale invasion against Australia, so our focus is on countering more realistic levels of threat. Our purpose is to deter any potential aggressor and, if deterrence fails, to defeat the enemy in the sea and air approaches *and on land*.

That objective is, and must be, the core business of the ADF. Additionally, the government will make an effective contribution to regional security. Australia's defence does not begin at the coast-line.

---

19   John Howard, Leader of the Opposition, *Australia's Defence*, 13 Feb. 1996, p. 14, s. 4.1.

20   Howard, *Australia's Defence*, p. 15, s. 5.5.

21   In the interests of full disclosure I should note that I was Ian McLachlan's chief of staff during his time as Defence Minister and soon took on the role of being his speechwriter.

On the contrary, Australia cannot be secure if the region is unstable. Defence is making a growing contribution to Australia's wider regional security aims.

One of the issues we need to examine is how far that particular role can and should be taken. Australia cannot be adequately defended only by guarding its territory and by merely looking on at the changes sweeping through Asia [emphasis added].[22]

The combination of product differentiation and strategic change crystallised in the December 1997 publication of *Australia's Strategic Policy*,[23] the unclassified version of a strategic assessment undertaken by Defence at McLachlan's direction. Tabling the document in parliament, McLachlan said:

The focus of our policy remains on our ability to defend Australia. Australia's strategic interests do not begin and end at our shoreline. It would be a serious mistake to think we could adopt a 'fortress Australia' strategy in the event of a deterioration of regional stability. We cannot be secure in an insecure region.

... We can no longer assume that forces able to meet low-level contingencies in the defence of Australia will be sufficient to handle conflict beyond our territory ...

The government, therefore, rejects the argument that we must choose between a Defence Force to defend Australia and one able within realistic limitations to operate overseas. The Defence Force must be able to do both. The issue Australia faces is how to build a Defence force able to ensure the security of the country and able to contribute to the security of our region.[24]

*Australia's Strategic Policy* was almost as blunt as the 1996 pre-election statement. The word 'proactive' was used as a slightly more benign formulation than 'pre-empt', but the military meaning was clear:

More proactive operations offer the opportunity to seize the initiative, impose real pressure on an adversary to stop attacking Australia, and

---

22  Ian McLachlan, 'Australian Defence Policy after the Year 2000', in Helen Hookey & Denny Roy (eds), *Australian Defence Planning: Five Views from Policy Makers* (Canberra: Strategic and Defence Studies Centre, 1997).

23  Commonwealth of Australia, *Australia's Strategic Policy* (Canberra: Department of Defence, 1997).

24  Ian McLachlan, 'Ministerial Statement: Australia's Strategic Policy', *House of Representatives Hansard*, 2 Dec. 1997.

provide better confidence that Australian lives and property would be protected. That is not to suggest we would contemplate attacking the population centres of an aggressor. Rather, we would attack — or threaten to attack — military assets and installations which could be used to attack Australia.[25]

Language as blunt as this about the potential use of offensive military capability wasn't seen again until the 2009 White Paper. The media reception was mixed, the *Australian*'s headline following the release of *Australia's Strategic Policy* was: 'McLachlan's defence force gears up for war offshore.'[26] Many commentators saw the policy as presenting a return to the 'forward defence' strategy of the 1960s. That critique was vigorously resisted by McLachlan on the basis that a critical change was the increasing military capabilities of countries in the Asia-Pacific.

Much of the political debate on defence in the 1990s and early 2000s was around just how far forward into the region should the 1986 DOA be allowed to extend. It was useful for commentators and others to play up somewhat the apparent differences between a supposed Labor disposition for a 'fortress Australia strategy' and a Coalition preference for 'forward defence'. In reality there is less to the debate than at first meets the eye. DOA and 'forward defence' meet at some point in the archipelago of islands to Australia's north and further into South-East Asia. Elsewhere I have referred to this as 'DOA plus', which is where, to the surprise of many, Australia found itself in 1999 when it deployed a large stabilisation force into East Timor.[27]

The extension of the DOA concept further into the region reflected not so much a change of Australian thinking as it did a deterioration of regional stability that forced an Australian response. It pointed to the need to rethink Defence's capacity to deploy and sustain joint forces at significant distances from Australia. Given Australia's geographic position, it became clear as a result of the East Timor deployment that the requirements for an effective 'DOA plus' policy are practically identical to what is needed to sustain an expeditionary force.

25  Commonwealth of Australia, *Australia's Strategic Policy* (1997), p. 46.
26  Don Greenlees, 'McLachlan's Defence Force Gears up for War Offshore', *Australian*, 3 Dec. 1997, p. 1.
27  Peter Jennings, 'The Politics of Defence White Papers', *Security Challenges*, Vol. 9, No. 2 (2013), pp. 1–14.

Writing in anticipation of the 2000 White Paper, Dibb made the following comment:

> there can be no doubt that we do need to transform the ADF into a different sort of defence force to meet the strategic challenges of the 21st century. My view is that the defence of Australia and the archipelago to our north and east are now one force structure planning problem. This is what I have termed 'the regional defence of Australia'.[28]

What seemed a relatively novel proposition in 1996 and 1997 became the new orthodoxy in 2000. The seismic shift in strategic thinking was, of course, prompted by the 1999 East Timor crisis.

## 2000 and the Timor Shock

Howard and McLachlan wisely held off producing a Defence white paper in the government's first term,[29] but the experience of mounting Australia's largest military operation since the Vietnam War — the International Force in East Timor (INTERFET) — profoundly shaped Howard's thinking on defence. He wrote in his autobiography:

> I realised that for a long time into the future Australia would need to spend a lot of money on Defence. We had mounted a hugely successful operation, but launching and sustaining it had put an enormous strain on our military resources, particularly our ground forces and strategic lift assets.[30]

The White Paper *Defence 2000: Our Future Defence Force*, set out a strategy for extending Australia's strategic interests more deeply into the Asia-Pacific region and equipping the ADF in ways that would support long-term stabilisation operations. The paper presented these objectives as an evolution of policy-thinking from the 1987 White Paper. It stated that 'the two highest tasks' for the ADF were:

---

28   Paul Dibb, 'Transforming the ADF's Force Structure For the 21st Century', *Australian Defence Force Journal*, No. 123 (Jul.–Aug. 2000), pp. 27–28.

29   This was notwithstanding my best efforts as McLachlan's chief of staff to have a white paper initiated. Howard was sceptical about the value of over-elaborate policy statements and McLachlan had a sense of the challenge that might be involved in getting Defence to develop one. McLachlan's view was that the business needed to be restructured first, which led him to initiate the Defence Efficiency Review.

30   John Howard, *Lazarus Rising: A Personal and Political Autobiography* (Sydney: Harper Collins, 2010), p. 357.

First, Australia will maintain maritime capabilities — mostly air and naval forces — that can defend Australia by denying our air and sea approaches to any credible hostile forces. Second, Australia will maintain land forces — including the air and naval assets needed to deploy and protect them — that can operate as part of a joint force to control the approaches to Australia and respond effectively to any armed incursion onto Australian soil. Both those sets of capabilities would also be able to support the security of our immediate neighbourhood and contribute to coalition operations.[31]

Notwithstanding the reference to operations on Australian soil, there is no doubt that the government's thinking was focused on what was needed to deploy forces offshore. Howard said the Timor experience 'never left me' and directly led to subsequent decisions to purchase additional C–17 lift capability and to expand the size of the Regular Army.[32]

A clear strength of the 2000 White Paper was the decision to establish a rolling 10-year defence-capability investment plan and to 'commit' — as far as any government can tie future administrations — to a decade-long funding profile. The paper also sought to set out a clear strategic basis for key defence capabilities. The structure of the Army was to build around sustaining a brigade on operations for extended periods with an additional augmented battalion group able to perform a simultaneous separate operation. Air combat forces were to be 'at least comparable qualitatively to any in the region' and maritime forces were 'to maintain an assured capability to detect and attack any major surface ships, and to impose substantial constraints on hostile submarine operations, in our extended maritime approaches'.[33]

The basic structure of the ADF as set out in the 2000 White Paper, right down to the numbers of key platforms, remained remarkably similar to that assessed by Dibb 15 years earlier. That said, the hard realities of Timor and following operations shifted the ADF's capabilities into more joint, better supported and more integrated capabilities. It may be true that there was no better articulated strategic grounds in 2000 than there had been in 1986 to explain why the RAAF had approximately

---

31  Commonwealth of Australia, *Defence 2000: Our Future Defence Force* (Canberra: Department of Defence, 2000), p. xii.
32  Howard, *Lazarus Rising*, 2000, p. 358.
33  Commonwealth of Australia, *Defence 2000*, 2000, p. xiii.

100 combat aircraft. But at least by the time a squadron of F/A–18s were deployed to the Middle East in 2003, this was a capability more ready to fight in higher level contingencies. The elements of Defence that were deployed and used in the decade after 2000 got sufficient investment to make them more operationally effective. Force elements that were not called on — anti-submarine warfare (ASW), for example — tended to atrophy. This points to two important principles of force structuring: first, what gets used gets funded; and, second, operations lends more rigour to capability decision-making.

Was Defence any better placed to develop the 2000 White Paper than Dibb found the organisation to be in 1986? The answer is clearly 'yes' because the 2000 statement was produced by the department, albeit by a team lead by Hugh White that removed itself from Russell to what is now the location of the Australian Strategic Policy Institute (ASPI) in Barton, Canberra. Like Dibb, White brought a focus to the task that wasn't to be diverted by departmental bickering. As an experienced prime minister by 2000, Howard knew what he wanted of Defence so he gave the White Paper the same purposeful momentum that Beazley provided 15 years earlier. The Timor experience created a Defence organisation with less time for internal gamesmanship. The senior leaders of the ADF were genuinely thinking of the entity more as 'the ADF' rather than a loose coalition of Services. Moreover, there was a broad (but never universal) agreement between the ADF and the civilian elements of Defence that supported the White Paper's outcomes.

Politically the Coalition Government benefited from encouraging a perception that it was strong on national security and better able than Labor to handle defence. In January 2001, the Newspoll organisation added defence to the list of policy areas over which it asked Australians which political party was the better manager. For that poll, 40 per cent nominated the Liberal/National Coalition and 23 per cent Labor.[34] The Coalition retained a similar lead as the party 'best able to handle defence' for the life of the Howard Government.

---

34  Newspoll findings for January 2001 are available at polling.newspoll.com.au/image_ uploads/cgi-lib.12728.1.1002issues.pdf (accessed 2 Sep. 2015). It is possible to search the Newspoll archives on defence and national security polling results at www.theaustralian.com. au/national-affairs/newspoll.

# Yet More White Papers: 2009 and 2013

The 2009 White Paper, *Defending Australia in the Asia-Pacific Century: Force 2030*, was Labor's first white paper since 1994. For Prime Minister Kevin Rudd, a former diplomat with a hard-edged strategic world view, the statement gave the opportunity to make his own definitive mark on defence policy. A key challenge was to differentiate the product from the Howard Government's claim to be the 'natural party' of national security. The White Paper started with a list of priorities, the first of which might have been lifted from its 1987 predecessor: 'Australia's most basic strategic interest remains the defence of Australia against direct armed attack.' But with this respect paid, it rapidly became clear that the statement was far more outward looking:

> The more Australia aspires to have greater strategic influence beyond our immediate neighbourhood — that is to say the ability to exert policy influence that is underpinned by military power — the greater the level of spending on defence we need to be prepared to undertake.[35]

The ability to 'exert policy influence' went at least as far as ensuring 'that no major military power … could challenge our control of the air and sea approaches to Australia, [or have] access to bases in our neighbourhood from which to project force against us'. This approach called for a 'more potent force', which lead to the key policy announcement in the White Paper:

> The major new direction that has emerged through consideration of current and future requirements is a significant focus on enhancing our maritime capabilities. By the mid-2030s, we will have a more potent and heavier maritime force.[36]

If this amounted to a variation of DOA, it was DOA on steroids — 'DOA plus, plus' perhaps. The centrepiece of the maritime program was to double the submarine fleet from six to 12 boats, with the new class of submarine planned to 'have greater range, longer endurance on patrol, and expanded capabilities compared to the current *Collins*-class submarine'.

---

35  Commonwealth of Australia, *Defending Australia in the Twentieth Century: Force 2030* (Canberra: Australian Government Publishing Service, 2009), p. 11.
36  Commonwealth of Australia, *Defending Australia* (2009), p. 13.

The grand conceptions of the 2009 White Paper were undermined by the leadership turmoil and administrative chaos of the Rudd Government and by the impact of the global financial crisis which started to bite hard as the document was being finalised. This forced a rather sad late inclusion as the second paragraph in the Executive Summary of the statement:

> The global economic crisis is the most fundamental economic challenge facing this Government. At times such as these, the Government must be fiscally responsible. It would be reckless to commit substantial new resources to Defence while uncertainty surrounding the crisis remains.[37]

In essence the policy was dead in the water before it went to the printers. Looking back on the experience a few years later, then Foreign Minister Bob Carr reported on a discussion with the White Paper's principal author, Michael Pezzullo:

> He said, 'take the 2009 Defence White paper. That was a case of over-hedging'. By this he meant the controversial chapter talking up Chinese strategic assertiveness and the prospects of major power conflict ... but the 2013 Defence white paper which pulled back a bit (but not in respect of its commitment to those defence acquisitions), that would be an example of plain hedging.[38]

The Defence White Paper 2013 was a curious policy in terms both of content and timing.[39] As Carr observed, it reasserted the 2009 Rudd force structure but without a convincing funding base. The release of the White Paper just a few months before the 2013 October election suggested that it was there as a place marker rather than a believable forward plan. As a relatively new prime minister with a self-confessed lack of deep interest in international affairs, Julia Gillard was not well placed to drive a white paper's development. Gillard also had an internal problem, which was to create a policy position able to distinguish her own leadership from that of Rudd. This Gillard did with her department's *Australia in the Asian Century* White Paper in October 2012 — an economically focused and overly optimistic

---

37 Commonwealth of Australia, *Defending Australia* (2009), p. 11.
38 Bob Carr, *Diary of a Foreign Minister* (Sydney: New South Publishing, 2014), p. 395.
39 Commonwealth of Australia, *Defence White Paper 2013* (Canberra: Department of Defence, 2013).

assessment of the long-term prospects for growth in Asia.[40] In some respects, this White Paper was developed using a similar approach to the 'Dibb model'. Ken Henry, an external expert and former Secretary of the Treasury, was brought in to develop the strategy. But Henry's report was not intended to present personal advice to government. The document received Cabinet endorsement as a complete statement of policy. Thus Gillard denied herself the opportunity to shape a more targeted policy after absorbing community reactions to the study.

The tide of Australian domestic politics in 2013 did not leave much time for a careful consideration of the more pessimistic assessment of regional security contained in Defence White Paper 2013 when contrasted with the considerably more benign assessments of the *Asian Century White Paper* and Gillard's January 2013 National Security Statement.[41] The same force structure was presented as the outcome of the different strategic analytical work that took place in 2009 and 2013, which pointed to a breakdown in strategic policy rigour and indicated the breadth of the conceptual gaps between the various policy statements on offer.[42] The 2013 Defence White Paper did, however, present a more nuanced assessment of regional security, including a more balanced assessment of China's role in the region and making the case for reinvigorated defence relationships with Indonesia, Papua New Guinea and Japan. The White Paper's lasting contribution to strategic thinking was to point to an important trend: 'a new Indo-Pacific strategic arc is beginning to emerge, connecting the Indian and Pacific Oceans through Southeast Asia.' That assertion helped to shape a stronger emphasis on defence posture in the White Paper, in addition to reiterating the capability development plan of 2009 and adding the acquisition of the 'Growler' electronic warfare equipped Super Hornet aircraft.

---

40  Commonwealth of Australia, *Australia and the Asian Century White Paper* (Canberra: Department of Prime Minister and Cabinet, Oct. 2012). With the change of government in October 2013, the *Asian Century White Paper* was quickly removed from the Department of Foreign Affairs and Trade's website, but it is helpfully still on the Defence website.

41  See a brief review of that statement here: Peter Jennings, 'National Security: The Decade after the Decade Before', *ASPI: Strategist*, 25 Jan. 2013, available at www.aspistrategist.org.au/national-security-the-decade-after-the-decade-before.

42  I review these policy statements in more detail in Peter Jennings, 'Ken Henry's Asian Century', *ASPI: Policy Analysis*, No. 104 (Aug. 2012). See also Peter Jennings, 'Defence Challenges after the 2013 White Paper', *Policy*, Vol. 29, No. 2 (Winter 2013).

Dibb's assessment of the 2009 and 2013 white papers is worth noting to assess the policy changes that had developed since 1986. On strategic geography, Dibb welcomed the emphasis the 2013 White Paper put on Australia's wider region as being the key likely priority for operations: 'the security of Southeast Asia as increasingly central to our own security':

> That means the ADF's primary operational area must encompass the eastern Indian Ocean, the waters of Southeast Asia (including the South China Sea), the South Pacific and the Southern Ocean. This amounts to more than 10 per cent of the earth's surface and poses a substantial challenge to a defence force of less than 60,000.

On force-structure priorities Dibb was less forgiving:

> When it comes to force structure priorities and the defence budget this white paper is on weaker ground. If we are no longer structuring the defence force to fight a major power in high-intensity combat why do we still need 12 large submarines? This was an idea spawned by prime minister Rudd's advisers without rigorous strategic analysis.[43]

Although there is widespread agreement that submarines are an increasingly important capability for Australia, no clear justification was presented in the 2009 or 2013 statements as to why 12 rather than, say, nine or 15 submarines, was the nominated target. After the 2009 policy announcement, explanations for the number of submarines were offered based on assessments of what was needed to keep one or two boats continuously on patrol while others underwent maintenance

---

43    Paul Dibb, 'Show us the Money for Defence Spending', *Australian*, 6 May 2013.

and preparation.[44] As soon as the number of 12 was released it was captured by an aggressive industry lobby in South Australia, which has politically made it very difficult for successive governments to change the policy setting.

Dibb described any implication from the 2009 White Paper that the submarine expansion was designed to impose substantial costs against a major power adversary (that is, China) as a 'dangerous indulgence', but stressed the importance of the capability in Australia's nearer region and South-East Asia.[45] His assessment (writing with Richard Brabin-Smith) was that:

> the policy focus on the defence of Australia and operations in our immediate region continues to be inviolable, especially with the expected continued growth of the economies and military potential of the major and middle powers of the Indo-Pacific. We have re-emphasised the centrality of a strategy that is maritime in focus.[46]

# Looking to the Future

The defence policy development process initiated by Beazley in 1985 and undertaken by Dibb in his 1986 *Review of Australia's Defence Capabilities*, followed by the 1987 Defence White Paper, became a model that subsequent governments followed, albeit with variations

---

44   When asked in 2012 about why 12 submarines had been identified in the 2009 White Paper, the following exchange took place in Senate Estimates Committee hearings:

> Rear Adm. Moffitt: When it comes to the academic analysis of the weight of forces necessary to defend a nation the size of Australia with its geography and population and the available budget to do that, the number we acquire of anything probably has more to do with the threshold of pain than it does with the absolute need to do the task.

> Senator JOHNSTON: Can you just explain that? I do not quite follow you. When you say 'the threshold of pain', you mean cost and time —

> Rear Adm. Moffitt: How much are we prepared to spend? It is a process of trading off our ability to invest in defence against the need.

> Senator JOHNSTON: Let us just be clear: the operational concept has yet to be finished and you are not sure where the number 12 comes from?

> Rear Adm. Moffitt: I cannot talk to the number 12 except that it is in the white paper.

> See Foreign Affairs, Defence and Trade Legislation Committee, *Estimates – Defence Portfolio*, *Senate Hansard*, 28 May 2012.

45   Paul Dibb & Richard Brabin-Smith, 'Australian Defence: Challenges for the New Government', *Security Challenges*, Vol. 9, No. 4 (2013), pp. 45–64, p. 58.

46   Dibb & Brabin-Smith, 'Australian Defence' (2013), pp. 62–63.

to the theme. The most successful of the various white papers were, in this author's view, the 1987 and 2000 statements. In both cases the white papers had sponsors — Beazley and Howard — who actively shaped the content and then stayed long enough in their jobs to see significant parts of the policy implemented. Dibb in 1986 and White in 2000 provided solid intellectual content and consulted sufficiently with the wider Defence establishment to get enough buy-in to give the policy a chance to succeed.

Other white papers were less successful. The 1976 statement was more a product of Tange's intellect than the Fraser Government's. Core concepts were implemented and funding — apart from a brief increase after the 1979 Soviet invasion of Afghanistan — was not sustained. The 2009 White Paper articulated a strong new policy direction with a maritime emphasis and presented a coherent and rather pessimistic account of the regional security outlook. But the policy's implementation faltered because of the chaotic nature of the Rudd Government and the bloody leadership handover from Rudd to Gillard. Without its chief sponsor, the 2009 statement lacked an advocate and planned funding did not materialise.

Will the 'Dibb model' survive as a favoured way of making defence policy? The answer is unequivocally 'yes'. The Coalition Government under Tony Abbott has made substantial use of externally led review teams to assist the 2016 White Paper project — the Defence 'External Expert Panel' — and to engage in a root and branch review of Defence organisational structure — the so-called First Principles Review by David Peever and his colleagues. The approach has become a standard trope of policymaking. Oppositions call for reviews of this type to draw attention to flaws in the government's approach. Governments undertake Dibb-style reviews to show their engagement and commitment to good policy outcomes.

Beyond the theatre of policy, the reality is that if external policy reviews are done well, they will help to shape good-quality outcomes. If anything, a tendency shown by recent governments of different political stripes has been to draw more heavily on advice that comes from sources outside of the Australian Public Service. Governments do this because they are looking for agility and for the intelligent fusing of policy objectives and political benefit, which is at the core of successful government. In the future we will see more rather than fewer 'Dibb model' reviews.

Has Defence got better at setting the conceptual basis for force structuring? Again, the answer is broadly 'yes'. It's still the case that there are important issues over which the Services and civilians will disagree — a recent example being over the level of capability required for the Sea 5000 project to replace the ANZAC-class frigates.[47] Dibb remained uncomfortable about the structure of the Army, agreeing with the Plan Beersheba to restructure the Army into three multi-role combat brigades, but not with the heavier elements of the Land 400 plan for Army vehicles. The biggest challenge for Army, Dibb and Brabin-Smith maintain, is to fully embrace the amphibious capabilities that are inherent in the new *Canberra*-class 'landing helicopter dock' ships.[48] For all of these differences over capability priority, current civil–military relations in Defence do not remotely approach the dysfunctionality of 1984–85.

It may be that operational experience and constant pressure for better performance from governments has meant that Defence has improved its ability to collaborate on complex policymaking and, arguably, to agree to sensible approaches to joint-capability development. However, it is noteworthy that the organisation has yet to effectively articulate, as Dibb observed, 'in any rigorous, analytical way' the precise basis for an Army structured around three regular brigades, and Air Force with around 100 combat aircraft and a Navy with six (or 12) submarines and 12 surface combatants. Several reasons may help to explain this apparent analytical gap. First, force structures are slow to change and are grounded in strong historical experience demonstrating the effectiveness of key capabilities. Second, outside of the major wars of the last century, the ADF remains a small force that is focused on the challenges of maintaining the viability of key force elements. A Navy with fewer than a dozen surface combatants is surely at the brink of viability.

---

47 See Cameron Stewart, 'Rebuff for Navy on Super Warships', *Australian*, 9 May 2015.
48 Dibb & Brabin-Smith, 'Australian Defence' (2013), pp. 60–61.

Further, the politics of reducing any military capabilities is difficult. While there was certainly a case to argue that the Army might not replace the Leopard tank, Howard was unwilling to make that call regardless of the case some strategists advanced to let the capability go. Force structures are 'sticky' — governments and Defence organisations tend to emphasise platform replacement, even though this can be a less than rigorous approach to designing new capabilities. Thus far disruptive new technologies have not really threatened the core assumptions of the 'balanced force' approach, although defence applications of cyber capabilities may do so in the future.

A concluding thought on politics is needed. It is often claimed that 'politics' is the enemy of good defence policy development, but as this survey has shown, politics *done well* is a critical component of delivering high-quality policy outcomes. Dibb's experiences in 1986 as well as the white paper process of 2000 were lucky to hit some 'sweet spots', where experienced political leaders engaged thoughtfully in policy design and then stayed on long enough to guide implementation. By contrast, dysfunctional politics produces poor policy outcomes. For the 'Dibb model' of policy development to work, an intelligent and pragmatic partnership needs to be struck between politicians and their professional advisers.

# 10

# The 'Priceless' Alliance: Paul Dibb and ANZUS

Benjamin Schreer

There is hardly a more important strategic question for Australia's defence policy than how close to position itself towards its American ally and how much support to expect from Washington, particularly during times of major changes in the geostrategic environment. As a result, the Australia–New Zealand–United States (ANZUS) alliance has been of singular importance to Paul Dibb's professional life. During the Cold War, he was directly involved in negotiating Australia's intelligence and defence arrangements with the US ally. For instance, as Deputy Secretary of Defence for Strategy and Intelligence, Dibb had a major role in running the policy on the alliance relationship with the United States. He was also closely involved with the alliance's joint intelligence and communications facilities at Pine Gap, Nurrungar and North West Cape. This first-hand experience deeply impressed upon Dibb a fundamental belief in the 'priceless' value of the alliance for Australia's security, derived from privileged access to US intelligence, weapons systems, logistics support and extended deterrence guarantees.[1]

---

1    Paul Dibb, 'Australia – United States', in Brendan Taylor (ed.), *Australia as an Asia-Pacific Regional Power: Friendships in Flux?* (London: Routledge, 2007), pp. 36–37.

Moreover, in his 'second life' as a strategic scholar, Dibb has been a constant contributor to Australia's contemporary debate on ANZUS. His writings on the alliance over more than three decades show an ambivalent strategist who, on the one hand, recognises the huge advantages of being a close US ally, but who also is at times deeply sceptical and wonders if the time has come for Australia to look for alternatives. The analysis also shows that Dibb is a 'classical realist' when it comes to alliance politics: he stresses the importance of values and traditions that tie the two allies together. Moreover, his writings are a testament to the enormous challenges ANZUS has encountered since the collapse of the Soviet Union, its remarkable resilience, and its ability to adapt to those changes. Indeed, after considerable concerns about a potential estrangement between Canberra and Washington, Dibb's answer to the core question of whether any credible alternative exists for Australia under the current geostrategic conditions is a resounding 'no'.

## A Unique Alliance

Nations enter into military alliances either to 'balance' against an external threat (current or future), or to 'bandwagon' with the most powerful actor in the international system.[2] In Australia's case, 'balancing' against a potentially hostile Asian major power has always been the major rationale behind ANZUS. As Dibb points out, a key role of the alliance for Australia is to sustain the United States' critical role as a 'balancer' in the Asia-Pacific region and to check against hegemonic ambitions of a hostile major power. In his words, 'Asia without the United States would be a much more dangerous place for Australia's strategic interests'.[3] Moreover, other traditional alliance functions for Australia include the twin pillars of reassurance and deterrence:

> The core of the ANZUS alliance has always been the need for protection by a great and powerful friend. The United States has reassured Australia in that regard, from providing extended nuclear deterrence through to an expectation that it would defend Australia in the event of a serious threat by a major power.[4]

---

2     Stephen Walt, *The Origins of Alliances* (Cornell University Press, 1987), ch. 2.
3     Paul Dibb, *Australia's Alliance with America*, Melbourne Asia Policy Papers, Vol. 1, No. 1 (University of Melbourne, Mar. 2003), p. 7.
4     Dibb, *Australia's Alliance with America* (2003), p. 37.

For Dibb, however, the 'real' value of ANZUS is 'the access it provides to US intelligence, defence science and advanced weapon systems'.[5] In combination with US security guarantees, including extended nuclear deterrence, against an existential threat, these factors deliver the 'unique nature of the alliance for Australia'.[6] Indeed, as a member of the UK–US intelligence-sharing agreement of 1946, Australia has enjoyed privileged access to highly classified US intelligence, even if this has not been risk-free. Dibb acknowledges that hosting the joint intelligence, early warning and communications facilities at Pine Gap, Nurrungar and North West Cape during the Cold War most likely made Australia a Soviet nuclear target but that 'this was the price to be paid for the alliance'.[7] Moreover, through the 'Five Eyes' framework (the intelligence alliance between Australia, Canada, New Zealand, the United Kingdom and the United States), Australia derives significant strategic advantages:

> In Australia's case, access to American signals and satellite intelligence and assistance with developing our indigenous intelligence capabilities has been priceless. I mean that in the sense that it is not possible to put a price on how much it would have cost Australia to go it alone and develop such capabilities — it would simply have been beyond Australia's indigenous research and development capabilities.[8]

Dibb is critical of voices in Australia arguing that more money should be invested in the development of a truly independent intelligence capability, stressing that 'frankly, world-class facilities such as Pine Gap cannot be replicated at any price'.[9] As well, for strategic reasons the intelligence relationship with the US ally remains indispensable:

> The very privileged access we have to intelligence of the very highest order is an important force multiplier for Australia, both in peace, to establish an essential transparency and to learn what is and what is not going on, and of course in conflict and war, to give us a leading edge over any potential regional adversary, who simply would not have that access.[10]

---

5    Dibb, *Australia's Alliance with America* (2003), p. 2.
6    Dibb, *Australia's Alliance with America* (2003).
7    Dibb, 'Australia – United States' (2007), p. 35.
8    Dibb, 'Australia – United States' (2007), p. 36.
9    Paul Dibb, 'Australia's Defence Relations with the United States', testimony to Joint Standing Committee on Foreign Affairs, Defence and Trade, Defence Subcommittee (2 Apr. 2004), FADT 58.
10   Dibb, 'Australia's Defence Relations with the United States' (2004).

The alliance is also essential for defence science cooperation and Australia's access to advanced US military weapon systems. Examples include access to US combat aircraft such as the F–111, the F–18 and, more recently, the Joint Strike Fighter. It also included advanced torpedoes and weapons systems for the *Collins*-class submarine; the future submarine is certain to have a US combat system on board. As well, the Navy's new air warfare destroyer is equipped with the US Aegis combat system. These are just the most prominent examples and, from Dibb's perspective, it is almost imperative to keep in mind the value of access to US military equipment since this has 'helped to ensure that Australia has maintained a distinct margin of technological superiority in its own region of primary strategic interest'.[11] In fact, as countries in the Asia-Pacific have started to catch up militarily in recent years, he expects Australia's reliance on US defence technology to increase — notwithstanding the fact that Washington remains reluctant to provide certain critical technologies to even its closest allies.[12]

As a consequence, for Dibb, the ANZUS alliance is in many ways 'irreplaceable'[13] for Australia, including for its future as a credible defence policy actor in the region and beyond. In this context, he often contrasts Australia with New Zealand's strategic choice:

> If Australia did not have access to US intelligence and high technology weapon systems we would have to spend much more on defence. And even then we would not have a credible defence capability — unless, of course, we decided to go down the New Zealand path of having little more than a lightly armed army.[14]

Finally, given his British heritage, one might be tempted to suspect that Dibb represents the tradition of Britain's Lord Palmerston, foreign secretary and two-time prime minister under Queen Victoria, who famously stated that 'Britain had no eternal allies and no perpetual enemies, only interests that were eternal and perpetual'.[15] In realist logic, US alliances, including with Australia, should therefore have suffered a terminal decline after the end of the Cold War and the

---

11   Dibb, 'Australia – United States' (2007), p. 36.
12   Dibb, 'Australia – United States' (2007), pp. 36–37.
13   Dibb, 'Australia's Defence Relations with the United States' (2004).
14   Dibb, *Australia's Alliance with America* (2003), p. 3.
15   Quoted in David Brown, *Palmerston and the Politics of Policy, 1846–1855* (Manchester University Press, 2002), pp. 82–83.

demise of a clear, existential threat.[16] Dibb, however, agrees with Stephen Walt that alliances are 'not merely the product of rational calculations of national interests'.[17] He emphasises that alliances 'involve shared values and belief systems and a shared history of doing things together. They also involve domestic politics.'[18]

Undoubtedly, the ANZUS alliance is an integral part of Australia's strategic culture.[19] This also helps to explain why the alliance has endured since the collapse of the Soviet Union. Yet, as will be shown later, Dibb has at times been bewildered by certain aspects of US culture and has even considered them as burdensome for the ANZUS alliance. Moreover, recently he has become concerned about the persistence of Australia's bipartisan consensus regarding the centrality of the alliance because of potential changes in public opinion.

One critical conclusion from Dibb's insistence on the fundamental importance of the alliance for Australia is that, despite much debate about his emphasis on Australia's 'defence self-reliance' in the context of the famous *Review of Australia's Defence Capabilities* (Dibb Review) in 1986, he has always been acutely aware that a degree of 'self-reliance' can only exist within a US alliance context — particularly since the strategic alternatives of 'armed neutrality' and 'non-alignment' have never been attractive for Australian policymakers and the larger public. Instead, Dibb points out that, as the smaller power, the policy of a protective alliance through ANZUS has been and will likely continue to be the preferred option for Australia.[20]

He acknowledges, however, that the lack of real strategic alternatives to the alliance with the United States brings challenges that need to be factored into Australian security and defence policymaking. According to Dibb, 'borrowing someone else's strength has disadvantages as well as advantages'.[21] The disadvantages have been most prevalent during periods when the larger ally is preoccupied with security problems

---

16   See Kenneth N. Waltz, 'The Emerging Structure of International Politics', *International Security*, Vol. 18, No. 2 (1993), pp. 44–79.
17   Stephen M. Walt, 'Why Alliances Endure or Collapse', *Survival*, Vol. 39, No. 1 (Spring 1997), p. 156.
18   Dibb, *Australia's Alliance with America* (2003), p. 4.
19   On strategic culture see Colin S. Gray, 'Strategic Culture as Context: The First Generation of Theory Strikes Back', *Review of International Studies*, Vol. 25, No. 1 (Jan. 1999), pp. 49–69.
20   Dibb, *Australia's Alliance with America* (2003), p. 3.
21   Dibb, *Australia's Alliance with America* (2003).

outside Australia's primary area of strategic interests (i.e. the Asia-Pacific) and when the 'unipolar moment'[22] in the international system led to hubris on part of the United States. His prescription as to what Australia could and should do to address such situations has, however, been less clear and emblematic of some unresolved challenges for the ANZUS alliance.

## ANZUS during the Cold War

Just like the North Atlantic Treaty Organization (NATO), the origins of ANZUS lie in the early days of the Cold War. As is well known, for Australia, the formation of the alliance with the United States and New Zealand in 1951 was a reassurance against the possibility of a resurgent Japan. Yet, the Korean War demonstrated the fact that the Soviet Union was the real security threat. Moreover, as Dibb points out, 'Moscow's naval deployments into the Indian Ocean and its acquisition of naval bases in Vietnam, as well as its intelligence activities in Canberra, brought the potential threat much closer to home'.[23] In this strategic context, Australia's value as an ally to the United States was considerable since the joint intelligence facilities were critical to 'US confidence in monitoring Soviet strategic nuclear-weapon capabilities and warning of nuclear attack'. From an Australian point of view, US security guarantees were considered essential not just against a possible Soviet aggression. Equally, if not more importantly, particularly during the 1960s the value of ANZUS for Australia was to guard against its bigger neighbour, Indonesia.[24]

During the 1970s and 1980s, however, the Australian strategic community, including Dibb, became concerned with the degree to which Australia could rely on US support in crises, particularly below the threshold of an existential threat. The 'Nixon doctrine' (also known as the 'Guam doctrine') of 1969 made it clear that the United States expected its Asia-Pacific allies to shoulder more of a burden for their own defence. As a consequence, the *Strategic Basis of Australian*

---

22   See Charles Krauthammer, 'The Unipolar Moment Revisited', *National Interest*, Vol. 70 (Winter 2002/03), pp. 5–17.

23   Dibb, 'Australia – United States' (2007), p. 34.

24   Stephan Frühling (ed.), *A History of Australian Strategic Policy since 1945* (Canberra: Commonwealth of Australia, 2009), p. 305.

*Defence Policy* paper of 1971 stated that 'Australia … cannot assume that the United States will necessarily provide assistance with the speed, of the type, and on the scale that we might think necessary'.[25] This assumption paved the way for Australia's thinking about 'defence self-reliance within the alliance' and Dibb played a major role in its conceptualisation.

Towards the end of the 1970 and early 1980s it became clear to Dibb that the threat perceptions of the two allies did not always align. In his words, during that period the United States:

> became ever more *obsessed* with the growing military capabilities of the Soviet Union. As late as 1984, the Central Intelligence Agency (CIA) was predicting that the Soviet Union would soon outstrip America in terms of its military might [emphasis added].[26]

The CIA's assessment was contrary to Dibb's own conclusion, articulated in the late 1980s, arguing that the Soviet Union was an 'incomplete superpower', unable to overcome the strategic advantages of the United States.[27] He was also puzzled as to why 'everything that the Soviet Union did in the Asia-Pacific region, including its trade and aid activities, was treated with potential hostile intent by the United States'.[28]

Moreover, during the 1980s Dibb also experienced the US ally as a hard-headed partner to deal with. For instance, he describes the Labor Government's decision to acquire 'full knowledge and concurrence' about US operations in the joint intelligence facilities, leading to one of the 'most difficult negotiations that Australia had with the United States … [which were] … [l]ong, drawn out and sometimes tense'.[29] Finally, Dibb witnessed how New Zealand became, in his words, the 'naughty boys'[30] in the 1980s when, in response to the ally's anti-nuclear stance, Washington excluded Wellington from access to the close intelligence-sharing arrangements.

---

25  Frühling, *A History of Australian Strategic Policy* (2009), p. 401.
26  Paul Dibb, 'America and the Asia-Pacific Region', in Robert Ayson & Desmond Ball (eds), *Strategy and Security in the Asia-Pacific* (Sydney: Allen & Unwin, 2006), p. 178.
27  Paul Dibb, *The Soviet Union: The Incomplete Superpower*, 2nd edn (London: International Institute for Strategic Studies and Macmillan, 1988).
28  Dibb, 'America and the Asia-Pacific region' (2006), p. 179.
29  Dibb, 'Australia – United States' (2007), p. 35.
30  Dibb, 'Australia's Defence Relations with the United States' (2004).

It is reasonable to assume that those experiences contributed to the 1986 Dibb Review, the first coherent document outlining the rationale and requirements for a self-reliant Australian defence policy. While Dibb recognised the importance of the alliance in terms of deterring against 'higher level threats', access to intelligence and defence technology, as well as military logistics, the review also reflected his reservations against relying too much on the United States:

> Our close relationship with the United States is significant for our security and the development of our defence capability, but for over a decade we have recognised that the United States is a global power with a variety of interests, none of them centred on Australia. There are potential situations where we would not expect the United States to commit combat forces on our behalf and where we need a demonstrably independent combat capability.[31]

Moreover, his review pointed out that the ANZUS Treaty did not entail an automatic obligation for the United States to defend Australia. Thus, it was 'realistic to assume that the parties will continue to approach each situation in accordance with their respective national interests'.[32]

Dibb's main conclusion in the report, however, was that possible alliance contingencies should not be the primary determinant for ADF force planning and equipment decisions.[33] Whilst the review stressed that Australia could not and should not aim for a fully independent defence policy, and that the ANZUS alliance remained a fundamental pillar of its strategic posture, Dibb's reasoning also demonstrates that, even before the Soviet Union collapsed in 1989, there was a cooling of the ANZUS alliance brought about by a relative divergence of strategic interests and the fact that, unlike NATO, the alliance was not highly institutionalised. That is, ANZUS does not have an integrated military command structure or a standing political committee akin to NATO's North Atlantic Council, which provides maximum flexibility but which can make effective consultations during periods of strategic drift more difficult. This drift became even more apparent in the immediate post-Cold War era.

---

31 Paul Dibb, *Review of Australia's Defence Capabilities*, report to the Minister for Defence (Canberra: Australian Government Publishing Service, 1986), p. 46.
32 Dibb, *Review of Australia's Defence Capabilities* (1986).
33 Dibb, *Review of Australia's Defence Capabilities* (1986), p. 47.

# In Search of a New Consensus: ANZUS in the 1990s

Following the rather sudden collapse of the Soviet Union, the alliance was left without an adversary. Australian strategic policymakers were particularly concerned with what Dibb later called a:

> rather surreal American attitude to international security and alliance relationship. We were not on the radar screen in the 1990s in Washington in the same way as we were undoubtedly in Cold War. There was a sense of drift and of, if not irrelevance, a lack of importance.[34]

In a 1993 address to the National Press Club in Canberra, Dibb impressed upon his audience that:

> naturally, with the end of the Cold War and the collapse of the Soviet Union, Australia has become rather less strategically important for the US. Australia is still seen as a valued ally, but Australia's strategic value to the US is necessarily affected by the lack of important US strategic objectives in our immediate region in the post-Cold War era.[35]

As a consequence, he called for the development of an *'order-based alliance'*[36] as opposed to the old threat-based alliance model. Echoing then Labor Foreign Minister Gareth Evans's approach to community building with Asian countries, Dibb saw the gradual emergence of a 'community of strategic interests' between Australia and the ASEAN countries, supported by the US administration of President Bill Clinton. Indeed, according to Evans, the new sense of purpose for the ANZUS alliance was that the 'United States should be encouraged to participate in a multilateral approach to the development of a new community of strategic interests in the 1990s. Such a community could be based on America's traditional regional allies and the ASEAN group.'[37]

---

34 Dibb, 'Australia's Defence Relations with the United States' (2004).
35 Paul Dibb, *The Future of Australia's Defence Relationship with the United States*, Working Paper No. 276 (Canberra: Strategic and Defence Studies Centre, 1993), p. 1.
36 Dibb, *The Future of Australia's Defence Relationship with the United States* (1993), p. 5. Italics in the original text.
37 Dibb, *The Future of Australia's Defence Relationship with the United States* (1993), p. 7.

By today's standards, this proposition reads as being rather ambitious. Yet, Dibb ended his talk with an even starker prediction:

> as we develop a more self-reliant defence policy and a community of strategic interests with our ASEAN friends, *the US will not be so central to our defence policy.* All this suggests to me that a much more equal alliance partnership will develop between Australia and the US in the coming decade [emphasis added].[38]

In hindsight, his prediction about a declining importance of the United States for Australia's defence policy did not materialise. Quite the opposite. The same is true for his envisaged 'community of strategic interest' with the Association of Southeast Asian Nations (ASEAN). Dibb's reasoning reflected, however, some common strands of thinking in international security circles at the time. One was uncertainty about the role the United States was willing to play in international affairs in general, and the viability of its alliance system more specifically. The other was cautious optimism about the opportunity to build new multilateral security arrangements, including in the Asia-Pacific. As such, Dibb's scepticism about the future of ANZUS and his pledge to look for complementary security arrangements were not unusual. But it also shows his ambivalent feeling towards relying too heavily on the larger ally.

Nevertheless, during the second half of the 1990s Dibb's assessment of ANZUS became less gloomy. Indeed, given the uncertainty surrounding the future security order in the Asia-Pacific, it was better, in his view, to maintain a close relationship with the Americans. Writing in 1997, Dibb warned about the challenges of a rising China for the regional security order: 'There is no more important question in Asia than the future role of China. Almost nothing is so destabilising as the arrival of a new economic and military power on the international scene.'[39]

He also stressed that while it was 'far from certain that the American alliance system will decay … America's alliance partners perceive that they will need to do more militarily for themselves'.[40] This referred to the old question about 'burden-sharing' within the alliance. For

---

38   Dibb, *The Future of Australia's Defence Relationship with the United States* (1993), p. 10.
39   Paul Dibb, 'The Emerging Strategic Architecture in the Asia-Pacific Region', in Denny Roy (ed.), *The New Security Agenda in the Asia-Pacific Region* (London: Macmillan, 1997), p. 110.
40   Dibb, 'The Emerging Strategic Architecture in the Asia-Pacific Region' (1997), p. 112.

Dibb, the ANZUS alliance was going to be one element of the emerging Asian 'security architecture', encompassing traditional alliances and multilateral security fora such as the ASEAN Regional Forum (ARF). Yet, while he still advocated the evolution of an Asian 'strategic community', he appeared less certain about its chances for success. One key reason in this respect was doubt over continued ASEAN cohesion. In what has become of great interest in current Asian strategic debate, Dibb pointed out in 1997 that China's growing power and influence had serious potential to split ASEAN.[41] Worse, some ASEAN countries might even 'bandwagon' with China. In such an environment, the 'case for strengthening Australia's own defence spending and seeking greater alliance commitments from the United States ... would become more compelling'.[42] Australia, therefore, needed 'to keep its traditional alliances in good repair'.[43] After all, for Dibb, the ANZUS alliance was critical to put some elements of restraint on China's potential quest for regional hegemony, particularly in South-East Asia, Australia's immediate strategic neighbourhood.[44] Despite its weaknesses, the US alliance remained the ultimate reassurance for the time when the period of 'strategic pause' in the Asia-Pacific might come to an end.

## Power and Hubris: ANZUS after 9/11

When President George W. Bush took office in 2001, Dibb was expecting that the new US administration would focus more on Asia and less on Europe.[45] Yet, his hopes quickly faded after the terror attacks on the United States on 11 September 2001. Subsequently, the United States launched its 'global war on terror' and expected its allies, including Australia, to support it in its wars in Afghanistan and Iraq. After 9/11, and for the first time in history, Australia invoked the ANZUS treaty to support its US ally. More controversially, the Coalition Government under John Howard also participated in the US-led campaign against Iraq in 2003.

41  Paul Dibb, *Alliances, Alignments and the Global Order: The Outlook for the Asia-Pacific Region in the Next Quarter-century*, Working Paper No. 317 (Canberra: Strategic and Defence Studies Centre, Dec. 1997), p. 11.
42  Dibb, *Alliances, Alignments and the Global Order* (1997), p. 12.
43  Dibb, *Alliances, Alignments and the Global Order* (1997).
44  Dibb, *Alliances, Alignments and the Global Order* (1997), pp. 6–7.
45  See Paul Dibb, 'New Defence Alignments', interview, *BBC AM*, 31 Jul. 2001.

In Dibb's view, 9/11 had a number of effects on the ANZUS alliance. First, the relationship became 'extremely close again — arguably even closer than in the Cold War'.[46] Second, Australia's larger ally enjoyed a unique power position in the international system and Dibb, in 2003, argued that the United States was 'unlikely to face a peer competitor, or even a combination of hostile powers, in the foreseeable future'.[47] Thirdly, and most importantly, Washington appeared to use this power in a different way. Dibb shared the view that the United States was 'no longer a status quo power, as it was in the Cold War. It has become very demanding of allies, including us, and … it is now inclined to be more interventionist, more unilateralist and more inclined to use force.'[48] It became quickly apparent that the Bush administration had a much more instrumental view of alliances, which led to an international debate about whether this might even be the end of traditional alliances.[49]

While Dibb did not go so far, he saw America's behaviour as a 'hyper power' as problematic for Australia. He was particularly critical of Washington's decision to intervene militarily in Iraq in 2003 and the Howard Government's willingness to support Operation Iraqi Freedom. On the eve of the operation, he warned that the alliance was now 'in more danger, and certainly under more pressure than at any time since the Vietnam War'.[50] Dibb was particularly worried that the bipartisan consensus on the importance of ANZUS would erode as a result of a war started without a United Nations Security Council resolution.[51] Moreover, he feared negative implications from Australia's unquestioning support for the US ally for Canberra's regional standing:

> Australia's very closeness to the US now threatens to complicate, if not challenge, some of our key relations in Asia. The initial outpouring of sympathy towards the US after September 11 has been replaced in some (but by no means all) parts of our region by a growing sense of unease that America is a unilateral power dismissive of the norms of international behaviour, except on its terms. The perception in

---

46   Dibb, *Australia's Alliance with America* (2003), p. 1.
47   Dibb, *Australia's Alliance with America* (2003), p. 2.
48   Dibb, 'Australia's Defence Relations with the United States' (2004).
49   See Kurt M. Campbell, 'The End of Alliances? Not So Fast', *Washington Quarterly*, Vol. 27, No. 2 (2004), pp. 151–63.
50   'ANZUS under Pressure from Iraq Conflict: Dibb', interview, ABC, 6 Feb. 2003.
51   Paul Dibb, 'Bipartisan Ties with the US are Critical', *Australian*, 15 Jun. 2004.

some parts of the region that Australia is America's deputy sheriff has also stuck … at least in some respects the alliance now threatens to divide us from some parts of our own region.[52]

As a consequence, he saw the alliance at 'a crucial point in Australia'[53] and argued that 'while still a close and loyal ally of the US, it is vital that Australia is seen to have an independent capacity when it comes to resolving security challenges in our own region'.[54] Critically for Dibb, America's (and Australia's) 'adventures' in the Middle East were distractions from the bigger strategic questions that were playing out closer to home. The terrorist threat for Australia, for instance, was more likely to come from neighbouring Indonesia. But, most importantly, by taking its eyes off the ball in the Asia-Pacific region, Dibb feared that the United States allowed China to fill some of the strategic vacuum created. Writing in 2006, he argued that America's 'singular obsession' with terrorism led to the risk that the 'second Bush administration will overlook or pay insufficient attention to more traditional security problems in Asia'.[55]

## ANZUS and the Rise of China

As mentioned before, China's rise was potentially the biggest of those emerging traditional security problems. In 2008, Dibb spelled out the coming strategic challenge posed by Beijing's economic and military growth for the regional order:

> I expect that by 2020 China will have a much more survivable strategic nuclear force (both land-based and sea-based intercontinental ballistic missiles) and — unless Japan spends a lot more on defence — the most potent naval and air forces of any Asian great power. It may well have an operational aircraft carrier capability in this timeframe, as well as advanced antisatellite capabilities and some form of ballistic missile defence. The strong growth of China's political and military power will enable it to dominate its maritime approaches and make survival much more hazardous for US naval forces, especially in the Taiwan Strait. We can expect to see China have more influence even

---

52   Paul Dibb, 'The Downside of being Too Close to the US', *Age*, 4 Apr. 2003.
53   Dibb, *Australia's Alliance with America* (2003), p. 9.
54   Dibb, *Australia's Alliance with America* (2003), p. 10.
55   Dibb, 'America and the Asia-Pacific region' (2006), p. 188.

than today in Southeast Asia, which it sees as its natural sphere of influence, and it may come to have more influence in South Korea than the United States.[56]

Most of these predictions ring true today. Interestingly, Dibb has more recently argued that China's military is largely a paper tiger, unable to pose a significant military operational challenge to the United States.[57]

Regardless, by 2010, China's growing power, the strategic quagmires in Iraq and Afghanistan, and the global financial crisis increased the realisation that America's 'unipolar moment' (if there ever was one) was quickly coming to an end. Dibb stated in 2009 that in an 'increasingly multi-polar Asia region and some uncertainty surrounding the issue of US strategic primacy', Australia had to become 'more self-reliant in its defence'.[58] He was therefore critical of Australia's 2009 Defence White Paper, which called for greater preparedness of the Australian military to fight alongside its US ally in distant theatres. On the other hand, however, Dibb conceded that in the area of military technology, for instance, Australia's dependence on the United States would only increase in the years ahead.[59]

In any event, the rise of China provided ANZUS with the new rationale that Dibb called for in the 1990s. That is, China's emergence as a serious challenger to the Asia-Pacific regional security order and the position of the United States as a guarantor of peace and stability has given the alliance a new sense of urgency. Importantly for Dibb, this situation has required the United States to refocus on Australia's own region. As a consequence, he has been a strong supporter for the administration of President Barak Obama and its 'strategic rebalance' of Asia, first announced in Canberra in November 2011. He defended the decision of the government of Prime Minister Julia Gillard to allow for the rotation of US Marines through Australia's bases in the north of the continent as an important step to enhance deterrence in times of strategic change. In this context, he argued that the terminal decline

---

56   Paul Dibb, *The Future Balance of Power in East Asia: What are the Geopolitical Risks?*, Working Paper No. 406 (Canberra: Strategic and Defence Studies Centre), p. 3.
57   See Paul Dibb & John Lee, 'Why China Will Not Become the Dominant Power in Asia', *Security Challenges*, Vol. 10, No. 3 (2014), pp. 1–21; Paul Dibb, 'Why the PLA is a Paper Tiger', *ASPI: The Strategist*, 15 Oct. 2015.
58   Paul Dibb, 'Is the US Alliance of Declining Importance to Australia?', *Security Challenges*, Vol. 5, No. 2 (Winter 2009), p. 38.
59   Dibb, 'Is the US Alliance of Declining Importance to Australia?' (2009), p. 39.

of the United States as a major power in Asia was far from given and that Australia could not provide China with a veto over closer alliance relations:

> We should not be in the business of accommodating China on key issues of our own security just because of some narrow mercantile views of the relationship. Neither should we eschew opportunities to enhance our longstanding alliance with the US because of premature notions of that great nation's decline.[60]

Since 2011, Dibb has consistently pointed out that the ANZUS alliance is crucial for upholding a regional order which benefits Australia (and the rest of the region) economically and security-wise. He has also been blunt in his criticism of Chinese strategic behaviour:

> The fact is that the Asia-Pacific region without the US would be a much more dangerous place for us. It is not in our interest to see a retraction of US military might. Nor do we want to see China develop the military capability to challenge decisively US military power in the western Pacific. China is becoming more assertive of late and shows little interest in maintaining order in a part of the world where arms races are occurring and where there are not the arms control and military confidence-building measures necessary for reassurance. It is the US and its allies that are largely responsible for supporting order and stability, which is so crucial to the economic wellbeing of the region — including China. It is China, however, that is now challenging multiple territorial claims in the South China Sea and elsewhere.[61]

China's rise, therefore, has also to some extent lessened the need for a more self-reliant Australian defence posture, which would be of limited value against a major power equipped with nuclear weapons. Instead, Dibb is now comfortable with ever deeper integration between US and Australian forces. Moreover, in the current dispute over China's creation of 'artificial features' in the South China Sea, he has been firm in his call for Australia to join the United States in challenging Beijing's unilateral claims by sending warships and military aircraft to

60   Paul Dibb, 'US Build-up no Threat to Peace', *Australian*, 15 Nov. 2011.
61   Paul Dibb, 'Modest US Military Presence is in our Interest', *Australian*, 4 May 2012.

these waters, even if that would draw a negative Chinese response.[62] In his logic, the alliance has regained the critical importance it had during the height of the Cold War.

## Conclusion

As Australia faces a more uncertain Asia-Pacific strategic environment, the national debate about the relative costs and benefits of remaining a close US ally is likely to intensify. After all, the decision whether and how to support the United States in regional theatres will be much more consequential than deploying Australian soldiers to the Middle East. Yet, in Dibb's logic the answer is clear: the biggest threat for the alliance is distraction by the United States and the absence of a clear challenger. As long as the United States retains a strong strategic footprint in the region, Canberra is well-advised to remain close to Washington in these times of strategic change. Dibb does not buy the argument that the price for standing up to China might well be too high.

As Rob Ayson points out in his contribution to this volume, for Dibb, geography is a key factor determining Australia's security.[63] In some sense then, the utility of the US alliance for Australia is tied to the geographic proximity of a potentially serious military challenge. In other words, in times when the US ally is preoccupied with secondary security challenges outside Australia's own region, the pressure on the alliance to maintain cohesion and purpose increases, and so does the need to develop a more independent defence posture. The moment when the US ally concentrates on keeping a potentially hostile major power in Australia's key area of strategic interest in check, however, the higher becomes the incentive for Australia to stay close to its ally and to eschew costly alternatives. Expect Dibb to be a strong supporter of the US alliance as China seeks to fundamentally change the Asia-Pacific security order.

---

62    Paul Dibb, 'Chinese Expansion Calls for Firm Challenge', *Business Spectator*, 5 Jun. 2015.
63    Rob Ayson, 'The Importance of Geography', ch. 6, this volume.

# 11

# 'Weak and Mighty': Unravelling the Enigma of Soviet Power

Hugh White

Paul Dibb was a devoted student of the Soviet Union before he ever became a student of strategy, and he made his mark as a leading analyst of Soviet military and strategic affairs long before he turned his attention to the questions of Australian defence policy and Asian strategic affairs with which his name has been so strongly associated over recent decades. Moreover, despite his leading contribution to policymaking, the intellectual discipline of intelligence analysis, honed on the Soviet target, has arguably always remained his preferred intellectual milieu.

Understanding his approach to the fascinating enigma of Soviet power is therefore central to understanding his approach to strategy, and his overall achievements as a strategist. It can be argued that, important though his contribution has been to Australian defence policy, his work as a Soviet analyst most clearly shows his formidable intellectual strengths. Moreover no one can doubt that Russia — before, during and after the Soviet era — remains his first and deepest professional love, even if it will always remain for him an intelligence 'target'. Dibb has never lost his passion for the sheer scale, grandeur and paradoxical mysteries of Russia, so neatly encapsulated in the lines he chose as the epigram for his major work on Soviet power:

> Wretched and abundant
> Oppressed and powerful
> Weak and mighty
> Mother Russia![1]

The pedestrian concerns of a small continent in the South Pacific could never quite measure up to this. Many people will have heard Dibb describe his initial reaction to Kim Beazley's invitation to shift the focus of his work from the Soviet Union to questions of Australian defence policy. 'Why would I bother with a country with 4 battalions, 100 tanks, 6 submarines, 11 warships, 75 fighters and 24 F–111s? I have been studying a country with 300 divisions, 50,000 tanks, 5,000 combat aircraft, 600 warships and 280 submarines … let alone 20,000 nuclear warheads!'

In view of the clear centrality of Soviet strategic analysis to Dibb's intellectual and professional trajectory, it comes as rather a surprise to realise that it was only in 1974, when he was appointed head of the National Assessments Staff (NAS) in what was then the Joint Intelligence Organisation (JIO), that he started to really focus on strategic assessments of the Soviet Union as his major job.[2] His interest in the Soviet Union germinated much earlier, in the 6th form of Kings School in Pontefract (founded, as Dibb is fond of recalling, in 1139, a century before the Mongol invasion of Rus), when a geography assignment on Russia first introduced him to the extraordinary extent of the country and the magic of its placenames. By chance, that seedling was nourished when he went on to study geography at Nottingham University. He shared digs with an ex-National Service Russian linguist, and his teachers included a leading expert on Russian geography, and this became his specialty as well.

It is therefore not surprising that he found his way into work on Russia soon after arriving in Canberra from the England in 1962. He was working in the Department of Overseas Trade under Sir John 'Black Jack' McEwan. With Britain's possible entry to the European Economic Community, McEwan was interested in exploring the

---

1    Paul Dibb, *The Soviet Union: The Incomplete Superpower*, 2nd edn (London: International Institute for Strategic Studies and Macmillan, 1988), p. vi. The lines are from a poem by Nikolai Nekrasov.
2    Biographical details in these paragraphs from an interview with Professor Paul Dibb, 13 Aug. 2015.

potential of the Soviet Union as an alternative market for Australian wheat, and he asked Dibb to study the Soviet wheat industry. This led in 1964 to his recruitment by Stuart Harris to the Bureau of Agricultural Economics (BAE) and then, in 1968, to his joining The Australian National University's (ANU) formidable band of Soviet specialists in the Research School of Social Sciences (RSSS) under the great Harry Rigby, where he produced his first book, *Siberia and the Pacific: A Study in Economic Development and Trade Prospects.*[3] And it was from there that he was recruited by Bob Furlonger to join the newly established NAS as director of economic intelligence in 1970. After only four years in that role, and obviously having proved his remarkable and formidable talents both for intelligence analysis and for bureaucratic politics, was Dibb promoted at the very young age of 34 to be head of the NAS. And only then did he really start to focus on the Soviet Union as a military and strategic power.

## The Soviet Target

This was an interesting time in the evolution of Australia's international and strategic outlook. Concerns about what Prime Minister Robert Menzies had a decade earlier called 'the downward thrust of Chinese communism between the Indian and Pacific oceans' had abated with the opening to China in 1972 and the consolidation of pro-Western regimes in South-East Asia. Fears about communism and adventurism in Indonesia had been dispelled by the replacement of Sukarno by Suharto and his New Order in Jakarta. The sense of a clear and present strategic risk in our immediate South-East Asian neighbourhood, which had characterised the postwar decades and inspired the forward defence policies of the 1950s and 1960s, was now passed, and Australians now felt more secure from direct local threats.

On the other hand, from the mid-1970s and for several reasons, the Soviet Union began to loom larger in Australia's strategic thinking. First, as local tensions in Asia began to reduce, the risk of a global superpower confrontation began to loom larger in Australia's threat perceptions. The reasonable view at the time was that, despite Australia's remoteness from the main theatres of conflict and the

---

3    Paul Dibb, *Siberia and the Pacific: A Study in Economic Development and Trade Prospects*, (New York: Praeger, 1972).

fact that we had no intention of building forces to take part in such a conflict, the possibility of a major superpower war posed the most serious military threat to Australia's wider security and national interests, especially in view of the unimaginable consequences of the global nuclear exchange that such a war would almost certainly entail.

Second, the risks of such a conflict appeared to grow in the later 1970s as Moscow took advantage of what it thought to be a period of American weakness in the aftermath of the Vietnam War and the Watergate political scandal to try to expand Soviet influence in areas that had hitherto been peripheral to US–Soviet rivalry, including the Indian Ocean and the Horn of Africa. Under Admiral Sergey Gorshkov, the Soviet Navy began to compete with the US Navy to establish a global maritime presence that included an unprecedented level of activity in the Indian Ocean. In 1974, for example, the Soviets established at Berbera in Somalia what was, for a time, the largest military base outside the Warsaw Pact area. This brought the reality of Soviet power somewhat closer to home for Australia than had earlier been the case.

More broadly, in the 1970s it began to appear that the Soviets were gaining the upper hand in its competition with the United States for global primacy. Its economy was thought to be doing well and it was thought by some to have achieved parity with the United States in military power, and to be bent on pushing ahead to achieve a clear measure of superiority. And, while the Strategic Arms Limitations Talks (SALT I and II) agreements of 1972 and 1979 showed that the superpowers could negotiate arms control agreements, at the same time nuclear arsenals on both sides were growing larger and more accurate, and the fears for the stability of the central deterrent balance grew accordingly.

All of this raised great concern in Washington and London, and created an often fraught atmosphere for the evaluation of Soviet capabilities and intentions. Moreover, after 1975 Australia's Prime Minster Malcolm Fraser took an active interest in strategic affairs and was focused on the Soviet threat to Australia's interests in the global order, so there was a lot of demand in Australia for assessments of Soviet strengths and weaknesses. All of this culminated in the crisis in US–Soviet relations that followed the invasion of Afghanistan in 1979, which led to the final surge of the Cold War in the 1980s.

Dibb was continually engaged as head of NAS and in subsequent roles in assessing these developments from 1974 up to the time he left Defence in 1981 to join ANU. Throughout this period he was the Australian Government's principal analyst of Soviet military and strategic affairs, and one of the recognised and respected voices on these questions in the wider Western intelligence community. It was not by any means an easy role. The intellectual challenges were formidable and the stakes were high. But there were also real political and personal pressures to contend with. Judgements about Soviet military capabilities and strategic intentions easily acquired ideological overtones and became indexes, in the minds of some, of policy and political orthodoxy, and even of loyalty. Careers could be made or marred. It was not a field for the faint-hearted. Not being faint-hearted himself, Dibb thrived.

The vast bulk of his work as head of NAS was of course highly classified and will not be publicly released for a long time yet, if ever. However, in 1981 Dibb left that role and moved to the Department of International Relations and then the Strategic and Defence Studies Centre (SDSC) at ANU. Between then and 1985, when he was recruited by Defence Minister Kim Beazley to undertake what became known as the Dibb Review, he published a great deal, and this very productive period culminated in the publication of his renowned book on the Soviet Union as an incomplete superpower (1986). From this book and his other writings in these years, and from one or two things he published even while head of NAS, we can learn a great deal about his approach to the central questions of Soviet power, both as an intelligence analyst and as an academic.

The big questions that Dibb addressed in this period included not just the nature and extent of Soviet power and the trajectory of Moscow's overall strategic intentions, but more specific questions about Soviet aims and capabilities in the Asia-Pacific region and the potential for this to affect Australia directly. These more specific issues are themselves interesting in retrospect, but the analysis that follows will focus on the broader questions of Soviet power and ambition, because Dibb himself always saw his work as aimed primarily at those issues. As well, they take on a special interest in retrospect because they touch on tantalising issues of the durability of the Soviet system, and the possibility that it might collapse. Looking back with the benefit of hindsight, it is intriguing to see how Dibb assessed this possibility at a time when so many people, including many of its bitterest enemies, saw the Soviet system as increasingly invincible. The natural focus for the study of Dibb's thinking about all this is *The Incomplete Superpower*, in which Dibb so clearly distilled decades of analysis of the Soviet target.

## The Incomplete Superpower

The book that Dibb began to write in 1982 was intended primarily as a contribution to a debate among Western analysts and policymakers that had raged with increasing intensity from the second half of the 1970s about the extent of Soviet power and the nature of Soviet intentions. On one side of this debate stood the 'hawks', who believed that 'the Soviet Union has achieved decisive military superiority over the United States',[4] and that Moscow as a result had confidence in its ability to fight and win both conventional and nuclear wars against the West, 'and so achieve its goal of global domination'.[5] In other words they saw the Soviets as having, or being on the way to having, both the capability and the intention to dominate and transform the global order.

On the other side of this debate stood the 'doves', who believed that the Soviets were under no illusion that they could win a war with the West, and who explained the Soviet military build-up 'largely in defensive terms'.[6] Dibb describes his own views as lying 'somewhere in the middle of the spectrum'[7] between the hawks and the doves but, in reality, his position is much closer to the doves than the hawks, and the argument presented in *The Incomplete Superpower* is in fact an impressively sustained and detailed rebuttal of the hawks' position.

The argument is based on a methodological premise that is critical to intelligence assessment and which underpins everything Dibb wrote about the Soviet Union. This is set out explicitly in the preface to his book, where he says that it aims to present 'a perception of the world as seen from Moscow'.[8] 'If we are to understand the Soviet Union,' he wrote, 'we should at least try to avoid imposing on it a Western

---

4   Dibb, *The Soviet Union* (1988), p. 141.
5   Dibb, *The Soviet Union* (1988).
6   Dibb, *The Soviet Union* (1988).
7   Dibb, *The Soviet Union* (1988).
8   Dibb, *The Soviet Union* (1988), p. xviii.

perspective', because 'the perceptions that the USSR has of the world around it are derived from unique cultural and historical traditions'. To avoid surprise, he says, one must 'see events from the perspective of the opposition'.[9] Following this precept, Dibb analyses Soviet actions and policies on the basis of how things might look from Moscow.

Looking back 30 years later, and across the ruins of the Soviet Union, it seems hard now to credit the strength of the views Dibb was attacking, or the scale of the issues at stake. This was no dry academic argument. The hawks' analysis of Soviet power and intentions was influential in Washington, as well as in London, and did a lot to shape the policies of the administration of President Ronald Reagan and the government of Prime Minister Margaret Thatcher. Partly as a result, the Cold War intensified sharply over the years when Dibb was writing his book, and the risk of a superpower conflict plainly grew. Robert Gates, then the senior Soviet analyst at the CIA, later called 1984 'the most dangerous year'.[10] These dangers were clear to Dibb at the time, and provide the mainspring for his argument. In the preface he wrote:

> If nuclear war is not to become a self-fulfilling prophecy we in the West need to understand the nature of Soviet power in a calmer, more objective way than is often the case at present. It seems to me rather too simplistic to divide the world, as some American commentators do, between the forces of good and evil. This is a dangerous attitude because it fosters a bellicose style, which can only raise East–West tensions. We should never be led by a false sense of moral self-righteousness into treating the Soviet Union as an 'evil empire', however much we may dislike the system that it stands for.[11]

And, a few lines later, he makes explicit the moral and policy implications of his analysis:

> With Herman Hesse, I believe that peace is an infinitely complex, unstable and fragile thing — more difficult to achieve than any other ethical or intellectual achievement. But if we wish to see peace continue, it does not make sense to face the Soviet leadership with

---

9    Dibb, *The Soviet Union* (1988), p. xix.
10    Robert Gates, *From the Shadows: The Ultimate Insider's Story of Five Presidents and How They Won the Cold War* (New York: Simon and Schuster, 1996). Gates refers specifically to the Abel Archer exercise that year which came close to triggering a US–Soviet conflict. Dibb also wrote about this.
11    Dibb, *The Soviet Union* (1988), p. xx.

either capitulation or confrontation. There is a middle path which, whilst not compromising the West's vital interest, or appeasing the Soviet Union, will ensure the continuation of non-violent competition with the USSR.[12]

Thus the basic argument of *The Incomplete Superpower* is that if we realistically assess the extent of Soviet power, and analyse the way that its leaders use that power in the light of the challenges they face as they see them, then the USSR looks less like a country set on a path to global domination, and more like a country struggling to deal with multiple threats and challenges from an inadequate and dwindling base of power. In other words, this is a country with which the West could and should learn to co-exist.

The starting point for Dibb's analysis is an assessment of Soviet power. Power is, as he says, a difficult concept: 'a concept at the heart of the relations between nations, yet few topics in strategic studies are so poorly understood.'[13] He offers an inclusive account of the elements of power,[14] including — not surprisingly for a geographer — a Mackinderian consideration of geopolitical location.[15] Dibb, however, gives most attention to four elements of Soviet power — the economy, its 'empire' in the Soviet Bloc, its domestic political position and, of course, its armed forces. Each of these he examines in some detail.

The account Dibb gives of the Soviet economy is detailed, nuanced and carefully balanced, but it springs from a simple experience. Visiting the Soviet Union as an official in the mid-1970s, he was struck by the poverty and deprivation that he saw around him, as people — even senior people — stood in line for tomatoes or meat. How, he asked, could this be reconciled with the image of a country on the threshold of global dominion?[16]

In exploring and answering this question, Dibb acknowledges the USSR's extraordinary achievements: growth averaged 4.8 per cent per annum from 1951–79, compared to 3.5 per cent for the United States,[17]

---

12    Dibb, *The Soviet Union* (1988).
13    Dibb, *The Soviet Union* (1988), p. xix.
14    Dibb, *The Soviet Union* (1988), pp. 16, 19.
15    Dibb, *The Soviet Union* (1988), p. 21.
16    Paul Dibb, interview with the author, 13 Aug. 2015.
17    Dibb, *The Soviet Union* (1988), p. 67.

recalling the time when serious people really did believe that it would overtake the United States to become the largest economy in the world. But, as he recounts, by the mid-1970s the growth had stalled and the economy overall was 'faltering'.[18] The Soviet economy peaked at little more than half the size of America's, and might soon be overtaken by Japan's, he suggested[19] — as indeed it was. There were particular problems in sectors like agriculture but, more broadly, Moscow seemed incapable of delivering the improvements in productivity that would be essential for sustained high growth. He suggested that 2 per cent was the most that could be expected over the longer term. He cautioned, however, against the more dire predictions of a looming disaster. 'Economic collapse', he wrote, 'is not in prospect'. The USSR had many resources and assets,[20] but it would remain what he called 'a semi-developed economy'.[21] Economic problems, he argued, would not compel cuts to defence spending[22] but this was not an economic power base from which Moscow could launch a bid for global domination.

Likewise what Dibb called the Soviet 'empire', especially in Eastern Europe, was seen as an uncertain strategic asset at best. Poor economic performance compared to the West was one key negative factor, nationalism and resentment of Soviet control was another. The increasing frailty of Moscow's hold over its east European satellites, as exemplified by developments in Poland in the early 1980s, and the very serious consequences for the internal stability of the USSR itself of any major unravelling of Soviet control there were clearly highlighted.[23] Dibb wrote presciently that:

> Should widespread rebellion break out in Eastern Europe, or if a major nationality group rose up in revolt, or if the territorial integrity of the far flung Soviet state were threatened, then Soviet state power would be seriously threatened ... Politically, the uncontrolled spread of disaffection and rebellion in its East European empire would have implications for the stability of Soviet rule in the homeland.[24]

18 Dibb, *The Soviet Union* (1988), p. 2.
19 Dibb, *The Soviet Union* (1988).
20 Dibb, *The Soviet Union* (1988), p. 95.
21 Dibb, *The Soviet Union* (1988), p. 71.
22 Dibb, *The Soviet Union* (1988), p. 97.
23 Dibb, *The Soviet Union* (1988), pp. 29, 36.
24 Dibb, *The Soviet Union* (1988), p. 29.

Not surprisingly, Dibb put most focus on the analysis of Soviet military power. There is no space here to do justice to the detail of his analysis, but his key point is simple and powerful. He argues that, by the early 1980s, the Soviet armed forces were indeed immense and, while their numbers had not grown since the early 1960s, their capability had developed steadily as a result of massive and sustained investments in equipment over several decades.[25] But to infer from this, as the hawks did at the time, that the Soviets were intent on using their armed force aggressively, and were in their own eyes close to achieving the capacity to fight and win a war for global domination, was to overlook the way Russia's strategic environment, the range of threats it faced and the forces needed to address them, looked from Moscow.

By the early 1980s the trends of the 1970s that seemed to be moving the 'correlation of world forces' in Moscow's favour had clearly started to reverse.[26] From that perspective, he argued, the Soviet's formidable military power was only just sufficient to keep looming threats at bay. For example, he calculated that in a full-scale conflict in the European central front, the Soviets could only expect a preponderance of 2:1 in ready combat divisions, which is well below the traditional rule of thumb that a margin of 3:1 is required on the main axis of advance to give reasonable assurance of swift victory.[27]

One key factor in Dibb's analysis is the need to assess Soviet and Warsaw Pact forces not just against US forces but against all those that might be mobilised to fight the Soviets in a general war, including North Atlantic Treaty Organization (NATO) allies in Europe, Japan and even China. Russia's army might have been twice the size of America's,[28] but the wider balance of forces was clearly America's way. Soviet strategic planners did indeed see a worst-case scenario in which it faced all these forces as credible.[29] In the early 1980s, Soviet leaders were saying plainly that they believed the threat of major war from the United States had clearly and sharply increased.[30]

---

25  Dibb, *The Soviet Union* (1988), p. 144.
26  Dibb, *The Soviet Union* (1988), p. 116.
27  Dibb, *The Soviet Union* (1988), p. 162.
28  Dibb, *The Soviet Union* (1988), p. 144, 159.
29  Dibb, *The Soviet Union* (1988), p. 140.
30  Dibb, *The Soviet Union* (1988), p. 112.

This encompassed, of course, the threat of nuclear war. While the Soviet leadership had itself abandoned the idea that nuclear war could profitably be fought and won, they remained unsure that the United States shared that view.[31] This fear was amplified by their perceptions of trends in the US nuclear posture, including the development of highly accurate and survivable 'counterforce' weapons, and of ballistic missile defences.[32] Thus, Dibb argued, the Soviets believed they had little choice but to continue to build up their own massive nuclear forces.

Dibb's basic conclusion is that 'the Soviet Union probably does not have more military power than it *thinks* it needs for defensive purposes'.[33] But he also said that Moscow was probably wrong about this: 'Does the Soviet Union have more military capability than it requires for defensive purposes? The answer is probably "yes"'.[34] His explanation for this misperception on Moscow's part is two-fold. One is the Russian military tradition of bigness. In responding to both nuclear and conventional threats, Russia's instincts, based on long historical experience including the Second Word War, was to go for scale.[35] For the Soviet military mind, Dibb argued, quantity still had a quality all its own. The other elements of the explanation lie even deeper, in Russia's traditional sense of inferiority and vulnerability.

## Soviet Intentions and the Weight of History

This brings us to the second key element of Dibb's analysis of the Soviet Union as a strategic actor — the question of intention. In the opening chapter of the book, he explores at some length the way our assessment of Soviet intentions must be influenced by an understanding of Russian history and the way that history has shaped Russia's view of itself and the world around it. In particular, he wrote, we have to grasp Russia's sense of its own weakness and vulnerability. The perception of weakness comes from a sense that Russia lags behind the West. Despite bravado, he says, there remains 'an uneasy

---

31 Dibb, *The Soviet Union* (1988), p. 110.
32 Dibb, *The Soviet Union* (1988), p. 122.
33 Dibb, *The Soviet Union* (1988), p. 175.
34 Dibb, *The Soviet Union* (1988), p. 176.
35 Dibb, *The Soviet Union* (1988), p. 145.

sense of the backwardness still of Soviet state power'.[36] The perception of vulnerability comes from a history of invasion — 'at least once a century for the last millennium', culminating in the German invasion of 1941.[37] And both are fed by a sense of Russia's uncertain identity, neither European nor Asian but somewhere between both.[38] The effect of this 'is to reinforce a sense of separateness which already exists for geographical and traditional political reasons', Dibb wrote, and helps feed a jingoistic Great Russian patriotism.[39] This leads him to what is, in some ways, the key passage in the book:

> It might thus be asked whether Russia's historical experience of invasion and war, its lack of spiritual identity with other states, and the extreme patriotism of the Russian people are a force for expansion or defence. One possible explanation is that the USSR's drive for security — whilst basically defensive because it feels menaced by the very presence of strong states and stands alone in the community of nations without any reliable friends — also has an expansionary impulse and is perceived in this way by other (especially neighbouring) countries. Soviet security can be achieved only at the expense of the security of others.[40]

This naturally fed a classic security dilemma on both sides, and drove what Dibb argues is a systematic overestimate by the West of the scale of Soviet military power[41] and the nature of its strategic intentions.

On the other hand, elsewhere in the book, Dibb writes of Soviet power and ambitions in terms closer to those of the anti-Soviet hawks. He says that the Soviet Union was 'the one power that might have the potential to supplant the United States as the dominant power over the international system', and that '[t]he Soviet Union has considerable strengths, which will sustain its bid for supreme power'.[42] He remains, in other words, somewhat ambivalent about the nature of Soviet power to the end.

---

36  Dibb, *The Soviet Union* (1988), p. 1.
37  Dibb, *The Soviet Union* (1988), p. 7.
38  Dibb, *The Soviet Union* (1988), p. 9.
39  Dibb, *The Soviet Union* (1988), p. 10.
40  Dibb, *The Soviet Union* (1988), p. 10.
41  Dibb, *The Soviet Union* (1988), p. 163.
42  Dibb, *The Soviet Union* (1988), p. 259.

# Predicting Collapse

This ambivalence shows perhaps most clearly in the way Dibb addressed what is in retrospect the most tantalising question of all — the potential for the whole Soviet system to collapse. Ever since the actual collapse Dibb has modestly averred that he failed to predict it, but this is at most only half true. Throughout *The Incomplete Superpower*, and in some other writings dating back to the 1970s, he thoroughly explored the vulnerabilities of the Soviet system and considered the possibility that they would prove fatal to it. For example, in 1983 Dibb wrote the following highly prophetic words:

> The coming two decades could well bring a coincidence of unrest and rebellion among increasingly restive populations in several Eastern European countries at the same time. At home, the Soviet leadership will have to grapple with increasingly serious economic problems, of a fundamental structural nature, which will bring about stagnant — or even declining — standards of living and great pressure to cut back defence spending … In the long haul, the very 'Russianness' of the Soviet multinational state is in question.[43]

As we have seen, *The Incomplete Superpower* correctly identified and extensively analysed the basic factors that were to lead so swiftly to the collapse of the Soviet Union and, at many points, raised the question of whether collapse loomed. Dibb nonetheless judged that the Soviet system itself was robust enough to withstand the resulting pressures. 'Above all,' he wrote,

> the Soviet political elite clearly has the will to rule the Soviet Empire by traditional means, including coercion. What has been built so painstakingly in the Soviet Union over the generations with much sacrifice, ruthlessness and conviction will not be allowed to disintegrate or radically change. The USSR has enormous unused reserves of political and social stability on which to draw, and in all probability will not in the next decade face a systemic crisis that endangers its existence.[44]

---

43  Paul Dibb, *World Political and Strategic Trends over the Next 20 Years — Their Relevance to Australia*, Working Paper No. 65 (Canberra: Strategic and Defence Studies Centre, 1983), p. 11.
44  Dibb, *The Soviet Union* (1988), p. 30.

Later in the book, Dibb confidently asserted that 'the Soviet Union is not now (nor will it be during the next decade) in the throes of a true systemic crisis'.[45] But, in the same section, he also wrote: 'What remains uncertain is whether the Soviet system is entering a prolonged period of atrophy and deepening crisis or whether sufficient reforms can be introduced to muddle through.'[46] And he made this clear prediction: 'it is possible that the USSR could eventually see its control of Eastern Europe begin to crumble later this century. A loss of control of Eastern Europe would probably strengthen centrifugal tendencies within the USSR itself.'[47]

So while it is true that Dibb did not see the Soviet collapse coming, he certainly saw very clearly the pressures that were so quickly to bring it about, and recognised the possibility that the Soviet system, for all its apparent strength, might prove vulnerable to these pressures sooner rather than later. Few if any analysts saw these factors and possibilities as clearly as Dibb, and he deserves credit for understanding the weakness of the Soviet Union as well, and perhaps better, than anyone else in the Western analytic community. This was a major intellectual achievement.

## The Bear is Back

Fortunately for Dibb, and for Australia, by the time the Soviet Union collapsed he had already shifted his attention to questions closer to home. But he has never lost his interest in Russia, and was among the first to detect the reappearance of some of the classic characteristics of Russian strategic outlook, which he had analysed so effectively in the Soviet era, when they reappeared in post-Soviet Russia.

In a series of writings from the early 2000s, Dibb warned that Russia should not be underestimated as a great power. It had the resources to maintain powerful forces and, above all, it had the resolve and determination, borne of the deep historical, cultural and geographic factors he had explained in *The Incomplete Superpower*, to pose

---

45   Dibb, *The Soviet Union* (1988), p. 260.
46   Dibb, *The Soviet Union* (1988), p. 264.
47   Dibb, *The Soviet Union* (1988), p. 261.

a serious challenge to the post-Cold War order in Europe and beyond, where it believed its interests were threatened. As Dibb wrote in *The American Interest* back in 2006:

> A resurgent Russia will not be a recycled Soviet Union, either in terms of messianic ideology or territorial conquests. The Cold War as such will not return. But make no mistake: This renewed Russia will be strong, assertive and probably increasingly undemocratic. Its human rights record will not be pleasant, and it will definitely not be a consistent or reliable partner of the West.[48]

And so it has proved.

---

48 Paul Dibb 'The Bear is Back', *The American Interest*, Vol. 2, No. 2, 1 Nov. 2006, www.the-american-interest.com/2006/11/01/the-bear-is-back/.

# 12

# Paul Dibb and the Asian Balance of Power

Brendan Taylor

For a medium-sized country, Australia has enjoyed an uncanny prominence when it comes to scholarship addressing the Asian balance of power. Such intellectual giants in the fields of international relations and strategic studies as Coral Bell, Hedley Bull and Hugh White have each contributed seminal works on this subject. Yet it would be by no means hyperbolic to describe Paul Dibb as *primus inter pares*, or 'first among equals', when referring to his scholarship in this particular area. Reviewing that scholarship, this chapter begins by providing a brief summary of work on the Asian balance of power and seeks to account for the prominence of Australian scholars within it. The chapter then analyses Paul Dibb's contribution to this scholarship, particularly his Adelphi Paper from the mid-1990s, which this chapter judges to be *the* classic academic treatment of the Asian balance. Finally, during an era when balance-of-power politics appears to be truly coming into fashion in Asia, the chapter concludes by asking what contemporary scholars and analysts can usefully take and apply from the Dibb approach.

# Australians and the Asian Balance

The balance of power is one of the oldest ideas in the theory and practice of international politics. Writing over 2,000 years ago, for instance, Thucydides attributed a fundamental shift in the balance of power between Ancient Greece's two leading city states — Athens and Sparta — as a precipitating cause of the Peloponnesian War.[1] Less often acknowledged is that power-balancing behaviour was also a central feature of Ancient China during the so-called Spring, Autumn and Warring States periods from 770–221 BC.[2] Balance-of-power theory was also evident in the work of political scientists and historians who studied relations between the Italian city states during the fifteenth and sixteenth centuries.[3]

The application of the balance of power in a specifically 'Asian' context has a similarly distinguished and enduring lineage. Writing over 100 years ago, for instance, the renowned American geostrategist Alfred Thayer Mahan broke with tradition to argue that the security of an emergent United States was intimately tied to the Asian balance of power as well as to that of Europe.[4] Writing more than half a century later, the father of realism, Hans Morgenthau, also identified the importance of the Asian balance to the United States, highlighting the critical importance to America of preventing 'any one European or Asian power from gaining control of the power potential of China, acquiring a monopoly for the exploitation of China'.[5]

Amongst Australian scholars, the work of Bell stands as a pioneering contribution to scholarship on the Asian balance. Writing also during the 1960s, Bell published one of the earliest papers in the then Institute for Strategic Studies' Adelphi series, in which she considered the

1    Robert B. Strassler (ed.), *The Landmark Thucydides: A Comprehensive Guide to the Peloponnesian War* (New York: Free Press, 2008), p. 16.
2    Victoria Tin-bor Hui, *War and State Formation in Ancient China and Early Modern Europe* (New York: Cambridge University Press, 2005).
3    Richard Little, *The Balance of Power in International Relations: Metaphors, Myths and Models* (Cambridge University Press, 2007), p. 4.
4    Alfred Thayer Mahan, *The Problem of Asia: Its Effect upon International Politics* (New Brunswick: Transaction Publishers, 2003).
5    Hans J. Morgenthau, *Truth and Power: Essays of a Decade, 1960–1970* (London: Pall Mall Press, 1970), p. 391.

applicability of the balance-of-power concept to an Asian context.[6] Writing in the prestigious American policy journal *Foreign Affairs* during the early 1970s, Bell's Australian contemporary Hedley Bull speculated about the emergence of a new, four-sided 'complex' balance of power in the Asia-Pacific that included the United States, the Soviet Union, China and Japan.[7] In recent years, Hugh White has picked up Bull's conceptual baton, writing of a slightly different four-sided balance comprising the United States, China, Japan and India. White's proposal that this balance can best be managed through a concert of power-type arrangement similar to that which existed in Europe throughout much of the nineteenth century has attracted widespread attention and an equal measure of criticism, including from the man whose work forms the focus of this chapter.[8]

What explains the prevalence of Australian scholars in writings on the Asian balance of power?

First and foremost, Australia's strategic geography and, in particular, this country's proximity to Asia have unquestionably played a role. As Bell observes in the opening stanzas of her Adelphi Paper:

> perhaps there is a certain appropriateness to an Australian examination of this question since Australians are the only group of Westerners who must remain fully and inescapably vulnerable to the diplomatic stresses arising in Asia, on whose periphery they live or die.[9]

At the same time, however, Australia's geographic remoteness and relative distant from Asia's major power machinations also go some way towards explaining the prominence of Australian scholarship in this area. Precisely for reasons of distance, a case can be made that Australians can look at the Asian balance more objectively and systematically than, for instance, scholars and practitioners from those countries that are geographically closer and whose very national existence is potentially contingent upon shifts in that balance. Japan, for instance, has historically also been acutely attentive to changes

---

6    Coral Bell, *The Asian Balance of Power: A Comparison with European Precedents*, Adelphi Paper No. 44 (London: International Institute for Strategic Studies, Feb. 1968).

7    Hedley Bull, 'The New Balance of Power in Asia and the Pacific', *Foreign Affairs*, Vol. 49, No. 4 (Jul. 1971), pp. 669–81.

8    Hugh White, *The China Choice: Why America Should Share Power* (Collingwood: Black Inc, 2012).

9    Bell, *The Asian Balance of Power* (1968), p. 1.

in the Asian balance. In Japan's case, however, the balance has been viewed more subjectively and in terms of what balance-of-power *policy* should be adopted either in anticipation or in response to those shifts.[10]

Second, links to the 'home country' Great Britain also have played a hand in the prominence of Australian scholarship addressing the Asian balance. While, as noted previously, balance-of-power thinking was in evident in ancient times, the concept had its formal beginnings in fifteenth-century Europe and really took root there from the late seventeenth century onwards.[11] The British embraced the concept with particular enthusiasm for, as Michael Sheehan notes:

> Britain was not in a position to play a significant role in determining the outcome of European politics except in conditions of equilibrium and ... it was therefore of paramount importance that she should strive always to maintain a balance of power on the continent.[12]

It is interesting to note here that each of the Australian scholars most prominently associated with the Asian balance of power have strong British links. Dibb, of course, was born in England and spent the first two decades of his life there. Bell and Bull both studied and worked in England for lengthy periods. White studied there also. Moreover, reflecting upon his time as an official in the Australian Department of Defence, White explicitly recalls the direct influence of British thinking:

> During the early 1990s some of us working in Defence began exploring this problem of defining Australia's wider strategic interests in the post-Cold War world. Our attention was caught by Lord Palmerston's famous line about 'Britain having no permanent friends and no permanent enemies, only permanent interests'. We started to look at how Britain defined these permanent interests, and what we might learn from them ... the British experience seemed worth examining, not because of historical or sentimental connections with the UK, but because of certain geostrategic similarities. Like Australia, Britain is an island lying offshore a continent of major powers.[13]

---

10 For further reading see Kenneth B. Pyle, *The Resurgence of Japanese Power and Purpose* (New York: Public Affairs, 2007).

11 Little, *The Balance of Power in International Relations* (2007), p. 4.

12 Michael Sheehan, *The Balance of Power: History and Theory* (Abingdon: Routledge, 1996), p. 51.

13 Hugh White, 'Strategic Interests in Australian Defence Policy: Some Historical and Methodological Reflections', *Security Challenges*, Vol. 4, No. 2 (Winter 2008), p. 69.

Third, the international prominence of Australian scholarship on the Asian balance is consistent with what Michael Wesley has termed the 'rich tradition of Australian realism'.[14] Wesley downplays the extent to which Australian international relations scholarship is derivative of that developed either in Britain or North America. Instead, he contends that, since the 1920s, a distinctly Australian strain of realism has developed and evolved in the antipodes. It is a form of realism that is highly pragmatic, a-theoretical in nature and influenced by practitioner–academics. That said, while balance-of-power theory may thus not appear explicitly as a central feature in Australian international relations scholarship, Wesley goes on to identify the analysis of 'power disparities' as one of the preoccupations of this body of work. He also points to an obsession with 'understanding the strategic mind of great powers' and a desire to prevent 'the domination of global decision-making by a great power cartel'. As the next section of this chapter goes on to discuss, each of these features is certainly evident in Dibb's work on the Asian balance.

## Dibb and the Asian Balance

Dibb's 1995 Adelphi Paper, *Towards a New Balance of Power in Asia*, sits comfortably alongside the seminal contributions of Mahan, Morgenthau, Bell, Bull and White, amongst others. Indeed, a strong case can be made that Dibb's Adelphi should be regarded as *the* classic treatment on the subject. It is certainly a widely cited work and one, as this chapter goes on to discuss, which exhibits a remarkable degree of prescience when seen in the context of the shifting power dynamics that are evident in Asia today.

In characteristic style, Dibb begins his classic Adelphi by immediately clarifying how he understands and applies the balance of power concept, thus dealing with the definitional debates that have weighed heavily upon other studies employing this term. While acknowledging the existence of those debates, with reference to his background as a practitioner, Dibb makes the observation that '[i]n the author's experience, the concept of the balance of power is much less contested among foreign policy and defence practitioners than among academics

---

14   Michael Wesley, 'The Rich Tradition of Australian Realism', *Australian Journal of Politics and History*, Vol. 55, No. 3 (2009), pp. 324–34.

and intellectuals'.[15] His definition 'assumes that nation-states will ensure that no one power is in a position to determine the fate of others' and he sees the balance of power as involving 'a rules-based system that limits both the ability of states to dominate each other and the scope of conflict'.[16] To borrow from Inis Claude's helpful taxonomy, Dibb thus regards the balance of power as a *system* rather than as a *situation* or a *policy*.[17]

Unlike Bull or White, the balance that Dibb saw emerging in Asia was a pentagonal one consisting of China, Japan, India, Russia and the United States. Dibb described this balance as 'new' to the extent that such a balance had not previously extended right across the entire Asian region. He saw this development of a new region-wide system of order as a potentially dangerous one, particularly given the lack of experience that any of the key players had had with the practice of balance-of-power politics. At best, Dibb observed, only local power balances were a feature of the international relations of Asia prior to this point.[18] At worst, he drew on the work of Henry Kissinger in this area (a consistent tendency in Dibb's work, as discussed below) to point out that the United States had never previously participated in a balance-of-power system.[19] Dibb pointed out that one possible exception to the Kissinger thesis might be America's experiences with Japan, China and Britain in East Asia during the 1920s and 1930s, which ended badly of course.[20]

While pointing to the emergence of a new balance of power system in Asia, Dibb was quick to observe that this arrangement would not be akin to a concert of power. This argument has again remained a consistent feature of his work during the period since and has been one of his key points of contention with White in their respective

---

15   Paul Dibb, *Towards a New Balance of Power in Asia*, Adelphi Paper No. 295 (London: International Institute for Strategic Studies, 1995), p. 75.

16   Dibb, *Towards a New Balance of Power in Asia* (1995), p.6.

17   In an attempt to streamline the innumerable applications of the balance of power terminology, Claude sought to categorise these into three broad groups. The balance as a 'situation' was a largely descriptive application, referring simply to the distribution of military power. The balance as a 'policy' referred to the approaches which individual states pursue when taking that distribution into account. The balance of power as a 'system' refers more broadly to the operation of international relations at a more systemic level, including the interactions between the states within that system. See Inis Claude, *Power and International Relations* (New York: Random House, 1962).

18   Dibb, *Towards a New Balance of Power in Asia* (1995), p. 10.

19   Dibb, *Towards a New Balance of Power in Asia* (1995), p. 38.

20   Dibb, *Towards a New Balance of Power in Asia* (1995), p. 12.

analyses of the contemporary Asian balance. Dibb's primary objection to the notion of a concert, both then and today, is that it would lead to the marginalisation of the small and middle powers in the system, including Australia. In a more recent critique of White's work, for instance, Dibb recalls that 'middle powers such as Poland either disappeared or were carved up' in the nineteenth-century concert of Europe. Dibb also makes the observation that the highly diverse and variegated Asian region of today lacks the common culture which facilitated the functioning of that concert.[21]

In his Adelphi, Dibb also makes the observation that the evolution of the Asian balance will occur gradually, perhaps even glacially. In his terms 'the redistribution of power between Asia and the rest of the world, as well as within Asia, will not be a sudden or catastrophic event. Change in the international status of nations rarely occurs quickly, except in the event of war.'[22] Again, this judgement is in keeping with Dibb's more recent work, especially that dealing with shifting power relativities between the United States and China. In a widely cited article co-authored with John Lee and entitled 'Why China Will Not Become the Dominant Power in Asia', Dibb argues that the US–China military balance still significantly favours America. He estimates that China is approximately 20 years behind the United States in high technology weaponry, pointing out also that the People's Liberation Army (PLA) is a force without any modern combat experience, including experience in the complexities of anti-submarine warfare operations. Even as China plays catch up, Dibb points out that the United States is not standing still militarily — even with the financial pressures that it has been experiencing over recent years — and that it continues to invest in technological 'game changers' that could actually shift the US–China military balance even further in America's favour.[23]

Consistent with this set of observations regarding the Sino–American military balance, while Dibb takes an explicitly systemic, state-centred approach in the Adelphi, he is also highly attuned to the importance of domestic dynamics and their capacity to shape inter-state power dynamics. In his terms, 'it would be a mistake to be complacent about

---

21   Paul Dibb, 'Why I Disagree with Hugh White on China's Rise', *Australian*, 13 Aug. 2012.
22   Dibb, *Towards a New Balance of Power in Asia* (1995), p. 21.
23   Paul Dibb & John Lee, 'Why China Will Not Become the Dominant Power in Asia', *Security Challenges*, Vol. 10, No. 3 (2014), pp. 15–19.

the underlying social stability of significant actors in Asia'.[24] In this respect, he would more accurately be labelled as a 'classical realist' rather than one of the 'neo-realist' variety, given the priority which the latter assigns to systemic and structural dynamics, virtually to the exclusion of domestic considerations.[25] This 'classical' approach has been a feature of Dibb's work throughout his career, as exemplified by his pathbreaking study *The Incomplete Superpower*, which rather presciently highlighted the domestic weaknesses and fragilities of the Soviet Union as Mikhail Gorbachev came to power.[26]

Dibb never claims to have predicted the demise of the Soviet Union, which came only a few years following the publication of *The Incomplete Superpower*, but he certainly came closer than most to doing so. This uncanny prescience is also a feature of his work on the Asian balance. Writing 20 years ago, for instance, he observed that '[n]o contemporary issue is more important than the rise of China'.[27] While that may seem a statement of the obvious today, it was much less so in that earlier period when just as many scholars were predicting the collapse or disintegration of China and where others were still talking up the rise of Japan.[28] On Japan, he predicted 'the emergence of a different sort of Japan', a country that would become 'more outward looking and assertive'.[29] He suggested that India had 'greater potential as a power of influence than its indicators would suggest', that 'it could emerge as a useful player in a multipolar Asian balance' and that it 'could attract American interest as a counterbalance to China'.[30] On Russia, he warned of the emergence of authoritarianism and a Moscow bent upon (re)establishing 'a powerful, nationalist Great Russian state that would reclaim its "rightful" role in the world'.[31] Finally, he envisaged a United States that would remain the single most important player in the new Asian balance of power, but that would create anxieties amongst its regional friends and allies as a superpower

---

24  Dibb, *Towards a New Balance of Power in Asia* (1995), p. 17.

25  See, for example, John J. Mearsheimer, *The Tragedy of Great Power Politics* (New York: Norton, 2001).

26  Paul Dibb, *The Soviet Union: The Incomplete Superpower* (London: International Institute for Strategic Studies and Macmillan, 1986).

27  Dibb, *Towards a New Balance of Power in Asia* (1995), p. 27.

28  See, for example, Gordon G. Chang, *The Coming Collapse of China* (New York: Random House, 2001).

29  Dibb, *Towards a New Balance of Power in Asia* (1995), p. 31.

30  Dibb, *Towards a New Balance of Power in Asia* (1995), pp. 33–34.

31  Dibb, *Towards a New Balance of Power in Asia* (1995), p. 36.

prone to 'domestic preoccupation and which has a foreign policy that merely reacts to events as they unfold'. In his view, 'the US will not be prepared with a grand strategy to advance its interests in Asia's emerging multipolar great-power competition'.[32]

Many analysts and commentators would regard this latter observation as a rather apt description of US grand strategy (or the lack thereof) during the presidency of Barak Obama.[33] Indeed, there is today remarkably little to quibble with in any of Dibb's assessments of the key players who constitute the new Asian balance.

Dibb concludes the Adelphi by contemplating how Asia's new power balance might function in practice. Again, his analysis of two decades ago has turned out to be remarkably prescient. Although viewing trends towards a deepening in economic cooperation and economic multilateralism as a 'force for peace',[34] Dibb was sceptical of arguments suggesting that interdependence would serve to dampen the prospects for great power rivalry. And while evidently seeing value in some of the confidence-building activities that were emerging at the time and calling for a deepening of these through, for instance, the introduction of a multilateral agreement on the avoidance of naval incidents — which remains a continuing theme in his work today[35] — Dibb was also dubious regarding the potential for emerging multilateral structures to manage or to militate power balancing behaviour. Again, the region was too diverse for such an outcome. In his terms:

> Multilateral institutions are weak in Asia and there is a reluctance to consider formal confidence-building measures and military transparency along the lines of the Organisation for Security and Cooperation (OSCE). These are seen as intrusive, technical arms-control measures that were appropriate to Europe but which do not reflect either the more complex security situation in Asia or the Asian way of doing business.[36]

Instead, what Dibb saw emerging in Asia was a more fluid and uncertain balance of power — or what he termed an 'unstable equilibrium'. Stability would be delivered through the major players acting to check

---

32  Dibb, *Towards a New Balance of Power in Asia* (1995).
33  See, for example, Michael O'Hanlon, 'How to Solve Obama's Grand Strategy Dilemma', *The National Interest*, 23 May 2014.
34  Dibb, *Towards a New Balance of Power in Asia* (1995), p. 53.
35  Paul Dibb, 'Treaty May Steer China, Japan to Safer Waters', *Australian*, 1 Apr. 2013.
36  Dibb, *Towards a New Balance of Power in Asia* (1995), p. 66.

the behaviour of one another, to ensure that none emerged as a regional hegemon. But, unlike in a concert-type arrangement, behaviour would be more competitive, self-serving and characterised by a lack of common interests. In such a setting, the prospect for a serious deterioration in Asia's security environment would, according to Dibb, remain considerable.[37] And with great prescience, once again, he identified Asia's territorial disputes as a potential trigger for such a deterioration. Of particular note is his observation that 'China's rise to great-power status will be accompanied by coercive levers of power, including the demonstration of a military presence in the South China Sea'.[38]

## The Asian Balance: An Idea Whose Time has Come?

At the time that Dibb published his Adelphi and for much for the period since, it has not been fashionable to discuss Asian security order in terms of balance-of-power politics. Indeed, just as Dibb himself discouraged the direct transplantation of Euro-centric multilateral frameworks into an Asian context, a general consensus seems to have emerged amongst scholars studying the international relations of Asia that the balance-of-power concept does not apply particularly well to this part of the world. In the main, these scholars have highlighted an absence of balancing behaviour during the period since the ending of the Cold War. They have pointed to a lack of evidence suggesting any effort on the part of the United States to 'contain' the rise of China through the establishment of an anti-Chinese balancing coalition. Equally, they see little evidence of China vigorously balancing against the United States or seeking to replace it as the region's dominant power.[39]

As widely accepted as these arguments have been for some time now, they have become increasingly difficult to sustain in recent years as signs of more overt balancing behaviour emerge in this region.

---

37    Dibb, *Towards a New Balance of Power in Asia* (1995), p. 55.
38    Dibb, *Towards a New Balance of Power in Asia* (1995), p. 40.
39    See, for example, Steve Chan, *Looking for Balance: China, the United States, and Power Balancing in East Asia* (Stanford University Press, 2012).

The United States under the Obama administration, for instance, has explicitly labelled its strategy for Asia as one of 'rebalancing', which is widely interpreted as a direct response to growing Chinese power and assertiveness.[40] A range of new initiatives in China, such as President Xi Jinping's 'Asia for Asians' security concept are too increasingly seen as part of a concerted effort on Beijing's part to challenge Asia's US-led security order and to undercut American influence in this part of the world.[41] Recent changes in Japan's force structure and a further intensification of the US–Japan alliance — as illustrated by the signing of a new 'vision statement' and revised set of 'defence guidelines' charting the future of that relationship during Japanese Prime Minister Shinzo Abe's May 2015 visit to America — have also been characterised as part of a Japanese 'counter-balancing' strategy in the face of China's rise.[42] Even in South-East Asia, where so-called 'hedging' strategies have long been regarded as the norm, there are clear signs of 'balancing' behaviour emerging, particularly on the part of those countries that feel most threatened by China's growing power and assertiveness, such as the Philippines and Vietnam.[43]

In this era of intensifying Asian balance of power politics, what can scholars and analysts today usefully take from the Dibb approach? First, Dibb's work on the Asian balance highlights the importance of having a clear and coherent conceptual framework. Having such a framework has been one of the defining features across all of Dibb's work. As he observes in one oft-cited analysis of Australian defence policy, for instance, 'planning without such a rigorous conceptual basis only serves to legitimise *ad hoc* equipment acquisitions'.[44] It is important to emphasise here that his utilisation of conceptual frameworks is never dogmatic or unduly prescriptive in nature. Rather, he uses conceptual frameworks more as a means for clarifying complex subject matter and for making this accessible to his readership, which routinely includes senior officials and policymakers. Such

40  See, for example, Robert S. Ross, 'The US Pivot to Asia and Implications for Australia', *Centre of Gravity* series, No. 5 (Canberra: Strategic and Defence Studies Centre, Mar. 2013).

41  Brad Glosserman, 'The Australian Canary', *PacNet*, No. 67 (21 Nov. 2011).

42  See, for example, Bjorn Elias Mikalsen Gronning, 'Japan's Shifting Military Priorities: Counterbalancing China's Rise', *Asian Security*, Vol. 10, No. 1 (2014), pp. 1–21.

43  Carl Thayer, 'The Philippines and Vietnam Forge a Strategic Partnership', *The Diplomat*, 10 Mar. 2015.

44  Paul Dibb, 'Is Strategic Geography Relevant to Australia's Current Defence Policy', *Australian Journal of International Affairs*, Vol. 60, No. 2 (June 2006), p. 255.

conceptual clarity and consistency is all the more important when dealing with such an ambiguous and potentially confusing term as the balance of power.

A second defining feature of Dibb's work that is of relevance to analysing the contemporary Asian balance is his reliance upon the highest quality sources. For this reason, a close reading of Dibb's footnotes is always rewarding in its own right. His Adelphi Paper, for instance, makes regular reference to other classic works of the day, including Henry Kissinger's magisterial work *Diplomacy* and Paul Kennedy's *Rise and Fall of the Great Powers*. Dibb combines this with an iron discipline when it comes to keeping up with leading media sources. He religiously reads all of the key Australian newspapers on a daily basis and for years he has been an avid consumer of such prominent international publications as the *Economist*, the *New York Times* and the *Wall Street Journal*. In an increasingly crowded environment where the proliferation of blogs and various forms of social media have resulted in an overabundance of sources of information, Dibb's judgement in selecting what to read and his discipline in reading it are characteristics that will each serve contemporary analysts of the Asian balance particularly well.

Finally, Dibb's experiences both as a leading scholar and as one of Australia's most significant policy practitioners have undoubtedly combined to benefit his work on the Asian balance and to enhance the benefit of this work to these so-called 'two worlds' — the policy world and the academic world.[45] While moving between these various worlds is relatively common practice in the United States — with the likes of Kissinger, Joseph Nye, Aaron Friedberg, Victor Cha and Thomas Christensen being particularly notable examples — it has been far less routine in Australia. As Dibb's intellectual home — the Strategic and Defence Studies Centre (SDSC) at The Australian National University (ANU) — celebrates its 50th anniversary in 2016, and as we honour his work in this volume, there may be no better time to rectify this situation. Perhaps the Australian Department of Defence and ANU could establish a new 'Dibb fellowship' which allows particularly gifted practitioners to spend a period of time undertaking high-quality, policy-relevant research at the SDSC.

---

45 For further reading see Christopher Hill & Pamela Beshoff, *Two Worlds of International Relations: Academics, Practitioners and the Trade in Ideas* (London: Routledge, 1994).

# 13

## Hard Power and Regional Diplomacy: The Dibb Legacy

Raoul Heinrichs and William T. Tow

To a much greater extent than their US counterparts, Commonwealth governments such as Australia's have maintained a sharp demarcation between both government agencies and those officials who manage their policies, and the independent strategic analysts in academia or in think tanks who provide independent assessments of government policy performance. There are examples of members of US foreign policy and strategic studies establishments who have excelled in manoeuvring between Washington's inner sanctums of policy formulation and prestigious independent venues providing policy commentary — Henry Kissinger, Zbigniew Brzezinski, Madeleine Albright and, more recently, Ashton Carter and Jeffrey Bader all come to mind — but few Australian equivalents. In this context, Paul Dibb is the Australian who has most resembled the American model of a policy practitioner. He has been sufficiently nimble and eclectic to bestride both the hard power world of strategic and defence policy analysis and the delicate and often ambiguous world of diplomatic counsel and has engaged in both pursuits with unquestionable excellence.

Tracing how Dibb has managed to do this, particularly during the late Cold War years and in the post-Cold War era, is the primary theme of this chapter. The narrative that follows reveals at least two fundamental strands that merit such a discourse. One is his ability to apply his unparalleled understanding of how great power dynamics work in the Asia-Pacific region to specific policy tasks and objectives. It has been no coincidence that Dibb has been tapped on the shoulder by successive Australian foreign ministers and corresponding defence officials to communicate his country's thinking about regional defence and security politics to key policymakers throughout Asia over more than three decades. In turn, he has gained a wealth of knowledge about how those regional actors perceive Australia's role as both a key US ally and a sovereign player in the Asia-Pacific and international security arenas. This has reinforced his reputation as one of the world's premier strategic and defence policy experts while providing him with the flexibility to broaden his growing profile as an accomplished diplomatic councillor. Second, he has orchestrated the strengths and weaknesses of bilateral and multilateral security politics in ways that have facilitated regional confidence-building and Australia's role in it.

Initially, a brief summary is offered on Dibb's background as it relates to Australia's efforts to come to grips with evolving regional security challenges from the late Cold War. The focus then shifts to cover his subsequent contributions as one of Australia's originators of regional confidence-building politics. Lastly, Dibb's latest diplomatic engagement with a 'Track 1.5' initiative (i.e. the Association of Southeast Asian Nations (ASEAN) regional forum (ARF) Eminent and Expert Persons (EEP) group), which was designed to infuse greater viability into that process, is offered as an example of how he has applied his understanding of hard power and regional diplomacy to a daunting implementation of regional dialogue.

## Hard-wired for Regional Security

Given his professional and intellectual background as arguably Australia's premier strategic studies analyst, Dibb's wide-ranging contribution to regional security cooperation is somewhat surprising. He has a long-standing involvement in the processes, discussions and confidence-building agendas of the region's evolving multilateral security architecture. So too has been his ongoing support of that architecture's transition from dialogue to practical cooperation. Dibb himself is the first to acknowledge the apparent contradiction between his strategic studies profile and his record as a diplomatic practitioner. 'I arrived at all this from a career in intelligence and defence planning', he notes.

> My focus was mostly on 'hard-power': military capabilities; nuclear developments, particularly in the Soviet Union; and the methodological basis of Australian defence policy. When (in the early 1990s) I was approached to help build an agenda for confidence- and trust-building exercises, it just wasn't my natural scene.[1]

In many ways, his misgivings about multilateral security processes are understandable. Like most of his contemporaries in national security policy during the Cold War, Dibb's world-view necessarily rested on a hard-edged, implicit form of *realpolitik*.[2] Conceptually, this was not conducive to an overly optimistic view of regionalism, cooperative security, or even, despite some demonstrable successes during detente, measures for resolving strategic mistrust — which many see as essential in the international system.[3] Yet these were concepts for which there was a newfound enthusiasm in the post-Cold War world, one suddenly liberated from the constraints of the bipolar geopolitical and ideological confrontations of the past 50 years.

There were other challenges. Dibb had been primarily outcome-oriented in his government service; he now faced a world in which process seemed to matter as much as, if not more than, the goals it was intended to produce. 'Patience, patience, patience', he recalls Australia's then Foreign Minister Gareth Evans counselling him before a Track 1.5 dialogue.[4] For Dibb, the precision and logic that typified his approach to national security, particularly his *Review of Australia's Defence Capabilities* in 1986,[5] might now be found to be

---

1    Paul Dibb, interview with the authors, The Australian National University, Canberra, 12 Aug. 2015.
2    See, for example, Paul Dibb, *The Soviet Union: The Incomplete Superpower* (London: International Institute for Strategic Studies and Macmillan, 1986); Paul Dibb, *World Political and Strategic Trends over the Next 20 Years — Their Relevance to Australia*, Working Paper No. 65 (Canberra: Strategic and Defence Studies Centre, The Australian National University, 1983). For a discussion of the characteristics of Australian realist thought, see Michael Wesley, 'The Rich Tradition of Australian Realism', *Australian Journal of Politics and History*, Vol. 55, No. 3 (2009), pp. 324–34.
3    See, for example, John Mearsheimer, 'The False Promise of International Institutions', *International Security*, Vol. 19, No. 3 (Winter 1994–95), pp. 5–49.
4    Dibb, interview (2015).
5    Paul Dibb, *Review of Australia's Defence Capabilities*, report to the Minister for Defence (Canberra: Australian Government Publishing Service, 1986).

less applicable to the amorphous concept of regional security. Linking strategic guidance to capability, optimising Australia's military for a range of credible contingencies, structuring the Australian Defence Force (ADF) in line with the Defence of Australia (DOA) doctrine, all reflected traditional national security policy in a world shaped by power politics. These approaches constituted Dibb's professional world. In terms of regional security cooperation in the era following the end of the Cold War, however, he now faced an ambiguous and daunting task — one over which he had less direct influence — not just responding to the forces of power politics, but exploring the means by which they could be fundamentally ameliorated.

As it happened, none of these challenges proved insuperable to Dibb, either during or after the Cold War. Indeed, at least in some cases, those factors that might otherwise have inhibited Dibb's contribution to regional security cooperation in fact propelled him in the other direction. A number of personal attributes made him suited to the task. Arguably the most important was credibility, defined by the combination of intellectual weight and political skill and the ability to formulate ideas and successfully translate them into policy. By the early 1990s, Dibb was as close to a household name in Australia as defence intellectuals can become. The Dibb Review, as it came to be known, had imposed unprecedented analytical rigour on Australian defence policy. His emphasis on Australia's quest for 'defence self-reliance' cut against a strategic culture of dependence on great and powerful friends that was so deeply ingrained in Australia's psyche it had come to be seen as constitutive of the national identity. Undoing this mindset was no easy feat. It meant, among other things, overcoming entrenched bureaucratic interests, not least within the Defence organisation and the Australian Army, whose traditional primacy among the military services had been upended in favour of a strategy that privileged air and maritime capabilities. If the process was transformational, so were the consequences. As Australia's then foreign minister wrote: 'This new confidence in our defence capability liberated Australian foreign policy. Australian foreign ministers are freer to think about their responsibilities more systematically, and more intricately, than ever before.'[6] It also compelled Australia to think

6    Gareth Evans & Bruce Grant, *Australia's Foreign Relations in the World of the 1990s* (Melbourne University Press, 1991), p. 30.

more systematically about how it would relate diplomatically and strategically with its regional neighbours. It provided a foundation for a broader national security approach that ironically led to Australia, over time, becoming a pivotal force in defining and shaping regional collective security politics.

Dibb's classical work on the Soviet Union, too, contributed to his credibility as an intellectual heavyweight as the transition from a bipolar world to a more complex multipolar one unfolded. No one foresaw the extraordinary confluence of events that brought about the demise of the Soviet Union and the end of the Cold War — but very few had come as close as Dibb. From the early 1980s, he had identified a set of potentially fatal underlying flaws in the Soviet Union: economic stagnation and decline leading to insurmountable pressure on Russian standard of living, Soviet military expenditures and doubt about the Soviet Union's overall political cohesion.[7] These, he argued, 'could see the Soviet Union's empire eventually begin to crumble ... In the long haul, the very "Russianness" of the Soviet multinational state is in question'.[8]

The clarity and foresight of these observations confirmed Dibb's prescience. Time and again, from intelligence to policy to academia, and from issue to issue, Dibb exuded a level of intellectual ability that bode well for his efforts in the world of regional security cooperation.[9] As Evans has observed, 'Enlisting one of our foremost minds in confidence-building and the Track 1.5 agenda, we felt, itself signified our seriousness and commitment to the tasks.'[10]

Finally, there is another, more innate characteristic that made Dibb a good fit for regional security cooperation. An old joke reveals that you can tell an extroverted defence intelligence analyst when they look at *your* shoes while talking to you. If there is any grain of truth in this, Dibb is a striking exception. As Hugh White explains: 'Paul is a natural diplomat. He has a disarming sense of charm and wit. When he pulls you aside, he has this way of making you feel like you're one of the

---

7   Dibb, *The Soviet Union: The Incomplete Superpower* (1988).
8   Paul Dibb, *World Political and Strategic Trends* (1983), p. 11.
9   Dibb has a long list of academic publications from his time in government. This is uncommon amongst members of the Australian Public Service, still less among members of the Australian intelligence community.
10   Gareth Evans, interview with the authors, Melbourne, 3 Sep. 2015.

only people in the room.'[11] Beyond this, Dibb is intuitively attuned to the way power and influence shape organisational dynamics. He has, as Australia's former 'defence supremo' Sir Arthur Tange once put it, 'a persuasive personality' without being abrasive.[12] He also has a sharp memory and an easy interpersonal style. Taken together, these attributes made him almost preternaturally disposed to cultivating the kinds of personal relationships that are important diplomatic currency in Asia.[13]

## Dibb goes to China

Much of Dibb's work on regional security cooperation occurred after the end of the Cold War, once he had left government to head the Strategic and Defence Studies Centre (SDSC) at The Australian National University (ANU) in 1991. It began, however, more than a decade earlier. Then in his 30s, Dibb was appointed by Tange as Deputy Director of the Joint Intelligence Organisation (JIO, the forerunner to today's Defence Intelligence Organisation) in 1978.[14] From this point to the early 1990s, Dibb was a central actor in two sets of official government-to-government contacts (or 'Track 1' exchanges) — the first with the People's Republic of China (PRC), the second with Japan. In both cases, these strategic relationships were in their infancy.[15] As a consequence, Australia's official contact with these two critical countries' military and security establishments was in most cases less substantive than procedural, and largely exploratory in nature. Nevertheless, these early contacts helped build the foundations for security relationships. Although not core business for Dibb at the time, they provided him with an entrée into the work that would become a preoccupation in the years to come.

---

11   Hugh White, interview with the authors, The Australian National University, Canberra, 13 Aug. 2015.

12   Sir Arthur Tange, *Defence Policy-Making: A Close-Up View, 1950–1980: A Personal Memoir*, Peter Edwards (ed.), (Canberra: ANU E Press, 2008), p. 82.

13   For a discussion of the importance of personal relationships to diplomacy, see Keith Hamilton & Richard Langhorne, *The Practise of Diplomacy: Its Evolution, Theory and Administration* (Abingdon: Routledge, 1995), p. 172.

14   Michelle Grattan, 'Dibb to be Intelligence Chief', *Age*, 10 Oct. 1986.

15   See James Reilly & Jindong Yuan (eds), *Australia and China at 40* (Sydney: UNSW Press, 2012). See also Desmond Ball, 'Whither the Japan–Australia Security Relationship?', Nautilus Institute for Security and Sustainability, *APSNet Policy Forum*, 21 Sep. 2006, nautilus.org/apsnet/0632a-ball-html/.

The 1970s was a period of considerable change in Australia's strategic landscape.[16] On the one hand, the public articulation of the 'Guam doctrine' (also known as the 'Nixon doctrine') (1969), the withdrawal of British forces from east of Suez, and defeat for the United States in Vietnam augured new uncertainties. On the other hand, new opportunities for Australian diplomacy were emerging as geopolitical shifts were underway in response to widening schisms in the communist world. For two decades since the communist victory in the Chinese Civil War (1949), Chinese foreign and strategic policy had been geared towards undercutting American power wherever it appeared, in the ultimate hope of removing the United States as a predominant player within the Asian balance of power. The resulting tension produced two wars — during Korea and Vietnam, Australia endured two anxious decades of bitter power rivalry in the region.

All of this was modified by Richard Nixon's visit to China and America's subsequent opening to that Asian country. At the heart of the Sino–American 'rapprochement' was a tacit alliance to preclude Soviet expansionism in Asia.[17] In practice, this meant that America would formalise its recognition of the Chinese Communist Party, while China would do nothing to aggravate the situation in Vietnam or Korea — and, more broadly, would reduce its contest of American power in Asia.[18] Eager to avoid hastening or strengthening Sino–US rapprochement, the Soviet Union soon accommodated itself to a new era of détente. As Kissinger has pointed out, 'Once America had opened to China, the Soviet Union's best option became seeking its own relaxation of tensions with the United States'.[19]

For Australia, such ongoing geopolitical developments had a soothing strategic effect, although one which took some time to internalise. More immediately, however, it provided the political context in which Australia's opening to China could proceed on the back of Prime Minister Gough Whitlam's historic October 1973 visit to Beijing. With relations established in 1972 and normalised in 1975, and with the

---

16   See Hedley Bull, 'The New Balance of Power in Asia and the Pacific', *Foreign Affairs*, Jul. 1971.

17   See Robert Ross, *Chinese Security Policy: Structure, Power and Politics* (London: Routledge, 2009), p. 25.

18   See Hugh White, *The China Choice: Why America Should Share Power* (Melbourne: Black Inc., 2012).

19   See Henry Kissinger, *Diplomacy* (New York: Simon and Schuster, 1994), p. 30.

relationship accelerating from that point onward, the strategic scene was at least partly set for Dibb's fascinating, if much less well known, 1978 visit to China.

Dibb crossed into mainland China from Hong Kong on 1 August 1978 — the first official visit of an Australian defence intelligence representative to the PRC. Early in the visit Dibb was shown fall-out shelters under Tiananmen Square. Despite Mao Zedong's notorious outward ambivalence to the threat posed by nuclear weapons, this was a potent reminder of the reality of China's strategic nuclear anxieties.[20] It was also, Dibb knew, intended as a prompt. For China, the purpose of his visit, beyond just 'feeling Australia out', was to garner any available information he may have and be willing to convey about the Soviet Union's strategic intentions and capabilities.[21] In particular, Dibb's Chinese interlocutors wanted to know anything he could offer on Soviet missile systems. 'They understood our intelligence-sharing arrangements with the United States', Dibb notes. 'They knew that we knew about them [Soviet missile systems], and they wanted to test whether we might be more forthcoming than the US. On that front, to their chagrin, they were bound to be disappointed.'[22] Chinese disappointment was compounded when a People's Liberation Army (PLA) divisional commander made the age-old mistake of trying to drink Dibb under the table. Hungover, they headed for the port city of Hangzhou, and from there to Shanghai, where he was a guest of the three-star garrison commander.

Shanghai turned out to be the setting for both the low point and high point of Dibb's visit: the former involved a night at the Chinese opera (an assault on Dibb's auditory senses); the latter, an unexpected visit to the PLA Navy's submarine building yard and an up-close view of a *Romeo*-class submarine — at the time, China's most potent naval platform. This was surprising because the physical characteristics of submarines are among states' most closely guarded military secrets.[23] Back in Canberra, Defence's naval intelligence wonks were

---

20  See Jeffrey G. Lewis, *The Minimum Means of Reprisal: China's Search for Security in the Nuclear Age* (Cambridge: MIT Press, 2007).

21  Dibb, interview (2015).

22  Dibb, interview (2015).

23  The question of whether Dibb was the first Westerner to tour a Chinese submarine base remains a matter of conjecture. According to James Lilley, then US ambassador to China, the honour belongs to him. Dibb disagrees.

disappointed to discover that, as a strategic rather than a technical analyst, the finer details of the *Romeo*'s properties had eluded him altogether.

In any case, this was not Australia's purpose in dispatching Dibb to China. Rather, it was for him to initiate strategic contacts at the official level, to begin the process of consolidating Australia's broader diplomatic relations with China, and to cultivate some personal linkages that might serve as a foundation for deeper engagement. In this sense, the visit was a success. While Australia's defence relationship with China remained tentative, defence attachés were formally swapped. This allowed for a gradual increase in contact between the two defence organisations, and for the incremental institutionalisation of a defence relationship that has further evolved today.

## Dibb and Japan

Dibb's next major foray into confidence-building and regional security cooperation helped lay the groundwork for the establishment of Australian mechanisms for regular official exchanges and dialogues with Japan on shared strategic challenges. It may seem strange to note the fundamentally underdeveloped nature until the early 1990s of Australia's security relationship with Japan against the backdrop of the dramatic acceleration of strategic relations in recent years.[24]

From the 1970s, however, the most pronounced feature of Australia's security relationship with Japan was, as Aurelia George Mulgan notes, 'a rather dull predictability, a relationship that appeared to have reached the limits of its potential, without much scope for dramatic expansion or diversification'.[25] While trade and investment ties increased through the 1970s and 1980s, politico-strategic relations

---

24   This has brought about the Joint Declaration on Security Cooperation (2007), a Defence Acquisitions and Cross-Servicing Agreement (2010), as well as the possibility of the acquisition by Australia of a variant of the Japanese *Soryu*-class submarine. If this latter step is realised, the deal would be Japan's first major postwar defence export agreement. See Malcolm Cook, 'The Quiet Achiever: Australia–Japan Security Relations', *Analysis* (Sydney: Lowy Institute for International Policy, 2011). See also Chris Brooks, 'Australia–Japan Security Relations: Improving on a Best-Friends Relationship', *Indo-Pacific Strategic Papers* (Canberra: Australian Defence College, 2014).

25   Aurelia George Mulgan, 'Australia–Japan Relations: New Directions', *ASPI Strategic Insights* (Canberra: Australian Strategic Policy Institute, Jul. 2007), p. 2.

continued to be inhibited by a range of factors: the absence of any compelling strategic requirement, the bitter legacy of the Second World War, growing Australian uncertainties about the intentions of an increasingly powerful Japanese economic actor, and Japan's own strict constitutional limitations on its external strategic relations.

Concrete interaction on security issues commenced in the mid-1970s at the instigation of the Australian Secret Intelligence Service (ASIS), but such cooperation was limited.[26] Although ASIS took the lead, bilateral cooperation expanded in the late 1980s into defence intelligence. As head of the National Assessments Staff (NAS) at Defence, this is where Dibb's exposure to Japan began in earnest. By the time Dibb had departed as Director of the JIO in 1986, incorporated agreements with the intelligence directorates of each of the branches constituting Japan's Self-Defense Force (SDF) were in place.[27]

At the same time, Australia's security cooperation with Japan began to evolve out of intelligence and into the world of policy. That this occurred in lock-step with Dibb's appointment as the Deputy Secretary for Defence in 1988 was no coincidence. The creation of regular mechanisms for dialogue on shared strategic challenges was seen by Canberra as an important confidence-building measure (CBM) and a crucial base on which to build the relationship.

In March 1990 Dibb, together with then Vice Chief of the Defence Force, Vice-Admiral Alan Beaumont, led an Australian delegation to Japan for the first Track 1 security dialogue between the two countries. On the Japanese side, discussions were facilitated by Dibb's friend, Yukio Satoh, then Director-General in the Analysis, Research and Planning Bureau of Japan's Ministry of Foreign Affairs (MOFA). The two had discovered that they shared a birthday, and Satoh began lightheartedly referring to Dibb as his 'blood-brother'. As Dibb explains, 'In Japan, personal connections really matter!'[28]

In spite of the obvious congeniality between these two key players, overall discussion about Australia–Japan security was still characterised by considerable Japanese sensitivity. 'Remember, this was the first time they had done anything like this with any country

---

26  Ball, 'Whither the Japan–Australia Security Relationship' (2006).
27  Ball, 'Whither the Japan–Australia Security Relationship' (2006).
28  Dibb, interview (2015).

other than the US', notes Dibb. Indeed, the Japanese delegation was limited to civilians from the Japan Defense Agency (JDA) and MOFA. Senior officials had proscribed attendance of uniformed personnel from the SDF, unwilling to risk transgressing Japan's normative and legal constraints by approving direct military-to-military talks with forces not from the United States.

While discussions remained exploratory rather than substantive, the agenda was nevertheless wide ranging. Issues included the future of the (by then beleaguered) Soviet Union and its implications, and the scope and limits of each country's respective alliance with the United States. In particular, Dibb's Japanese interlocutors were eager to learn more about Australia's 'full-knowledge-and-concurrence' arrangements at the joint facilities at Pine Gap, Nurrungar and North West Cape.[29] This came as no surprise to Dibb. Entrapment dilemmas as a result of US sovereignty over bases throughout the Japanese archipelago had for decades been a vexed issue in Japan, and it remained a matter of ongoing concern. For Australia's part, the talks were an opportunity to canvass Japanese views of north-east Asia. A resident power, Japan could be expected to have a more nuanced understanding of China, Taiwan, North Korea and South Korea, and the Russian far east.

The Dibb–Beaumont talks, as they came to be known, continued until 1995, when they were supplanted by annual Track 1 political–military and military–military discussions. Yet the success of the initial round — and of Dibb's leadership — was reflected in swift developments in the Japan–Australia security relationship from that point on. In May 1990, Japanese Defence Minister Yoso Ishikawa became the first to visit Australia. The visit was reciprocated by Australian Defence Minister Robert Ray in 1992, and relations gathered steady momentum throughout the 1990s.

Today, Australia–Japan security relations span the full range of strategic issues and forms of cooperation.[30] The intelligence relationship has been nurtured to unprecedented intimacy. Official dialogues have spawned annual 2+2 ministerial (defence and foreign minister) talks, and leadership summits are a regular occurrence, often

29  For a detailed discussion, see Desmond Ball, *A Suitable Piece of Real Estate: American Installations in Australia* (Sydney: Hale & Iremonger, 1980).
30  See Australian Department of Foreign Affairs, 'Japan Country Brief', Canberra, 2015, dfat. gov.au/geo/japan/Pages/japan-country-brief.aspx.

on the sidelines of the region's major multilateral meetings. A trilateral strategic dialogue has been institutionalised between Australia, Japan and the United States, including regular joint military exercises. The Joint Declaration for Security (2007) provides a broad foundation for cooperation on everything from counterterrorism and border security to maritime security, counter-proliferation and disaster relief operations.

In 2013, when Prime Minister Tony Abbott openly declared Japan to be Australia's 'closest friend in Asia', it appeared possible, perhaps likely, that relations might even coalesce into a formal alliance.[31] This remains a highly contentious issue in Australian strategic policy[32] as to whether it would be a prudent move for Australia in light of Japan's uncertain strategic future. Whatever the case, it is ultimately not Dibb's problem, or even his legacy. Dibb's task was to get Australia–Japan security relations off the ground floor. To that end, he executed his mission with trademark skill, energy and finesse.

## World in Flux: After the Cold War

Like the 1970s, the post-Cold War world of the early 1990s presented itself as a dizzying one for the makers of Australian foreign and strategic policy. Once again, elements of continuity and discontinuity interacted to produce a range of conflicting trends in Australia's security environment.[33] As Dibb pointed out in the inaugural Melbourne Asia Policy Paper, a sense of policy drift had overtaken the traditional rationales for the United States to value Australia. Expectations for a 'new world order' underwritten by globalisation and democracy (and, by implication, to be shaped by multilateral approaches to order-building) were running high in Washington.[34] The sudden disintegration of the Soviet Union removed the primary sources of global ideological and geopolitical confrontation. For the first time in almost 50 years, the world appeared to have been freed

---

31   See Mark Kenny, 'Tony Abbott says "Japan is Australia's Closest Friend in Asia"', *Sydney Morning Herald*, 9 Oct. 2013.

32   See Hugh White, 'Abbott Should Think Twice Before Becoming Friendly with Japan', *Age*, 8 Jul. 2014.

33   See Evans & Grant, *Australia's Foreign Relations* (1991).

34   Paul Dibb, *Australia's Alliance with America*, Melbourne Asia Policy Papers, Vol. 1, No. 1 (University of Melbourne, Mar. 2003), p. 9.

from the ever-present spectre of apocalyptic nuclear war. Regionally, the lead times on development of military capabilities by other regional powers remained far enough over the horizon not to cause alarm.[35] Australia's ally, the United States, suddenly found itself alone at the top of the international pecking order.

The United States was facing momentous choices.[36] Whichever direction it took would have profound implications for Australia. If the United States eventually chose to remain deeply engaged in Asia, if it retained its alliances and deployed its now overwhelmingly preponderant military power in support of them, Australia could probably 'breathe easy'. Canberra could continue to enjoy the region's strategic quiescence, with all the benefits and opportunities that entailed. At the time, however, that outcome felt far from assured. The dissolution of the Soviet Union had robbed the Asia-Pacific of what many reasonably assumed was the only compelling reason for Far East assignment of American power. Again, it was Dibb that best posed the obvious question: 'What does alliance mean when the discipline of a common threat has gone?'[37] The 1994 Defence White Paper offered a less than emphatic response: 'The United States will remain a major contributor to security over the next fifteen years, but it will neither seek nor accept primary responsibility for maintaining peace and stability in the region.'[38]

The possibility of a significantly diminished US role loomed as a frightening one. In the worst case, US retrenchment from Asia threatened to create a vacuum, bringing into play the full range of strategic risks to Australia that American power had hitherto suppressed: the resumption of Sino–Japanese rivalry, the attainment of dominance by one or the other, or worse still, a war followed by the emergence of a new hegemon.[39] There were other uncertainties too: the potential realisation of North Korea's nuclear ambitions and its unresolved conflict with the South, territorial disputes in the South

35   See Paul Dibb, *The Regional Security Outlook: An Australian Viewpoint*, Working Paper No. 262 (Canberra: Strategic and Defence Studies Centre, The Australian National University, 1992), p. 1.
36   See Charles Krauthammer, 'The Unipolar Moment Revisited', *The National Interest* (Winter 2002/2003).
37   Dibb, *The Regional Security Outlook* (1992), p. 9.
38   Commonwealth of Australia, *Defending Australia: Defence White Paper 1994* (Canberra: Australian Government Publishing Service, 1994), p. 9.
39   See Thomas Christensen, 'China, the US–Japan Alliance, and the Security Dilemma in East Asia', *International Security*, Vol. 23, No. 4 (1999), pp. 49–80.

China Sea, an Indo–Pakistani conflagration, Taiwan's indeterminate status, or the possible proliferation of weapons of mass destruction to offset asymmetric conventional military balances. Each of these could have serious implications for Australian security.[40] Even if worst cases did not eventuate, there was still a sense that Australia needed to better develop a strategic environment shaped by the attitudes and approaches of regional countries themselves.[41]

In terms of regional security cooperation, the uncertainties of this new era created the impetus for two overlapping sets of objectives. The first involved exploring new bilateral avenues for security cooperation with regional states in order to directly augment Australian national security — for example, exchanges in personnel or intelligence, or joint military exercises (this kind of cooperation was Dibb's forte). The second, which was more ambitious and more multilateral, involved taking the lead in processes that, it was hoped, could temper the forces of power politics unleashed by a new strategic order.

While the objectives were distinct, the means of pursuing them were similar. Each would require CBMs to overcome initial suspicion and mistrust and to develop necessary habits of cooperation. Each would have to avoid becoming impeded by excessive formality or held up by diplomatic sensitivities. In that sense, they would benefit from the use of unofficial channels, at least in the early stages. And each would involve a role for Dibb, albeit in slightly varying capacities.

The first objective saw Dibb, now in academia at ANU, reprise his diplomatic role to lead Australian delegations in a series of semi-official Track 1.5 dialogues throughout the region. These included follow-up discussions throughout the early to mid-1990s with China and Japan, and later establishing new forms of dialogue and security interaction with such regional actors as South Korea and Vietnam. The Track 1.5 format was a kind of 'Goldilocks option'. It was structured so as to avoid falling into the realm of abstraction, which was a risk of a fully unofficial (or Track 2) process, but less rigid than Track 1 engagements. Track 1.5 dialogues were officially sanctioned, and they included a substantial number of Australian officials and their regional counterparts acting in their official rather than private

---

40   See Dibb, *The Regional Security Outlook* (1992), pp. 1–4.
41   Australian Department of Defence, *Defending Australia* (1994), p. 85.

capacities, in contrast to the more informal Track 2 dialogues.[42] Dialogue was intended to fulfil a number of intermediate purposes: foster personal relationships, bolster transparency and trust, explore mutual perceptions of the regional security environment and take early steps to carve out some mutual understandings about the potential direction of future strategic cooperation.

For the architects of these dialogues, Dibb's lead role made good sense. He was now an academic, so at liberty to be more open, but still highly attuned to government priorities and requirements. He had personal networks in Australia and overseas and on all sides of politics. As a former intelligence specialist, he was particularly adept at probing his interlocutors on the most salient issues while steering discussions away from more trivial aspects. Behind the scenes, he could process information and assimilate it into a broader strategic framework to convey useful, actionable information to Canberra. According to White:

> These talks were not designed to push strong policy agendas. They were exploratory kind of intelligence gathering missions on how changes in Asia's order were being interpreted by countries we didn't have a long track-record of talking to about these things.[43]

## Practical Proposals

Dibb's efforts in relation to the second objective centred around his role in drafting the *Australian Paper on Practical Proposals for Security Cooperation in the Asia Pacific Region* (1994). He had been designated for this role by his co-author, Foreign Minister Evans. In seeking to further the paper's objectives, Dibb also chaired a major Track 1.5 meeting in Canberra in November 1994. This was an intersessional seminar comprised of officials from the foreign and defence ministries of the 18 members of the ASEAN ARF, as well as a number of leading regional academics. The key outcomes were to be carried forward at the 1995 ARF Senior Officials Meeting in Brunei. The conclusions

---

42  See Desmond Ball & Brendan Taylor, 'Regional Security Cooperation', in Desmond Ball & Robert Ayson (eds), *Strategy and Security in the Asia-Pacific* (Crows Nest: Allen & Unwin, 2006), p. 273.

43  White, interview, (2015).

drawn by this study and the dialogue processes it elicited proved to be a substantial component of the region's subsequent CBM politics. Accordingly, it is assessed in some detail here.

The *Australian Paper* treatise had its origins in the 1993 ASEAN Post-Ministerial Conference on regional CBMs. It was submitted for discussion at the ARF Senior Officials Meeting (May 1994), and from there went before the first ministerial-level meeting of the ARF, in Bangkok, later the same year. While the formal terms of reference for the ARF were set out in a concept paper, adopted in August 1995, the organisation's general approach to CBMs — an emphasis on sensitivity and trust as an essential precondition to deeper forms of cooperation — reflected many of the key themes and principles outlined in Evans's and Dibb's submission.

The *Australian Paper*, in turn, built on the scholarly contributions to the field of CBMs that Dibb was making as head of The Australian National University's SDSC.[44] The document was designed, first, to be 'strategic', embedded firmly in concerns about the evolution of Asia's security environment after the Cold War. Second, it was intended to be diplomatic. The terminology used in the paper was deliberately employed to distinguish it from the traditional language of arms control and international security, which harked back to the previous era of superpower confrontation. According to Evans, 'Cold War language and concepts were not appropriate to the entirely different political, cultural and strategic situation in the Asia Pacific'.[45] Third, the paper was geared to be realistic. It explicitly precluded the possibility of addressing 'Asia Pacific security cooperation in all its dimensions', instead limiting its focus to 'military cooperation and defence issues'.[46] It adopted a graduated approach, categorising specific trust-building measures not on their urgency, but rather by how easily they might

---

44   See, for example, Paul Dibb, *Focusing the CSBM Agenda in the Asia-Pacific Region: Some Aspects of Defence Confidence Building*, Working Paper No. 256 (Canberra: Strategic and Defence Studies Centre, The Australian National University, 1992). Also see Paul Dibb, *How to Begin Implementing Specific Trust-Building Measures in the Asia-Pacific Region*, Working Paper No. 288 (Canberra: Strategic and Defence Studies Centre, The Australian National University, 1994).

45   Gareth Evans & Paul Dibb, *Australian Paper on Practical Proposals for Security Cooperation in the Asia Pacific Region* (Canberra: Strategic and Defence Studies Centre and Australian Department of Foreign Affairs and Trade, 1994), p. 1.

46   Evans & Dibb, *Australian Paper* (1994), p. 3.

be implemented. It deliberately avoided setting out time frames, and it included a specific list of 'areas where information-sharing is unlikely'.[47]

Finally, the paper was intensely practical. '[D]ialogue', noted Evans in his remarks to the 1994 conference, 'must have a specific focus and content.'[48] CBMs were divided into three categories based on the level of trust needed to implement them. Category 1 initiatives were the principal focus and included proposals for a limited exchange of military information, which would build transparency; a regional security studies centre to serve as a centralised repository for government-supplied information; a maritime information database, which would house data on all areas pertinent to shipping; strategic planning exchanges, which would create a regular mechanism in which defence planners could share perceptions on regional security developments; observers at military exercises; and peacekeeping training, which would focus on the 'peculiar requirements' of these kinds of military operations. Categories 2 and 3 involved more complex and structured forms of confidence-building — such as maritime cooperation, a regional arms register, and an incidents at sea agreement. These were contingent on the kind of trust which, it was hoped, would result from the institutionalisation of Category 1 CBMs.

Twenty years on, the legacy of the *Australian Paper* is mixed. This has less to do with the quality of the paper or the practicality of its proposals than with institutional constraints. In terms of direct influence on the ARF, the paper's impact has been limited to establishing the incremental approach that the organisation would take to building confidence. The intersessional meeting held in Canberra is noted in the ARF chairman's statement issued at the second annual ARF meeting convened at Brunei in August 1995. But any direct proposals flowing from it seem not to have gone much further than that.

Some progress has been made by the ARF in areas that reflect the paper's proposals. A range of enhanced contacts have occurred, including high-level visits, and exchanges between military academies and staff colleges. Defence white papers, especially about north-east Asia, are

---

47  Evans & Dibb, *Australian Paper* (1994), p. 5.

48  Gareth Evans, 'Address to the Seminar on the Building of Confidence and Trust in the Asia Pacific', Canberra, 24 Nov. 1994.

being promulgated more regularly, in part to serve the purposes of transparency.[49] Disaster relief exercises have become an important component of the agenda. The organisation has also spawned a number of smaller, more focused dialogues. But overall, the ARF's record on practical cooperation has been impeded by organisational malaise. The overriding emphasis on consensus and non-interference as the guiding principles have imposed structural limits on the ARF's capacity to progress beyond preliminary CBMs, much less tackle the more exacting tasks of preventive diplomacy or conflict resolution. By 2007, Dibb himself was evincing increasing despondence, declaring the ARF little more than a 'talk-shop'.[50]

## Eminent and Expert Persons Group

Despite these frustrations, Dibb did not give up. His next contribution to regional security cooperation involved representing Australia at the ARF EEP group every year from 2006 to 2015. Each member state could nominate up to five experts. Once again, Dibb was an obvious choice for Australia given his credentials in the field.[51] His nomination by the Department of Foreign Affairs and Trade (DFAT) found ready acceptance from its then Minister, Alexander Downer. He had appointed Dibb a member of his Foreign Policy Advisory Council for the nine years it existed from 1998.

The EEP group was created in 2002 as a Track 1.5 complement to the ARF. It was established as a professional repository of ideas, research and advice for the ARF's Track 1 processes. The meeting is open to all countries that are members of the ARF. Chairmanship rotates annually, with the co-chair designated host of the following year's meeting. The outcome is a chairman's report, including recommendations that are carried into the official ARF ministerial process.

---

49   See Ball & Taylor, 'Regional Security Cooperation' (2006), p. 273.

50   Paul Dibb, 'A New Defence Policy for a New Strategic Era?', in Clive Williams & Brendan Taylor (eds), *Countering Terror: New Directions Post 9/11*, Canberra Papers on Strategy and Defence No. 147 (Canberra: Strategic and Defence Studies Centre, The Australian National University, 2003), p. 64.

51   The other Australian participants nominated were Hugh White, Ivan Shearer, Sam Bateman and Alan Dupont.

Three factors underpinned the EEP group's creation. The first was a recognition of the scale of emerging regional strategic uncertainties in the twenty-first century: the rise of China and India, the North Korean nuclear issue, the emergence of terrorism as a central issue after the September 2001 attacks in the United States, and the war in Afghanistan. The second factor was the creeping sense of stagnation at the Track 1 level, especially the inability of the ARF to evolve beyond preliminary CBMs into the realm of preventive diplomacy. The third was concern about the potential emergence of competing new regional institutions.

Although the EEP group was established in 2002, it did not meet for the first time until 2006. Dibb was, to borrow Dean Acheson's landmark phrase to describe his own role at the inaugural EEP group meeting held in South Korea, 'present at the creation'.[52] The first three meetings focused largely on procedural matters but, with basic processes established, the group still seemed to lack clear direction. A breakthrough occurred at the fourth meeting, in Bali, when, at the direction of ARF ministers, the EEP group began to focus on establishing priorities for preventive diplomacy. A year later, in Timor-Leste, a modest set of initiatives for preventive diplomacy was brought forward, including a proposal for what would arguably become the EEP group's most concrete achievement to date: dispatching an election observation team for Timor-Leste's 2012 general elections.[53] Dibb was the Australian EEP group representative at those elections.

If the EEP group had taken a step forward, from that point onward, it seemed to take two steps back — even as the regional security environment deteriorated in the context of China's newly muscular approach in the East and South China Seas. Ministerial guidance and feedback to the EEP group became more sporadic and less specific. With the exception of Dibb and a few other EEPs, the lack of continuity in terms of EEP group member representatives compounded the problem, depriving the organisation of 'corporate memory'. The attendance of new representatives each year meant spending a substantial amount of time in meetings revisiting old issues rather than progressing on new ones. Geopolitically, divisions began to emerge. Substantively,

---

52   Australia co-chaired the 2016 meeting in Singapore and will host the event in 2017.
53   Many South-East Asian members did not participate, due to sensitivities about interference in internal affairs.

the traditional inhibitors of multilateral security cooperation in Asia became more pronounced. In particular, at a time when the need for practical proposals for ameliorating increasing strategic competition among the region's great powers had become more urgent than ever, the norms of non-interference and consensus were asserted to block sensitive discussions and hamper the advancement of key preventive diplomacy initiatives. For Dibb, this was a source of perennial frustration. Created as a Track 1.5 process to develop ideas in the face of these kinds of constraints, the EEP group seemed instead to be headed for the kind of lack of focus that many observers perceived as undermining the ARF.

As for Dibb, his personal contribution to the EEP group process stands in stark contrast to the overall performance of the organisation. Having attended every meeting since its founding and been one of its most active participants, he has served as a crucial source of continuity and corporate memory. From the earliest meetings, and in the face of reluctance, Dibb insisted that institutional relevance, at a minimum, necessitated a focus on 'hard' security issues. Year in and year out, through speeches, working papers (oddly referred to as 'non-papers'), briefings and negotiations on the margins of meetings, Dibb has helped to lead the EEP group both in critical self-examination and the more substantive work of developing a practical agenda for preventive diplomacy. Displaying immense patience, he has worked assiduously to gain support for a regional 'incidents at sea' accord as a viable component of regional maritime security. He has been a tireless agitator for the need to approach Asia's multilateral security architecture in ways that lead from dialogue to practical cooperation to serve the goals of peace and stability in the region.

## Conclusion

Only a few individuals are able to combine the pragmatism gained from cutting-edge policy experience with the aspirational motivations required to persist in advancing the normative agendas underlying multilateral approaches to regional security politics. Dibb has demonstrated such a dual capacity and, in doing so, has served his nation ably at a transitional time in its history. He was instrumental in advancing Australia's interest in cultivating strategic relations with

China and Japan at a crucial juncture in the evolution of the Asia-Pacific's contemporary security environment. He has been a critical player in developing Australia's role as an effective and active middle power in shaping that region's multilateral security dialogues. He has simultaneously contributed to his country's strategic policy thinking in ways that few of his peers have matched.

The most significant lesson that Dibb's career provides to us is that the very best analysts are those who are willing to apply their intellectual talents to actively shaping those policies that are of vital concern to themselves and to their country. His willingness to contribute to the conceptualisation and development of Australia's approaches to Asia-Pacific order-building, especially in the area of regional confidence-building, will be remembered as a benchmark for all those who aspire to think about and influence national security policy.

# Appendix: Paul's Publications

## Books

*The Soviet Union: The Incomplete Superpower* (London: International Institute for Strategic Studies and Macmillan, 1986, reprinted 1987, 2nd edn, 1988).

*Siberia and the Pacific, a Study in Economic Development and Trade Prospects* (New York: Praeger, 1972).

## Edited Books

*America's Asian Alliances* (with Robert D. Blackwill) (Cambridge: MIT Press, 2000).

*Australia's External Relations in the 1980s, The Interaction of Economic, Political and Strategic Factors* (New York: Croom Helm Australia and St Martin's Press, 1983).

## Monographs

*The Geopolitical Implications of Russia's Invasion of Ukraine*, Centre of Gravity Series No. 16 (Canberra: Strategic and Defence Studies Centre, Canberra, June 2014).

*The Nuclear War Scare of 1983: How Serious Was It?*, ASPI: Special Report (Canberra: Australian Strategic Policy Institute, October 2013).

*A Sovereign Submarine Capability in Australia's Grand Strategy*, Centre of Gravity Series No. 3 (Canberra: Strategic and Defence Studies Centre, December 2012).

*Essays on Australian Defence,* Canberra Papers on Strategy and Defence No. 161 (Canberra: Strategic and Defence Studies Centre, 2006).

*Australia's Alliance with America*, Melbourne Asia Policy Papers, Vol. 1, No. 1 (University of Melbourne, March 2003).

*Does Asia Matter to Australia's Defence Policy?* (The National Institute for Asia and the Pacific, 2002).

*Planning a Defence Force Without a Threat: A Model for Middle Powers* (Canberra: Strategic and Defence Studies Centre, 1996).

*Strategic Guidelines for Enabling Research and Development to Support Australian Defence* (with Ken Anderson), Canberra Papers on Strategy and Defence No. 115 (Canberra: Strategic and Defence Studies Centre, 1996).

*Towards a New Balance of Power in Asia*, Adelphi Paper No. 295 (London: International Institute for Strategic Studies, 1995).

*Australian Paper on Practical Proposals for Security Cooperation in the Asia Pacific Region* (with Foreign Minister Gareth Evans) (Canberra: Department of Foreign Affairs and Trade and the Strategic and Defence Studies Centre, 1994).

*The Conceptual Basis of Australia's Defence Planning and Force Structure Development*, Canberra Papers on Strategy and Defence No. 88 (Canberra: The Australian National University, 1992).

## Major Government Reports

*Review of Australia's Defence Capabilities*, report to the Minister for Defence (Canberra: Australian Government Publishing Service, 1986).

*Restructuring the Papua New Guinea Defence Force: Strategic Analysis and Force Structure Principles for a Small State* (with Rhondda Nicholas), report to the Minister for Defence of Papua New Guinea (Canberra: Strategic and Defence Studies Centre, 1996).

# Other Government Reports

*A New Policy for Defence Industry*, report to the Minister for Defence, April 2001 (this report became the basis of a Cabinet Submission on the same subject in October 2001).

*Report of the Defence Consultation Team* (co-authored with AVM B. O'Loughlin), report to the Secretary of the Department of Defence and the Chief of the Defence Force, October 2000.

*The Strategic Priorities for Australian Defence Industry*, report to the Department of Defence (Canberra: Australian Government Publishing Service, 1992).

*The Economics of the Soviet Wheat Industry: An Economic Study of the Structure, Trends and Problems from 1953 to 1965 with a Perspective to 1970* (Canberra: Bureau of Agricultural Economics, 1966).

# Book Chapters

'Managing Australia's Maritime Strategy in an Era of Austerity', in Andrew Forbes (ed.), *Naval Diplomacy and Maritime Power Projection* (Sea Power Centre, 2014), pp. 111–20.

'Defence Policymaking', in Peter Ream, Stephan Frühling and Brendan Taylor (eds), *Australia's Defence Policy: Towards a New Era* (Melbourne University Press, 2014), pp. 165–83.

'The Self-Reliant Defence of Australia: The History of an Idea', in Ron Huisken and Meredith Thatcher (eds), *History as Policy: Framing the Debate on the Future of Australia's Defence Policy*, Canberra Papers on Strategy and Defence No. 167 (Canberra: ANU E Press, 2007), pp. 11–26.

'Australia and the United States', in Brendan Taylor (ed.), *Australia as an Asia-Pacific Regional Power* (London and New York: Routledge 2007), pp. 33–49.

'SDSC in the Nineties: A Difficult Transition', in Meredith Thatcher and Desmond Ball (eds), *A National Asset: Essays Commemorating the 40th Anniversary of the Strategic and Defence Studies Centre (SDSC)* (Canberra: Strategic and Defence Studies Centre, The Australian National University, 2006), pp. 83–98.

'America and the Asia-Pacific Region', in Robert Ayson and Desmond Ball (eds), *Strategy and Security in the Asia-Pacific* (Sydney: Allen & Unwin, 2006), pp. 173–90.

'The Arc of Instability and the North of Australia: Are They Still Relevant to Australia's New Defence Posture?', in Tess Lea and Bill Wilson (eds), *The State of the North* (Darwin: Charles Darwin University Press, 2005), pp. 137–48.

'The Future of International Coalitions: How Useful? How Manageable?', in Alexander T. J. Lennon (ed.), *The Battle for Hearts and Minds* (Cambridge: MIT Press, 2003), pp. 29–44.

'A New Defence Policy for a New Era?', in Clive Williams and Brendan Taylor (eds), *Countering Terror: New Directions Post '911'* (Canberra: Strategic and Defence Studies Centre, 2003), pp. 59–68.

'Strategic Trends in the Asia-Pacific Region', in Paul D. Taylor (ed.), *Asia and the Pacific: US Strategic Traditional and Regional Realities* (Newport RI: Naval War College Press, 2001), pp. 9–28.

'The Strategic Environment in the Asia Pacific Region', in Robert D. Blackwill and Paul Dibb (eds), *America's Asian Alliances* (Cambridge: MIT Press 2000), pp. 1–17.

'The Relevance of the Knowledge Edge to Australia', in Desmond Ball (ed.), *Maintaining the Strategic Edge: The Defence of Australia in 2015*, Canberra Papers on Strategy and Defence No. 133 (Canberra: Strategic and Defence Studies Centre, 1999), pp. 141–69.

'Australia's Defence Policies in the Post-Cold War Era', in James Cotton and John Ravenhill (eds), *Seeking Asian Engagement: Australia in World Affairs, 1991–95* (Melbourne: Oxford University Press in association with The Australian National University, 1997), pp. 61–77.

'The Emerging Strategic Architecture in the Asia-Pacific Region', in Denny Roy (ed.), *The New Security Agenda in the Asia-Pacific Region* (London: Macmillan, 1997), pp. 99–120.

'The New Balance of Power in the Asia Pacific Region: A Source of Peace or Conflict', in J. Mohan Malik (ed.), *The Future Battlefield* (Melbourne: Deakin University Press in association with the Directorate of Army Research and Analysis, 1997), pp. 27–39.

'The Asia Pacific Strategic Environment — Implications for Defence Planners', in J. McCaffrie and D. Sherwood (eds), *The Navy and Regional Engagement* (Canberra: Australian Defence Studies Centre, 1996), pp. 3–11.

'International Security and Australia', in A. Stephens (ed.), *New Era Security: The RAAF in the Next Twenty-Five Years* (Canberra: RAAF Air Power Studies Centre, 1996), pp. 31–42.

'The Evolution and Future of Australian Defence Policy', in Coral Bell (ed.), *Nation, Region and Context: Studies in Peace and War in Honour of Professor T. B. Millar*, Canberra Papers on Strategy and Defence No. 112 (Canberra: Strategic and Defence Studies Centre, 1995), pp. 31–48.

'Intelligence and Australian Defence Policy', in A. Bergin and R. Halls (eds), *Intelligence and Australia's National Security* (Canberra: Australian Defence Force Academy, 1994), pp. 45–48.

'The Potential for Conflict and the Possibilities for a UN Response', in Hugh Smith (ed.), *Peacekeeping: Challenges for the Future* (Canberra: Australian Defence Studies Centre, Australian Defence Force Academy, 1993), pp. 177–84.

'Australia's Defence Strategy', in Sam Bateman and Dick Sherwood (eds), *Strategic Change and Naval Role: Issues for a Medium Naval Power,* Canberra Papers on Strategy and Defence No. 102 (Canberra: Strategic and Defence Studies Centre, 1993), pp. 93–103.

'Australia's Defence Policy: The Impact on the Asia-Pacific Region', in David Horner (ed.), *The Army and the Future: Land Forces in Australia and South-East Asia* (Canberra: Directorate of Departmental Publications, Defence Centre, 1993), pp. 115–28.

'The CSBM Agenda in the Asia-Pacific Region: Some Aspects of Defence Confidence Building', in Rohana Mahmood and Rustan A. Sanu (eds), *Confidence Building and Conflict Reduction in the Pacific* (Kuala Lumpur: Institute of Strategic and International Studies (ISIS) Malaysia, 1993), pp. 167–76.

'Australia's Regional Security Policy in the 1990s', in C. Coulthard-Clark (ed.), *The Qualitative Edge: A Role for Air Power in Regional Cooperation* (Canberra: Australian Government Publishing Service, 1993), pp. 3–18.

'Whither Strategic and Defence Studies', in Desmond Ball and David Horner (eds), *Strategic Studies in a Changing World* (Canberra: The Australian National University, 1992), pp. 408–29.

'New Directions in Australian Defence Policy', in Gregory R. Copley (ed.), *The Era of Great Change* (Washington DC: Defense & Foreign Affairs, International Media Corporation, 1990), pp. 47–55.

'One Strategic Entity: An Australian Defence Perspective on the South Perspective', in David Hegarty and Peter Polomka (eds), *The Security of Oceania in the 1990s*, Canberra Papers on Strategy and Defence No. 60 (Canberra: Strategic and Defence Studies Centre, 1989), pp. 66–70.

'Australia's Defence Capabilities', in Desmond Ball (ed.), *Air Power — Global Developments and Australian Perspectives* (Pergammon Press, 1988), pp. 17–45.

'The Global Context of North Pacific Security', in Andrew Mack and Paul Keal (eds), *Security and Arms Control in the North Pacific* (Sydney: Allen and Unwin, 1988), pp. 8–26.

'The Soviet Union's Security Outlook', in D.H. McMillen (ed.), *Asian Perspectives on International Security* (London: Macmillan, 1984), pp. 195–214.

'Comments', in Stuart Harris (ed.), *Australia's Antarctic Policy Option* (Canberra: Centre for Resources and Environmental Studies, The Australian National University, 1984), pp. 124–33.

'The Interests of the Soviet Union in the Region: Implications for Regional Security', in T. B. Millar (ed.), *International Security in the Southeast Asian and Southwest Pacific Region* (Santa Lucia: University of Queensland Press, 1983), pp. 44–77.

'Australia's External Relations: An Introduction', in Paul Dibb (ed.), *Australia's External Relations in the 1980s, The Interaction of Economic Political and Strategic Factors* (New York: Croom Helm Australia, 1983), pp. 11–16.

'World Political and Strategic Trends and their Relevance to Australia', in Paul Dibb (ed.), *Australia's External Relations in the 1980s, The Interaction of Economic Political and Strategic Factors* (New York: Croom Helm Australia, 1983), pp. 28–43.

'World Economic Nationalism: Its Relevance to Australian Foreign Policy in the 1970s', in B.D. Beddie (ed.), *Advance Australia — Where?* (Oxford University Press of Australia, 1975), pp. 196–222.

'International Trade, the Export Base and the Location of Rural Industries' in J. Powell (ed.), *The Making of Rural Australia* (Melbourne: Sorrett Publishing, 1974), pp. 151–60.

'Soviet Agriculture Since Khruschev — an Economic Appraisal', in Marshall I. Goldman (ed.), *Comparative Economic Systems: A Reader* (New York: Random House, 1971), pp. 361–87.

'International Trade, the Export Base and the Location of Rural Industries', in G.J.R. Linge and P.J. Rimmer (eds), *Government Influence and the Location of Economic Activity* (Canberra: Department of Human Geography, Research School of Pacific Studies, The Australian National University, 1971), pp. 115–40.

'The Soviet Far Eastern Fishing Industry' in R.H. Osborne (ed.), *Geographical Essays in Honour of K.C. Edwards* (University of Nottingham, 1970), pp. 149–60.

## Journal Articles

'Why China Will Not Become the Dominant Power in Asia' (with John Lee), *Security Challenges*, Vol. 10, No. 3 (2014), pp. 1–21.

'Australian Defence: Challenges for the New Government' (with Richard Brabin-Smith), *Security Challenges*, Vol. 9, No. 4 (2013), pp. 45–64.

'The Importance of the Inner Arc to Australian Defence Policy and Planning', *Security Challenges*, Vol. 8, No. 4 (2012), pp. 13–31.

'The Soviet Experience in Afghanistan: Lessons to be Learned?', *Australian Journal of International Affairs*, Vol. 64, No. 5 (2010), pp. 495–509.

'Is the US Alliance of Declining Importance to Australia?', *Security Challenges*, Vol. 5, No. 2 (2009), pp. 31–40.

'The Resurgence of Russia as a Great Power?', *Bear on the Prowl: The Return of Russia as a Great Power*, Australian Institute of International Affairs (AIIA) Policy Commentary (November 2008), pp. 11–22.

'Indonesia in Australian Defence Planning' (co-authored with Richard Brabin-Smith), *Security Challenges*, Vol. 3, No. 4 (November 2007), pp. 67–93.

'Colder Warrior — What is Rising from the Ashes of the USSR', *The Diplomat*, Vol. 5, No. 6 (February/March 2007), pp. 30–32.

'Is Strategic Geography Relevant to Australia's Current Defence Policy', *Australian Journal of International Affairs*, Vol. 60, No. 2 (June 2006), pp. 247–64.

'The Bear is Back (A Resurgent Russia?)', *The American Interest*, Vol. 2, No. 2 (November/December 2006), pp. 78–85.

'US–Australia Alliance Relations: An Australian View', *Strategic Forum*, No. 216 (August 2005), pp. 1–6.

'Has Australia Gone Soft on Communist China', *Defender: The National Journal of the Australian Defence Association* (Spring 2005), pp. 16–18.

'Security Problems in a Global Age and the Future Course of the Transformation of the Military: Australian View', *National Institute for Defense Studies (NIDS) International Symposium on Security Affairs 2004*, Tokyo (March 2005), pp. 7–16 (in English and Japanese).

'The Future of International Coalitions', *The Washington Quarterly*, Vol. 25, No. 2 (2002), pp. 131–44.

'Strategic Trends: Asia at a Crossroads', *Naval War College Review*, Vol. 54, No. 1 (Winter 2001), pp. 22–38.

'Indonesia: The Key to South-East Asia's Security', *International Affairs*, Vol. 77, No. 4 (October 2001), pp. 535–48.

'Indonesia's Grim Outlook' (co-authored with Peter Prince), *Orbis*, Vol. 45, No. 4 (Fall 2001), pp. 1–16.

'Australia's Best Defence White Paper?', *Australian Defence Force Journal*, No. 147 (March/April 2001), pp. 28–30.

'Transforming the ADF's Force Structure for the 21st Century', *Australian Defence Force Journal*, No. 143 (July/August 2000), pp. 27–28.

'A Trivial Strategic Age', *Quadrant*, Vol. 44, No. 7–8 (July/August 2000), pp. 11–17.

'ANZUS: cette alliance a-t-elle un avenir?', *Géopolitique* (Revue de l'Institut International de Géopolitique, Paris), No. 70 (July 2000), pp. 49–55.

'Asia's Insecurity' (with David D. Hale and Peter Prince), *Survival*, Vol. 41, No. 3 (Autumn 1999), pp. 5–20.

'Force Structure Priorities: The Need For Greater Self-reliance', *Dissent*, No. 2 (Summer 1999–2000), pp. 9–11.

'The Relevance of the Knowledge Edge', *Australian Defence Force Journal*, No. 134 (January/February 1999), pp. 37–48.

'Australia's Policy Options — Beyond Defence of Australia?', *Australian Security in a New Era: Reform or Revolution?*, conference proceedings, 11–12 November (Australian Defence Studies Centre, 1998), pp. 107–11.

'Regional Security Implications of the East Asian Economic Crisis', APEC Economics Program, Australia–Japan Research Centre, The Australian National University, Report No. 27 (September 1998), pp. 2–4.

'The Strategic Implications of Asia's Economic Crisis' (with David D. Hale and Peter Prince), *Survival*, Vol. 40, No. 2 (Summer 1998), pp. 5–26.

'The Revolution in Military Affairs and Asian Security', *Survival*, Vol. 39, No. 4 (Winter 1997–98), pp. 93–116.

'O Planejamento da Forca de Defesa na Auscencia de Ameacas: Um Modelo para as Potencias Medias', *Parcerias Estrategicas*, Vol. 1, No. 4 (December 1997), pp. 117–41.

'Unbreakable China', *The International Economy* (May/June 1997), pp. 50–53.

'Defence Force Modernisation in Asia', *Contemporary Southeast Asia*, Vol. 18, No. 5 (March 1997), pp. 347–60.

'A New Balance of Power in Asia?', *The Asia-Pacific Magazine*, Vol. 1, No. 1 (April 1996), pp. 28–32.

'The Future Military Capabilities of Asia's Great Powers', *Janes Intelligence Review* (May 1995), pp. 229–33.

'Space Surveillance Seminar — Keynote Address', *Australian Maritime Warfare Journal*, Edn 18 (1994), pp. 13–18.

'The Regional Security Outlook: The Australian Viewpoint', *Tomorrow's Pacific*, Current Issues, Institute of Public Affairs, Melbourne (February 1993), pp. 17–26.

*The Future of Australia's Defence Relationship with the United States* (Sydney: Australian Centre for American Studies, 1993).

*The Outlook for the Former USSR* (Sydney: Pacific Security Institute, 1992).

'Insecurity in the Asia-Pacific Region', *IPA Review*, Vol. 45, No. 3 (1992), pp. 43–48.

'Is Soviet Military Strategy Changing', *The Changing Strategic Landscape*, Adelphi Paper No. 235 (Spring 1989), pp. 35–47.

'Soviet Influence in East Asia and the Pacific in the Coming Decade', *East Asia, the West and International Security: Prospects for Peace*, Adelphi Papers No. 217 (Spring 1987), pp. 43–55.

'The Dibb Report: Review of Australia's Defence Capabilities', *Current Affairs Bulletin* (July 1986), pp. 4–18.

'Soviet Strategy Towards Australia, New Zealand and the Southwest Pacific', *Australian Outlook* (August 1985), pp. 69–76.

'Australia's Security Environment and Defence Policy', *Journal of the Royal United Services Institute* (June 1985), pp. 16–22.

'The Soviet Union as a Pacific Military Power', *Pacific Defence Reporter* (November 1984), pp. 19–25.

'Issues in Australian Defence', *Australian Outlook* (December 1983), pp. 160–66.

'The Soviet Union as a Pacific Power', *International Journal* (Spring 1983), pp. 234–50.

'What's Wrong with Australia's Intelligence Community?' (with R.H. Mathams), *Pacific Defence Reporter* (April 1983), pp. 10–16.

'New Soviet Line Likley to be Tough but Pragmatic', *Pacific Defence Reporter* (March 1983), pp. 7–9.

'Australia Cannot Plan for a No Threat Future: Challenges in the 1990s and Beyond', *Pacific Defence Reporter* (February 1983), pp. 15–19.

'Soviet Capabilities, Interests and Strategies in East Asia in the 1980s', *Survival*, Vol. 24, No. 2 (July/August 1982), pp. 155–62.

'Military Power and Soviet Global Influence', *Current Affairs Bulletin*, University of Sydney (July 1982), pp. 4–13.

'Siberia and the Soviet Presence in East Asia', *Strategic Survey 1981–82*, International Institute for Strategic Studies (1982), pp. 104–08.

'China's Strategic Situation and Defence Priorities in the 1980s', *Australian Journal of Chinese Affairs*, No. 5 (1981), pp. 97–115.

'The Strategic Inter-relations of the U.S., the U.S.S.R. and China in the East Asia-Pacific Area', *Australian Outlook* (August 1978), pp. 160–81.

'The Balance of Power in Northeast Asia', *Current Affairs Bulletin* (August 1976), pp. 4–17.

'Wheat Production in the Soviet Union and the Five Year Plan' (co-authored with F.M. Collins), *Quarterly Review of Agricultural Economics* (April 1967), pp. 95–104.

## Working Papers

*Australia's Security Relationship with Japan: How Much Farther Can It Go?*, Working Paper No. 407 (Canberra: Strategic and Defence Studies Centre, 2008).

*The Future Balance of Power in East Asia: What are the Geopolitical Risks?*, Working Paper No. 406 (Canberra: Strategic and Defence Studies Centre, 2008).

*The War on Terror and Air Combat Power*, Working Paper No. 369 (Canberra: Strategic and Defence Studies Centre, June 2002).

*The Utility and Limits of the International Coalition Against Terrorism*, Working Paper No. 365 (Canberra: Strategic and Defence Studies Centre, December 2001).

*Strategic Trends in the Asia-Pacific Region*, Working Paper No. 350 (Canberra: Strategic and Defence Studies Centre, August 2000).

*The Prospects for Southeast Asia's Security*, Working Paper No. 347 (Canberra: Strategic and Defence Studies Centre, June 2000).

*Will America's Alliances in the Asia-Pacific Region Endure*, Working Paper No. 345 (Canberra: Strategic and Defence Studies Centre, May 2000).

*Defence Strategy in the Contemporary Era*, Working Paper No. 337 (Canberra: Strategic and Defence Studies Centre, 1999).

*The Relevance of the Knowledge Edge*, Working Paper No. 329 (Canberra: Strategic and Defence Studies Centre, 1998).

*The Remaking of Asia's Geopolitics*, Working Paper No. 324 (Canberra: Strategic and Defence Studies Centre, 1998).

*Alliances, Alignments and the Global Order: The Outlook for the Asia-Pacific Region in the Next Quarter-Century*, Working Paper No. 317 (Canberra: Strategic and Defence Studies Centre, 1997).

*Force Modernisation in Asia: Towards 2000 and Beyond*, Working Paper No. 306 (Canberra: Strategic and Defence Studies Centre, 1997.

*The Emerging Geopolitics of the Asia-Pacific Region*, Working Paper No. 296, (Canberra: Strategic and Defence Studies Centre, 1996).

*How to Begin Implementing Specific Trust-Building Measures in the Asia-Pacific Region*, Working Paper No. 288 (Canberra: Strategic and Defence Studies Centre, 1994).

*The Political and Strategic Outlook 1994–2003: Global, Regional and Australian Perspectives*, Working Paper No. 282 (Canberra: Strategic and Defence Studies Centre, 1994).

*The Future of Australia's Defence Relationship with the United States*, Working Paper No. 276 (Canberra: Strategic and Defence Studies Centre, 1993).

*The Regional Security Outlook: An Australian Viewpoint*, Working Paper No. 262 (Canberra: Strategic and Defence Studies Centre, 1992).

*Focusing the CSBM Agenda in the Asia-Pacific Region: Some Aspects of Defence Confidence Building*, Working Paper No. 256 (Canberra: Strategic and Defence Studies Centre, 1992).

*Soviet Strategy Towards Australia, New Zealand and Oceania*, Working Paper No. 90 (Canberra: Strategic and Defence Studies Centre, 1984).

*The Soviet Union as a Pacific Military Power*, Working Paper No. 81 (Canberra: Strategic and Defence Studies Centre, 1984).

*World Political and Strategic Trends over the Next 20 Years — Their Relevance to Australia*, Working Paper No. 65 (Canberra: Strategic and Defence Studies Centre, 1983).

*Soviet Capabilities, Interests and Strategies in East Asia in the 1980s*, Working Paper No. 45 (Canberra: Strategic and Defence Studies Centre, 1982).

## Other

'The Death Knell of the Defence of Australia?', 'What Are the Real Existential Threats?', 'Why did America get Iraq so Badly Wrong?', 'A Resurgent Russia?' in Barbara Nelson and Robin Jeffrey (eds), *Capturing the Year 2007: Writings from the ANU College of Asia and the Pacific* (Canberra: ANU College of Asia and the Pacific, 2007), pp. 66–68, 69–72, 201–03 and 208–14.

'Radical new Defence Policy or Hill's Smoke and Mirrors?', 'What the New Defence Minister Should Do, and Not Do', 'As one Nuclear Flashpoint Reaches a Lull, Another Simmers Sway' in Barbara Nelson with Robin Jeffrey (eds), *Capturing the Year 2006: Writings from the ANU College of the Asia and the Pacific* (Canberra: ANU College of Asia and the Pacific, 2006), pp. 139–42, 145–47 and 190–92.

'A Defence Industry Development Strategy', in *The Business of Defence: Sustaining Capability*, CEDA Growth Report No. 57 (Melbourne: Committee for Economic Development of Australia, August 2006), pp. 10–19. (A summarised version is in *Australian Chief Executive* (Melbourne, CEDA, September 2006, pp. 24–27.)

'Implications of the New Defence Capability Plan for Industry', in *Tackling Future Capabilities*, Proceedings of the Australian Defence Magazine's 3rd Annual Congress, Canberra, 14 March 2006, available on CD.

*Australia's Strategic Circumstances and Possible Calls on its Defence Capabilities*, Proceedings 72nd National Conference of Legacy Clubs of Australia, Canberra, September 2001, pp. 10–17.

*Proceedings from Shaping the Future of the Australian–American Alliance Seminar, held on 23 February 1995*, The Australian Centre for American Studies, Discussion Paper No. 4, Sydney, pp. 27–32.

*The Global Political and Strategic Outlook: 1994–2003* (Commonwealth Funds Management Ltd, 1994).

*Soviet Agriculture since Khruschev*, Occasional Paper No. 4, Department of Political Science, Research School of Social Sciences (Canberra: The Australian National University, 1969).

*Soviet Siberia and Australia, Prospects for Pacific Trade*, Issue Paper 2, Wagga Wagga Teachers College, Area of Humanities, 1968.

www.ingramcontent.com/pod-product-compliance
Lightning Source LLC
Chambersburg PA
CBHW040142270326
41928CB00023B/3316